CONTENTS

ILLUSTRATIONS

Acknowledgments

SEVERAL PEOPLE HAVE made this project possible and deserve recognition. My husband, Howard, and our families have always been unyielding in their love and support throughout my education and career. Ronald G. Walters, my adviser, and several faculty members at Johns Hopkins University—John Spitzer, Tobie Meyer-Fong, Judy Walkowitz, and Toby Ditz—have also been limitless in their guidance and have given me the tools to pursue *Yellowface*. There were also several people from a number of institutions who helped me find resources and conceptualize this project: the Special Collections staff at Johns Hopkins University, especially Mary Campbell, Joan Grattan, and Cynthia Requardt; Fath Davis Ruffins and Franklin Odo at the Smithsonian Institution; Joyce Botelho at the John Nicholas Brown Center for American Civilization and Rosemary Cullen at the John Hay Library at Brown University; Roger Horowitz at the Hagley Museum and Library; Neville Thompson at the Winterthur Museum; Cathy Cherbosque at the Huntington Library; Lorraine Dong and Jeannie Woo at the Chinese Historical Society of America; Caroline Sloat, John Hench, Joanne Chaison, and Gigi Barnhill at the American Antiquarian Society; Miriam Smith, historian to the Immigration and Naturalization Service at the National Archives and John Celardo at the Northeast Region (New York) Office of the National Archives; Esther L. Mes and Rick Watson, collection assistants at the Harry Ransom Humanities Research Center at the University of Texas at Austin; and the staffs at the California Room of the California State Library, the Performing Arts Division of the Library of Congress, and the Newberry Library.

Yellowface

Introduction

THE SYNCHRONIZED PLATE THROWING of the Wesselys, a troupe of five jugglers, received an enormous round of applause as they bowed and walked off the stage. With the stage completely empty, Lee Tung Foo, arguably the first Chinese American in vaudeville, stepped out and positioned himself in front of the primarily white audience. The band struck up Dave Reed Jr. and Ernest R. Ball's "Love Me and the World Is Mine" (1906), a popular ballad that year, and Lee began to sing: "I wander on as in a dream . . ." From what we know of Lee's act from reviews and his own writings, he then gave a comedic monologue, sang an unnamed song in Cantonese, and broke out into an Irish brogue for his rendition of another 1906 hit, William Jerome's "My Irish Molly, O" (1906). His act ended with "Im Tiefen Keller" (In the Deep Cellar), a drinking song he sang in the original German.[1]

During the last week of December 1906 and into January 1907, Lee Tung Foo performed at Keith's Theater in Providence, Rhode Island, and received fulsome praise. Local critics in New England dedicated whole columns to Lee's act not only because it was original but also because it was a direct challenge to American perceptions of the Chinese. Lee, however, was not from China. As an American of Chinese descent, he knew what it meant to be Chinese only through what he saw in immigrant communities and in American caricatures, and he combined this material to create an image of what it meant to be Chinese. But it was all an "act" (see ill. 1). Novelty was important to Lee, and through it he drew attention to the incongruity between fixed preconceptions of race and his capacity to impersonate non-Asian characters, speak English without an accent, and sing American and European popular songs. As one critic wrote, "Not only has he an excellent voice, which he uses with such amazing intelligence, that one almost forgets his race, but he sings and speaks fluently in English and with an evident sense of humor that is surprising."[2] By all accounts, audiences were stunned at witnessing firsthand a Chinese American performing in an American idiom, a feat they had to see to believe. Indeed, his very presence on the stage challenged widely held beliefs about performers of Chinese descent and heralded the emergence of scores of other Chinese American vaudevillians.

I

Ill. 1. Portrait of Lee Tung Foo in a Chinese costume. Courtesy of the California History Room, California State Library, Sacramento.

LEE TUNG FOO'S ARRIVAL on the vaudeville stage marked an important transition in the relationship between American music and identity. His act may have led the Providence reviewer to "almost forget [Lee's] race," but in fact his act had everything to do with race. Since the nineteenth century, several important shifts had occurred in musical and theatrical performances about and by Chinese and Chinese Americans. Large numbers of performers and writers participated in circulating images of China and its people via print media and the stage, which eventually hardened into stereotypes. These individuals, who came from a variety of backgrounds, created certain images on the stage and in music not for the sake of accuracy but to help define and understand themselves as well as others around them. Many Euro-American musicians and writers created race-based distinctions between music and noise, used attitudes about race to question whether the Chinese could participate in Western music and performance, and finally, circulated anti-Chinese stereotypes. They, however, also turned to China to address other issues in the United States, such as gender relations, the definition of citizenship, working-class identity, the effects of modernity, and the development of new modes of musical expression. At the same time, Chinese and Chinese Americans had their own reasons for performing on the stage. Some came lured by stories of success and huge profits only to be left penniless by their American managers. Several Chinese immigrants, imbued with an entrepreneurial spirit, employed music and theater in hopes of maintaining their heritage among fellow immigrants and promoting cultural understanding with outsiders. Finally, the desire of Chinese American vaudevillians, such as Lee Tung Foo, to perform in an American popular idiom confronted established stereotypes by demonstrating that race was a performance. Together, these diverse voices, although unequal in their access to mainstream media, shed light on the complexity of constructions of race in the United States and the important role China played in the generation of an American identity and popular culture.

Although several historians have addressed the relationship between African American and Euro-American musical traditions, few have studied the connections between China and the United States through popular music, and of these, even fewer have gone beyond lyrics and staging to look at musical notation and instrumentation. Music and its performance, however, give us a window into the ways in which information circulated in the nineteenth and early twentieth centuries and how various groups saw their world. Because it requires listening, music operates differently from written or visual cultural products. This is not to say that a historical analysis of music does not rely on written or visual objects, but that music, in order to participate in the construction and circulation of meaning, must be performed to be consumed. Through its ephemeral and at times improvisational qualities, music cuts in several directions, depending on the body of the performer, performance strategies, musical notation, instrumentation, and lyrics. Moreover, music's performativity is not one-sided and functions more like a conversion among the producers (who consist of two coexisting groups—the songwriters and the performers) and the consumers. As argued by John Fiske in *Understanding Popular Culture,* consumers have a limited number of ways in which to respond to cultural products: they can reinforce the meaning generated by producers, partially accept it, or completely subvert it.[3] Furthermore, because the performers are not always the same as the songwriters, they too alter the materials they are singing or playing on a musical instrument in ways that fit more with their own ideas. It is by looking at all these sources and the contradictions among them that historians can begin to understand the complexity of representation and insert China into discussions of American identity and culture.

As a form of performance, music appeared in several types of venues. Although the phonograph and radio were growing in popularity at the beginning of the twentieth century, the majority of American audiences frequented concert halls, parks, or theaters in order to listen to music during this period. Because some instruments were portable (such as the harmonica or the human voice), musicians broke out into song almost anywhere they could; many Americans also played musical instruments in their homes.[4] Even silent films were not silent; "mood" music (what later became known as the soundtrack in talkies and television) was played by a pianist or a small orchestra to set the scene and to generate a certain atmosphere. Although certainly not limited to "Americans" or to the nineteenth and early twentieth centuries, musical performances were a main form of entertainment in the United States at this time and, as such, a potential purveyor of knowledge and communication.

The performative qualities of music resulted not only from the performance venues (after all, recordings are performances) but also from the disjuncture between music and everyday life. Of course, people whistle a tune or turn on the radio/CD player while working or relaxing, but music still functions as an alternative to what is perceived as "real" (most notably as a form of escapism and as a tool for relaxation). As Judith Butler maintains in her discussion of theater, audiences and performers share an understanding that what is going on is an "act" distinct from everyday activities and that the actor/actress has taken on a role that is not his/her "own."[5] Or put another way (and more closely tied to music), a conversation between two persons relies on the spoken word, not the sung word (imagine a board meeting conducted in recitative). The act of singing exists in a distinct space separate from what we consider normal, daily communication.

Music, however, as a form of performance can be separated from theater because it is primarily defined as a succession of tones or pitches guided by certain rules or values. The concepts that guide music making, such as harmonic movement and notational systems, are important in understanding the meaning behind these kinds of artistic works. Even with lyrics, music ultimately relies on sounds (sometimes organized into patterns, but also spontaneous) to relay meaning. Most listeners tie the meaning of music to feelings and emotions; however, music, like other forms of cultural production, is part of larger systems of thought. Rationality, constructions of gender, and national and racial identity are all manifested in music.

Edward Said has described Orientalism as a "western style of dominating, restructuring, and having authority over" the non-Western world. Imaginings of the "Orient," including China, function in opposition to whatever symbolized the West, and often portrayed the "sensuality, promise, terror, sublimity, idyllic pleasure, [and] intense energy" of this region of the world.[6] By the end of the eighteenth century, many European and American writers, realizing that what they saw as the "laws" of music and drama were not the same throughout the world, began systematically to marginalize non-Western traditions. China's performing arts traditions at this time were diverse, depending on region, type of ceremony or celebration, sex, and class. Government officials and literati, following Confucian teachings, studied music and played the *qin* (a zither) as a means of worship, character development, and good government. Regional operas flourished, some of which came together to create Beijing Opera in the nineteenth century. Women performed at court and in teahouses and brothels; blind musicians also played in the streets for spare change or food.[7] Westerners, as with other aspects of Chinese culture, saw and heard something else. Borrowing from the language in which the emerging middle classes distinguished themselves from the working classes and peasants, European and American writers obscured the diversity of traditions in China and described Chinese culture, with few exceptions, as devoid of anything musical.

Stereotypes circulated by the majority of American and European writers about China's inferior culture led many to the conclusion that the Chinese were incapable of understanding or producing something that Westerners perceived to be more sophisticated—Western music and theater. Racial inferiority, supported by popular beliefs and a growing scientific literature, was manifested in culture—both in the making of certain types of productions and in the doubts pertaining to the level of Chinese comprehension. Nevertheless, as Homi Bhabha contends in his analysis of race-based stereotypes, the belief that the Chinese were unable to sing and play in a Western fashion was seen, on the one hand, to be fixed and natural, and on the other hand, "ambivalent."[8] A few European and American missionaries believed that the Chinese could be uplifted from their current state of depravity through Christianity and become their equals; music was one of the ways they tried to prove this point. Here, a belief in universal brotherhood, which supported their prose-lytizing in nonwhite communities, conflicted with biologically based racist ideas.[9]

Although still tied to what was going on in Europe, nineteenth-century Americans developed their own brand of Orientalism in response to American–Chinese trade relations, immigration, and scientific racism. As argued by James Moy, John Kuo Wei Tchen, and Robert G. Lee, these attitudes perme-ated the highly commercial and often spectacle-driven musical and theatrical productions that began to appear during the antebellum period, which, in turn, supported certain kinds of Chinese portrayals.[10] Anti-Chinese stereo-types appeared mostly in lyrics and dialogue, sets, and the "yellowed-up" white body, and ignored the areas of musical notation and instrumentation until the latter part of the century. Lyrics and dialogue often relayed contem-porary social and political attitudes that were similarly found in newspapers, travel narratives, poetry, and popular fiction. The visual excesses of staged spectacles, which became more elaborate over the nineteenth century as new theatrical technologies appeared, worked hand in hand with the allure of the exotic, especially Chinese export goods, brightly colored sets, and lush fab-rics. Yellowface, a term used primarily during the twentieth century to de-scribe the ways in which white actors portrayed Asians, manifested degrading images of Chinese immigrants on the stage—images that were also appearing in contemporary political cartoons and magazine covers. As with blackface, which emerged in the 1830s as a popular way to parody African Americans, dialect, makeup, posture, and costuming comprised yellowface; when com-bined, these items marked the Chinese body as inferior and foreign.

The combination of these devices did not necessarily create a unilateral anti-Chinese image; both allure and repulsiveness coexisted in these perfor-mances. Peter Stallybrass and Allon White make the case in their analysis of the European bourgeoisie of the nineteenth century that "what is *socially* peripheral is so frequently *symbolically* central." Furthermore, "these low domains, apparently expelled as 'Other,' return as the object of nostalgia, long-ing and fascination."[11] This, too, appears in the United States in that what was seen as innately foreign and racially inferior (namely, Chinese immigrants and their cultural practices) not only marked the boundaries of American identity but also was a site of desire for those things and ideas that had been lost to "progress" or were seen as beyond conventional social mores. As a result, Chi-nese and Chinese Americans, and by extension all persons of Asian descent, were vital to the conception of American culture and the boundaries of racial and national identity.

Musical representations of the Chinese developed at a slower pace in com-parison to other aspects of performance, in part because of the lack of information about Chinese music but also because of the common dismissal of Chinese music as noise. Aside from a handful of attempts to use gongs and to incorporate early transcriptions of Chinese melodies, Chinese musical tokens did not emerge on a consistent basis in popular music until the latter part of the nineteenth century. Since the seventeenth century, however, composers had been working with musical representations of other parts of the "Orient," especially Turkey, in ways that reinforced stereotypes of exoticism and difference while also fostering musical experimentation.[12] American songwriters often turned to these earlier attempts to embody the "Orient," but they also used transcriptions of Chinese music as more material became available, along with two quite different but familiar types of musical otherness in the United States—blackface minstrelsy and African American musical traditions.

Although many scholars have focused on the black–white dyad in music, both blackface minstrelsy and African American music have much more complex positions in American culture—positions that become further muddied when mixed with Chinese musical tokens. Some cultural elites considered each, with some modifications to make them more sophisticated and civilized, to be uniquely American and therefore integral in the delineation of the United States from European nations. Similar arguments were also made for Native American and European-based folk music from Appalachia. There were, however, clear differences. White male performers had created blackface, which, although often employed to address a variety of social and political issues, co-opted African American melodies and openly denigrated African Americans through a combination of visual and aural devices.[13] African American music, while also a mixture of European and African elements, was a product of the African American experience in the United States, often functioning as a release from the prejudices that blackface embodied.[14] With an understanding that both African American music and blackface minstrelsy were tied to markers of racial inferiority, white songwriters applied these traditions to Chinese immigrants. Yet unlike African Americans, who were seen by some as a way to differentiate the U.S. population from that of Europe, the Chinese were not seen as Americans but as foreigners. Musically, however, composers frequently used the same devices to capture the "nonwhiteness" of both groups. This phenomenon, too, was filled with contradictions. By grouping these particular nonwhite groups together through music, songwriters opened up the possibility that Chinese immigrants too could lay claim to an American identity.

Aside from combining musical and theatrical signifiers in ways that could undercut Chinese stereotypes, the appearance of "real" Chinese bodies, like Lee Tung Foo's at the beginning of the twentieth century, further complicated the American musical landscape. As noted by Josephine Lee in *Performing Asian America*, performers of Asian descent "rob[bed] the stereotype of its power to substitute for the natural or essential being and reveal[ed] it as a social construct, the product of specific historical and social circumstances."[15] White audiences, who often saw yellowface as authentic and true to life, expected Chinese and Chinese Americans to reaffirm the caricatures that whites had previously produced in print media and on the stage. The flatness and limits of stereotypes, however, could not control Chinese and Chinese Americans on the stage (even those who reenacted American caricatures) because what they produced was "unreal" and distinct from their "real" selves, which were supposed to be the same as these stereotypes. For many Chinese visitors and immigrants, performance was a way to promote the appreciation of their heritage, question racism, and gain control over images generated on the stage. Those who went into vaudeville also demonstrated the musical ability of men and women of Chinese descent and the instability of race and nation as fixed categories. Although with mixed results, they ultimately employed a range of strategies on the stage in hopes that audiences would reevaluate anti-Chinese attitudes and their own conceptions of what it meant to be American.

THE LOOSELY CHRONOLOGICAL CHAPTERS in this book focus on the ways in which Chinese stereotypes were continually generated and reworked in musical performances by a wide array of writers and performers during the nineteenth and early twentieth centuries. Chapter 1 lays out the common perceptions of Chinese music and theater, and the ways in which songwriters depicted the Chinese at the beginning of the nineteenth century. For the most part, European and American commentators viewed Chinese music as unmusical and questioned whether the Chinese could understand Western culture. Musical productions set in China or with Chinese characters emphasized what was exotic and different between China and the West primarily through lyrics, dialogue, sets, costumes, and the cover designs of sheet music. The emergence of Chinese immigrants as musical subjects, first in California during the 1850s and then, by 1870, on the national level is addressed in chapter 2. These acts borrowed several devices from blackface minstrelsy, which previously had been used to put down African Americans and certain European immigrant groups. With few exceptions, songs from this period reinforced attitudes that led to the passage of the Chinese Exclusion Act in 1882 by framing Chinese immigrants as racially inferior and un-American. Chapter 3 looks at Chinese performers in the United States who first appeared at dime museums, Chinese theaters, and, by the end of the century, world expositions. These actors and organizers often used their musical and theatrical traditions to maintain their heritage for immigrant communities as well as to question American stereotypes of Chinese culture, opening up the possibility for alternative understandings of their civilization. For many white observers, however, their acts only reinforced anti-Chinese attitudes. The ways in which composers used musical notation and instrumentation by the end of the nineteenth century to represent China is discussed in chapter 4. Although reinforcing difference and inferiority as expressed in lyrics and the "yellowed-up" body, the use of Chinese-inspired sounds based on Orientalist operas, African American music, blackface minstrelsy, and transcriptions of Chinese music also gave American songwriters a new source of musical inspiration and innovation. It also undercut the perception that Chinese music was noise by putting these melodies into Western musical notation. Chapter 5 explores the heterogeneity of Chinese images produced in the United States from the mid-1880s through the 1920s, many of which did not necessarily promote notions of inferiority as they had appeared in previous decades. The quaintness, potential danger, and exoticism of Chinatowns and the sexual allure of Chinese women became central. At this time, African Americans and white women also began to impersonate the Chinese on the stage, but with their own motives that related to Euro-American conceptions of race, gender, and modern life. Finally, chapter 6 gives the final word to Chinese and Chinese American vaudevillians, who, with their appearance on the popular stage, at least partially upset the structures of racism that were meant to confine them.

Chinese and Chinese Americans as both musical subjects and performers helped to stimulate the continual shifting and reworking of anti-Chinese stereotypes and the conception of national and racial identity in the nineteenth and early twentieth centuries. Like other cultural productions, musical performances participated in the creation of a system of meaning that pushed Chinese and Chinese Americans physically and symbolically to the margins of American life. At the same time, the fact that these stereotypes were being performed and were separate from "reality" allowed for the possibility of multiple readings by producers and audiences. In particular, acts generated by Chinese and Chinese Americans contested stereotypes that excluded them from the stage (and by extension, American society and politics) and tried to offer alternatives. This wide array of people shaped the ways in which the Chinese appeared musically for over a century and, in so doing, reflected, reinforced, and challenged how all Americans imagined themselves.

CHAPTER 1

Imagining China

EARLY NINETEENTH-CENTURY WRITINGS AND MUSICAL PRODUCTIONS

BY THE BEGINNING OF THE NINETEENTH CENTURY, Americans and Europeans struggled with how to understand Chinese music and how to portray the Chinese in their own traditions. The majority of Western visitors to China drew on a long and relatively stable practice that described Chinese music as "noise" and, more broadly, saw this particular aspect of China's culture as inferior to that of Europe. Industrialization, contact with Chinese people (including performers), and the rise of scientific racism reinforced how these commentators understood the distinction between music and noise and between European and Chinese culture in general. Although travelers and other observers were clear about their opinions of Chinese music, the situation was different for composers and librettists. Songwriters were primarily concerned with entertaining and bringing in audiences, and to do this they relied on more exotic aspects of Chinese culture that went well with staged spectacles. It was both the descriptions of Chinese music and the depictions of China on the stage and in music that influenced attitudes toward Chinese culture. More importantly, however, these developments created a musical vocabulary of race that shaped, and would be reshaped, by further American contact with Chinese abroad and Chinese immigrants in North America.

As argued by Jacques Attali, sound, despite its ephemeral qualities, participates in the organization of human relations.[1] Specifically, the division of sound into two categories—music and noise—signifies the organization of social hierarchies and formulations of power. The boundaries between these two categories were frequently the subject of debate, depending on the listener's worldview and relationship to the subject. Nineteenth-century distinctions between music and noise arose out of a combination of forces tied to class tensions, gender relations, and intercultural contact. In previous centuries, composers and philosophers had developed a set of rules for music based on harmonic movement, which they saw as tied to the rationality and universality of the natural world.[2] Eighteenth-century writers, however, soon realized through information gathered primarily by French Jesuit missionaries that the traditions of non-Western peoples whom they saw as either closer to nature or, in a few instances, more refined (such as the Chinese, who were often seen as both) did not follow these rules. In response, Europeans and Americans did not alter their attitudes to allow for the coexistence of a variety of sophisticated musical traditions based on different sets of principles but instead chose to see their own practices as the pinnacle of human development and all others as inferior. This attitude, in turn, worked together with other racist ideas that emerged in the late eighteenth and nineteenth centuries.

The language that developed in response to these experiences was inextricably tied to what Edward Said has called Orientalism, and it helped to delineate China as Other. There were material differences between Chinese and Western traditions—musical notation, instrument construction, scales, vocal techniques, intellectual interests, orchestration, use of percussion, social organization of musicians and actors, theatrical traditions, and the social context of performances—but it was the way in which Westerners interpreted Chinese music that supported their more generalized belief in Chinese inferiority. In many cases, because Chinese traditions did not conform to the values of these writers, they were perceived to be lacking in "musical" qualities and therefore in need of containment and reform. Questions also arose about the ability of the Chinese to produce and understand what Westerners believed was a more complicated and sophisticated form of music.

Unlike American and European commentators on Chinese culture, composers and librettists had different inspirations and goals. During this same period, musicians, hoping to create more alluring and exotic images that would appeal to audiences, turned to the Chinese vogue of the time known as chinoiserie.[3] Although mainly associated with the decorative arts and landscape design, chinoiserie also informed the aesthetic sensibilities of the theater arts. Musical and theatrical producers were primarily concerned with the spectacle of what they were creating and only loosely borrowed from what limited information there was on Chinese clothing, objects, and architecture. As with the visual aspects of these productions, librettists recycled a limited number of previously published stories based on Western fascination with China and translations of Chinese and other Asian texts. These plotlines were also a conflation of "Chinese" and "Oriental" signifiers that librettists believed were marketable to European and Americans audiences and worked well with Chinese-stylized stage trappings.

Musically, most compositions set in China or containing Chinese subjects were similar to pieces based on European or American materials. Whether this was partially tied to attitudes about Chinese music making is not exactly clear; however, the conceptualization of Chinese music as un-musical probably did influence songwriters, who, with few exceptions, avoided imitating Chinese melodies or instrumentation. The limited number of analytical studies and the general lack of contact between Western and Chinese musicians almost certainly contributed to this phenomenon. The absence of exotic musical tokens during the early part of the nineteenth century undercut those aspects of music that emphasized difference and instead made the Chinese more like "us." This allowed for alternative attitudes, often generated by the Chinese themselves, toward Chinese culture. Only later in the century would composers focus on musical notation and instrumentation to create a more totalizing image of the Chinese as Other.

The ways in which writers and composers—primarily during the first half of the nineteenth century—conceptualized the Chinese had wide-ranging implications. Here, devices used by both Europeans and Americans are particularly significant. At first, Americans drew on European materials from the eighteenth and early nineteenth centuries; however, as the nineteenth century progressed, they turned to their own distinct experiences with the Chinese, especially those involving immigration. That story is told in chapter 2. Older attitudes from Europe and the eastern seaboard of the United States generated a vocabulary of signifiers and speculation about the relationship between culture and what was seen as the stages of human development. Ultimately, this "language" would lay the foundation for how Americans would perceive the Chinese in music over the next century.

NINETEENTH-CENTURY AMERICAN AND EUROPEAN WRITERS

The majority of nineteenth-century writers about China expanded on the musical attitudes generated by previous visitors from the seventeenth and eighteenth centuries.[4] For example, Johan Nieuhoff, steward to the 1656 Dutch embassy to Canton, wrote that a band during the celebration of the Dutch–Chinese trade agreement "made a hideous noise" such that "there was no hearing one another speak."[5] In part, increased disenchantment sustained these attitudes during the nineteenth century. The problems that the Chinese people faced (dynastic instability, Western encroachments, opium, rebellion, floods, and famines) and the increase of disillusioning information about Chinese culture and society led to rising concerns about the current state of Chinese civilization. Tensions surrounding trade relations and the sluggishness of religious conversion frustrated merchants and missionaries, who expressed these feelings to readers at home. These points of friction were the basis of many negative sentiments toward China.[6]

Many commentators stated that Chinese music was devoid of all principles that Americans and Europeans believed to be integral to musical composition and performance, and wrote about their dislike of Chinese music, especially operas, in the most hyperbolic terms. Aside from the term "noise," they described what they heard as a "din," "racket," or "universal hubbub."[7] A few authors even questioned whether the use of the word "music" or "musical" was appropriate for what they had heard. Sir Henry Ellis, the third commissioner of the British embassy to China from 1816 to 1817, chronicled his attendance at a performance in Canton. He noted that the "annoyance of a sing-song," an English term used to described Chinese operatic traditions in general, was a "mass of suffering" that he never wanted to experience again. "The noise of the actors and instruments (musical I will not call them) is infernal."[8] Somewhat later, Martha Noyes Williams, wife to the U.S. commissioner at Shantou, wrote about a similar performance during a visit to an island off the coast of that city. Besides the overwhelming heat, "the noise of the performers, together with the clangor of their musical (?) instruments," almost drove Williams "mad."[9]

Others expanded upon this attitude, focusing on singing, a major component of all Chinese theatrical productions. British army officer Sir William Tyrone Power complained that Chinese singers used "an unnatural falsetto key," which was "pitched as high as possible." These tones were "more hideous and ludicrous" than can "scarcely be imagined," which he compared to a "tom cat caterwauling on the pantiles."[10] The allusion to a tom cat marked the Chinese not only as racially inferior but also as oversexed and feminine, thus undermining the masculinity of all Chinese actors, who played both male and female parts. American missionary John L. Nevius also found that he disliked the high pitch of Chinese recitative. "Performers recite[d] their parts in a high, drawling, falsetto tone," which he also thought was "unnatural." In a reference to Western theatrical realism, a style wherein actors delivered their lines as they would everyday speech, Nevius went on, noting that this sort of delivery was "never used in common conversation" but only in the theater.[11]

Writers not only framed Chinese music through the binary relationship of music and noise but also drew comparisons with other non-European traditions. This was another way for Europeans and Americans to mark non-Western nations as inferior and to obscure the uniqueness of these diverse communities. French missionary Evariste Regis Huc wrote that Chinese music was similar to "the chants of savages," a reference to all peoples he saw as less civilized and un-Christian.[12] After Commodore Matthew Perry opened Japan to American trade and missionary interests in 1853, others created musical hierarchies between China and Japan. Despite its Chinese roots, Japanese music was seen by some travelers as superior to its antecedent. In *Dwight's Journal of Music,* an elite nineteenth-century music periodical from Boston, an anonymous author wrote that he had mixed feelings about performances in Japan, but that they were definitely better than what he had heard in China. Although the singer was attractive and graceful, she sang in a "species of a whine, not altogether so discordant as that of the Chinese, yet merely bearable from its strangeness."[13] Of course, regardless of the relative enjoyment of Japanese music, especially in contrast to that of the Chinese, European-based traditions were still on top.

Nineteenth-century Europeans and Americans also heard similarities between Chinese music and that of various European folk traditions. The association of China and European folk was based on music from more rural regions that industrialization and scientifically based music had not greatly affected. This too had racial implications, affirming the preeminence of certain groups of Europeans and creating a racial/ethnic hierarchy among these peoples. It also allowed for the possibility of equating the Chinese with Europeans in ways that undermined the rigidity of racial categories.

Although a few writers saw parallels between Chinese music and Spanish and Irish traditions, the majority associated the Chinese with the Scots.[14] During the nineteenth century, Scottish music was still seen as connected to both a pre-industrial world and an ethnic minority on the British Isles that, relatively speaking, did not pose a threat to English cultural preeminence. Large numbers of Scottish immigrants also came to the United States during the eighteenth and early nineteenth centuries, bringing their musical traditions with them.[15] This connection brought China much closer to home and broke down the suggestions that China was completely alien. For some, Scottish bagpipes sounded similar to the *suona,* often described as a Chinese version of a clarinet or oboe. John E. Duer, a member of the U.S. Navy stationed in China in the years before the Civil War, wrote that "one [wind instrument] resembles a clarionet in shape, and bagpipes in tone."[16] The use of the pentatonic scale in both Chinese and Scottish melodies was also significant. The late eighteenth-century music histories by Charles Burney, a British organist and music critic, were frequently reprinted or paraphrased in nineteenth-century writings on musical development throughout the world. One such article in the June 1835 edition of the *Family Minstrel* argued that the "similarity" between Chinese and Scottish music "proved them all to be more natural than they at first seem to be, as well as more ancient."[17] Burney's use of the terms "ancient" and "natural" expressed his belief that neither tradition had developed past a primitive stage. The term "natural," however, also contradicted the beliefs of many Western musicians and critics, including Burney himself, who saw Western art music to be closer to nature (despite alterations to the overtone series and the tempering of scales). Here, Burney saw "natural" as a mark of inferiority.

Aside from criticizing singing and musical accompaniment, writers also disliked Chinese theatrical practices, which reinforced their negative attitudes about the music. At the core of these comments were the differences in Western and Chinese performance styles. With the rise of neoclassicism in the seventeenth century, some European playwrights emphasized the importance of theatrical realism. Dramas were to have a unified sense of time and place, rational and systematic plotlines and characterizations, clear divisions between tragedy and comedy, the avoidance of supernatural beings and extraordinary circumstances, and a moral (with good always triumphing over evil). By the mid-eighteenth century, Europeans began to accept theatrical romanticism, a concept that developed in reaction to neoclassicism and promoted another variation of realism, allowing for tragedy and comedy to mix, more freedom of time and place, and the inclusion of the supernatural. Movement and speech, although exaggerated in order to communicate to audiences, were to be more conventional and individualistic than before.[18]

Nineteenth-century visitors emphasized the differences between Western and Chinese theatrical traditions, especially the lack of realism in the latter. British missionary and later diplomat G. Tradescant Lay, in *The Chinese as They Are,* argued that Chinese productions were "rude and inartificial," by which he meant inartistic or without skill. "Instead of allowing characters and events to be developed in the course of the piece, each performer on his first entry addresses the audience, and informs them who and what he is, what remarkable deeds he has performed, and what are his present views and intentions." He continued, noting that "the unities" found in "classic drama are completely trampled under foot."[19] Aristotle had first coined the term *unities,* also known as the three unities, to express the notion that theatrical productions needed to have a realistic sense of time, space, and action. Lay, like other nineteenth-century observers, supported this concept, and any deviance from it was second rate.

In explaining their belief in Chinese theatrical inferiority, authors formulated a "stages" view of human development—that the Chinese were located on a lower rung on the evolutionary ladder when compared with Europeans. Many wrote that Chinese productions were similar to those from sixteenth-century Europe, especially the dramas of William Shakespeare. Like Chinese practices, sixteenth-century English dramatics did not maintain the three unities, actors were sometimes seen as paupers and thieves, only men could perform on the stage, and few troupes had permanent theaters.[20] The implication of equating the Chinese theater with that of Shakespeare, however, was a dangerous game for those who endorsed race-based notions of civilization. On the one hand, this perspective enabled writers to locate the Chinese at a lower level of human development. On the other hand, once writers put the Chinese into the same category as Shakespeare, some of the distance between Chinese and European/American culture vanished, and the Chinese became connected to someone who was seen as one of the greatest English playwrights.[21]

As in sixteenth-century Europe, men still played female characters (*dan*) on the Chinese stage, which led many authors to hone in on what they saw as the effeminacy of Chinese men. Heavily ornamented costumes, stylized gestures and movements, and falsetto were integral to the portrayal of female characters, but for observers who were accustomed to women performing on the stage (a tradition that did not come into its own in Europe until the mid to late seventeenth century), this was problematic. Osmond Tiffany Jr.'s 1849 travel narrative, *The Canton Chinese, or the American's Sojourn in the Celestial Empire,* discusses the femininity of female impersonators in an opera given in Canton. He noted that young men from the ages of seventeen to nineteen played female parts with a "womanly way of moving, talking, and even thinking." Although there was "no indecency committed," these female impersonators were "natural" and "sentimental," and even portrayed "the belle and the mother much better than nine tenths of the European actresses."[22] The rise of anti-immigrant sentiments only a few years later in the nineteenth century also promoted the feminization of Chinese men living in the United States.

Chinese troupes also used nonrealistic stage properties, another tradition found in Europe before the eighteenth century. In her serialized recollection of her visit to China, Caroline Butler cited a description of the English stage by Sir Philip Sidney in 1583 to demonstrate the resemblance between English and Chinese stage properties. Sidney noted that "a *rock*" functioned in one moment as a "shipwreck" and then later "a *cave*" where "a hideous monster" lived. Later, "two armies fly in, represented with *four swords* and *bucklers,* and then what hard heart will not receive it for a *pitched battle?*"[23] Like Butler, an anonymous writer in the journal *All the Year Round* in 1865 wrote that Chinese staging reminded him of a scene in *A Midsummer Night's Dream.* In the opening of act 3, Bottom and his company are rehearsing a play version of *Pyramus and Thisbe,* when, on realizing that they need a wall with a hole, decide to have one man stand between the couple with his fingers in the shape of a circle through which the lovers speak. This scene, however, was a burlesque of rural bumpkins, further adding to the devaluation of Chinese theatrical practices.

European and American writers during most of the nineteenth century used a set number of tropes to construct Chinese musical inferiority. For most of these authors, Chinese music was not musical at all; at the same time, it was similar to sounds produced by other non-Western peoples, folk cultures in Europe, and animals. Chinese theatrical traditions, which always included music, reinforced these sentiments. Overall, these writings delineated the boundaries between music and noise, marking Chinese traditions as the latter, and supported the notion of Chinese cultural inferiority. Later, these same attitudes also justified anti-Chinese policies in the United States. This view was widespread and relatively stable over a long period of time, with only some minor changes such as the association of Chinese music with the raucous sounds of urbanization and industrialization and questions about the behavior of Chinese audiences.[24] Ironically, even these deeply held stereotypes would change by the end of the century, and in some surprising ways.

EXCEPTIONS

A few European and American travelers dissented from the generally negative view of their contemporaries and enjoyed listening to Chinese music making. Although their descriptions were clearly a minority view and often were mixed with more derisive comments, they did not portray Chinese music in terms of its supposed lack of musical qualities or as noise. For many such authors, these performances were still exotic, but they contained something that differentiated them from other experiences that most writers associated with cultural inferiority. A few wrote that religious music and specific kinds of secular performances, although simplistic, were pleasurable. With the growth of Protestant missions in China in the nineteenth century, others noted their amazement at the ability of Chinese converts to sing hymns based on Western tunes. Although hymn singing proved that missionaries were able to uplift the Chinese, it also demonstrated the ability of the Chinese to learn what was believed to be a much more civilized form of music and thus to challenge racist assumptions.[25]

Chinese religious ceremonies, despite being equated with heathenism, had a profound effect on a few writers. Sir William Tyrone Power wrote in *Recollections of a Three Years' Residence in China* that the chanting of Buddhist monks, along with the playing of bells and drums, was "awe-inspiring." Their chanting, however, was still basic, and Power compared it to earlier stages of Western music—the chants of medieval European monks or the worship of ancient Greek oracles. Once again, Chinese music, even the most agreeable to the European or American ear, was not as sophisticated as contemporary Western traditions.[26]

Authors also relayed the pleasure they found with performances on the *qin*, a ten-stringed zither with a short soundboard and no bridge, and the *yangqin*, a trapezoidal-shaped hammer dulcimer with metal strings. These instruments were recognized for their ability to create simple harmonies, which many authors complained were missing in Chinese music. In a village called Sang-yuen, where the British embassy stopped in 1817 on its return to Canton from Beijing, Sir Henry Ellis described listening to a blind musician play the yangqin and compared it to a harpsichord. "We all agreed that the performance was superior in harmony to any that we had before heard."[27] In a paper presented to the Royal Asiatic Society in London, which was then reported in the American press, G. Tradescant Lay described the origin and history of the qin. He noted that Chinese scholars studied and performed on this instrument in ways similar to European intellectuals. Performances on the qin were "very graceful" and included a variety of methods "of touching the strings."[28] Lay, however, believed that melodies produced on this instrument were "simple" and that the intervals they used were similar to those found in Scottish music.

Most positive writings about Chinese music making came from visitors who listened to Chinese converts singing in Protestant missions and schools. This music, imported by missionaries, was important to European and American listeners and readers who were concerned about uplifting the Chinese through religious conversion. By learning these hymns, the Chinese proved to missionaries and their supporters that they were able to sing and play what Westerners believed to be a more sophisticated form of music, thus countering more racist attitudes about Chinese musical ability. Missionaries ultimately hoped that through conversion they could improve Chinese culture and align it more with the West.

The divergence between Chinese and Euro-American perceptions of music making meant that missionaries often found teaching Western music to the Chinese was difficult—as difficult as converting them. First, there was the social stigma attached to professional singers and actors in China, who occupied the lowest rungs of Chinese society. Many missionaries found that wealthier families and government officials refused to participate in activities that originally had been performed primarily by slaves, prostitutes, or paupers. Nevertheless, members of the civil service and literati did study music and performed on the qin. In his quest to convert the Chinese near Shanghai, American missionary Edward W. Syle noted that members of some wealthy families pursued music as an intellectual activity and that they also enjoyed listening to Christian hymns and organ playing. However, they did not join in.[29]

Because of the different intervals used in Chinese and Western music, some missionaries found that the Chinese had trouble hearing and reproducing the diatonic scale. In an article in *Dwight's Journal of Music,* members of the London Missionary Society in Hong Kong stated that the Chinese, even after learning Western scales, were still "painful" to listen to. Most converts, they reported, learned simple melodies well, but few were able to progress further; some were unable to sing hymns at all. Debates began to circulate about the importance of using Western tunes in conversion. American missionary Erastus Wentworth suggested that because conversion was the priority and not good hymn singing, missionaries should translate hymns or psalms into local dialects and use Chinese melodies with which converts would be much more comfortable and familiar.[30]

Despite these difficulties, which reaffirmed the racialization of music ability, many missionaries believed that the Chinese, especially young children, could learn hymns. Because children had had less exposure to Chinese culture, missionaries argued, they would more easily absorb the missionaries' teachings. In many ways, these missionaries saw Chinese children as tabulae rasae on which they could imprint not only Christianity but also the traits of a more developed civilization. In *Dwight's Journal of Music,* Syle wrote about the success with local children at the Presbyterian and Episcopalian missions in Ningbo and Shanghai. He also noted that the organist at his mission was Chinese.[31]

European and American visitors praised Chinese children's music, which they saw as a relief from the cacophonous sounds found everywhere else in China. In his travel narrative, *Life among the Chinese,* Robert S. Maclay, a member of the American Methodist Episcopal mission, cited a letter from another missionary, Stephen L. Baldwin, who had visited a Christian school run by a married couple named Gibson in Fuzhou. Baldwin noted that one day after school, a group of ten boys stopped by the missionaries' home and asked Mrs. Gibson to play the melodeon, a small organ, and to sing for them. After Mrs. Gibson performed a few songs, she began to teach the children. Their ability to pick up music quickly impressed Baldwin. They ended the evening by singing a hymn in Chinese to the tune "Balerma," a melody found in both Protestant and Catholic hymnals. Baldwin went on to explain that these boys were currently singing at the local church and, he believed, should visit other missions to teach "the brethren and fathers there a few lessons," especially to stop the "merciless slaughter of Old Hundred [a melody sung to the Hundredth Psalm in the Bible] as takes place there every Sunday."[32]

During the nineteenth century, Western writers found a few particular kinds of Chinese performances to be enjoyable, although still simple and foreign. Some noted the beauty of Chinese sacred music and performances on the qin and yangqin. Most important to Western visitors was the ability of Chinese converts, especially children, to sing hymns. Although not indigenous to China, these songs proved to missionaries and others that the Chinese were able to perform in what Europeans and Americans perceived to be a superior musical tradition. This attitude did not counter the denigration of Chinese music in general but helped to undermine beliefs in Chinese inferiority and to hint at alternative possibilities for understanding Chinese music.

EARLY AMERICAN VISIONS OF CHINA IN MUSIC

During the first half of the nineteenth century, American composers had little if any contact with the Chinese, relying instead on over a century of European productions and writings for inspiration. As was the practice of the time, many American songwriters and playwrights rewrote European works for American audiences. European songs and musical plays were also brought to the United States and were frequently reproduced on the stage and as sheet music. Unlike Western writings on Chinese music, Western songs and productions with Chinese characters or set in China did not necessarily support the denigration of Chinese culture and played on those aspects that had previously appealed to consumers in the marketplace—chinoiserie and Chinese trade goods. These were still stereotypes, but they portrayed what Americans saw as attractive about China, not repugnant. More acerbic images of China increased in frequency as diplomatic and cultural tensions rose during and after the Opium War (1839–1842) and later with the arrival of Chinese immigrants in the Far West. Cultural differences were part of China's appeal, and usually they were embedded in the spectacle and lyrical aspects of performance.

The first of such songs appeared in the early 1800s, in Benjamin and Joseph Carr's *Musical Journal for the Pianoforte,* the first weekly music periodical in the United States. The Carrs, who had emigrated from Great Britain in 1793, began to publish the *Musical Journal* in 1800 to cater to elite families interested in current music from Europe and to feature newly written American works.[33] Quickly they published "Twelve Variations to Ching Chit Quaw" (ca. 1800), based on a trio from Rayner Taylor's musical play *The Mandarin; or, Harlequin Widower,* which had appeared at Sadler's Wells in London during the 1788–1789 season. *The Mandarin* was closely tied to the chinoiserie vogue in Great Britain during the latter part of the eighteenth century, and although no libretto exists, it was probably loosely based on travel narratives, Chinese histories, and design motifs on Chinese export goods. It is also possible that Taylor himself wrote "Twelve Variations to Ching Chit Quaw" for the *Musical Journal* in that he had also left London for Philadelphia and knew the Carrs.[34]

The two songs most associated with China during the nineteenth century—"The Peyho Boatmen; or, Higho Highau" (1796) and "Moo–Lee–Chwa" (1796)—also appeared in the *Musical Journal* sometime between 1802 and 1803 (see ill. 2). A year after the return of the first British embassy to China (1793–1795), the embassy's physician, a Dr. Scott, revamped his transcriptions of these tunes with help from small-time London composer Karl Kambra and published them.[35] Ironically, fellow embassy member John Barrow criticized Scott's changes, particularly to "Moo-Lee-Chwa," which he saw as so radical "that it cease[d] to be a speciment of the plain melody of China." Nevertheless, "Moo-Lee-Chwa" and "The Peyho Boatmen" were reportedly quite popular at the beginning of the nineteenth century.[36]

Perhaps the Carrs published "The Peyho Boatmen" and "Moo-Lee-Chwa" in the United States because of the songs' popularity. They too made alterations—framing the call and response in "The Peyho Boatmen" more clearly as a chorus and removing Scott's original transcription at the beginning of "Moo-Lee-Chwa."[37] The Carrs' publication, however, did not represent the last time either of these songs was reproduced as sheet music or performed in the United States. Both songs, but especially "Moo-Lee-Chwa," appeared in European and American books and articles on national music traditions and Chinese culture. In 1868, *The Western Musical World* reported that Patrick S. Gilmore's band played "Moo-Lee-Chwa" during the visit of the Chinese embassy to Boston. The German-language newspaper *Sonntag-Schul* from Cincinnati printed "Moo-Lee-Chwa" on its front page in 1881. Finally, Giacomo Puccini used "Moo-Lee-Chwa" throughout his last opera, *Turandot* (1926).[38]

During the first half of the nineteenth century, few pieces of sheet music with Chinese themes were published in the United States or imported from Europe until songs in response to Chinese immigration appeared in the Far West in the 1850s. Aside from "Moo-Lee Chwa" and "The Peyho Boatmen," those songs that existed made no attempt to imitate or allude to Chinese music but relied on visual or textual cues that would be well known to American consumers through literature and the marketplace. The majority of these songs were solely instrumental to be played on the piano, and they relied on the sheet music's cover design and title to do the work of denoting "Chineseness." In 1828, music publisher A. Fleetwood of New York City published British composer Mathias von Holst's "The Chinese Rondo."[39] Although this song was written for the piano, Holst tried to imitate other instruments in the introduction (clarinets, horns, flutes, trumpets, and a gong), presumably to

Ill. 2. Karl Kambra and Dr. Scott's "Moo-Lee-Chwa" (1796). Courtesy of the Eda Kuhn Loeb Music Library of the Harvard College Library.

make it more Chinese sounding. Only the gong, however, was clearly an instrument that would have been found in China. Furthermore, "The Chinese Rondo" (including the introduction) did not include orientalized sounds, as in the pentatonicism of later Tin Pan Alley tunes, to differentiate between European and Chinese musical traditions. The anonymous cover designer, however, must have had some exposure to information on Chinese costuming and instruments, in that a procession of Chinese men playing musical instruments, including a *yunluo* (a series of ten small gongs placed in a frame and hit with a stick), *suona* (a double-reed instrument with a flared metal bell), *luo* (gong), and *tongjiao* (a long, copper horn) was depicted. One musician near the front held a Turkish crescent, also known as a Chinese pavilion or *pavilion chinois,* which was used in Janissary and early European military band music. The Turkish crescent had been introduced to Europe from Turkey but was often called Chinese because the metal pieces attached to the rod looked like a conical hat, often found in European and American depictions of the Chinese. Thus, because of the instrument's name, perhaps the illustrator thought it was also from China.

Although only a few pieces of sheet music appeared at this time, there were several more staged musical productions. With the increasing emphasis on spectacle in the nineteenth century, American and European composers, librettists, and producers found that Chinese exoticism worked well on the stage. To a certain extent, these productions were similar to Chinese festivals and masques held in Europe starting in the seventeenth century and continuing throughout the nineteenth century.[40] A large number were also European musical plays or operas that were brought to the United States and produced by American or European touring companies. One of the earliest productions was *The Travellers; or, Music's Fascination* (1806), a musical play that its composer, Domenico Corri, hoped would introduce audiences to "the national melody of various kingdoms" and create a musical hierarchy with the English on top.[41] First premiering in London, *The Travellers* appeared at Philadelphia's New Theatre in 1807 but was not mounted elsewhere, which perhaps alludes to its lack of success with American audiences. To fit Corri's ideas on music, librettist Andrew Cherry created a story about Prince Zamphimri of China (a name borrowed from Arthur Murphy's *The Orphan of China* [1759]), who travels to England to study law. The opening act, which was set in China, included several songs in a European fashion; only the "Grand Chorus" or the "Chinese Chorus" used music from the "Hymne en l'honneur des ancêstres," a melody recorded by French Jesuit missionary Joseph-Marie Amiot, who had lived in Beijing during the eighteenth century.[42] On his way around the world, Prince Zamphimri and his retinue stop in Turkey and Italy before traveling to Great Britain. *The Travellers,* with its exotic settings and an aristocratic protagonist, had all the elements for an elaborate spectacle; however, the role of music makes this production say something quite different. By organizing *The Travellers* as a progression from lowest to highest in musical development, Corri and Cherry created a hierarchy similar to that found in European and American writings on Chinese culture. Yet, as with travel narratives and other texts, this formulation also located China on a spectrum with Great Britain rather than presenting it as utterly foreign.

In the early nineteenth century, fantastical musical plays were much more common than were productions such as *The Travellers*. *Aladdin*, which most people today associate with Persia and the Middle East thanks to films such as *The Thief of Bagdad* (1924) and Disney's *Aladdin* (1992), was one of the more popular nineteenth-century productions set in China because of its romantic and moralistic storyline and its potential as a spectacle.[43] Originally from Antoine Galland's eighteenth-century translation of *One Hundred and One Arabian Nights,* the story of "Aladdin" was set in western China, with scenes in North Africa.[44] Composers and librettists sometimes chose Persia as the setting for the tale because *One Hundred and One Arabian Nights* was from that region of the world and, like China, was a popular imaginative space for Americans and Europeans. As with the Orientalist tradition of obscuring Asia's diversity, some even combined Chinese and Persian objects together on the stage and thus amplified the novelty of their production.

Early adaptations of "Aladdin" were first produced in Great Britain before coming to the United States. In 1813, Charles Farley directed and produced *Aladdin; or, The Wonderful Lamp* (1813) at Covent Gardens in London.[45] Set in Central Asia, also known as "Tartary" during the eighteenth and nineteenth centuries, Farley's *Aladdin* included Chinese-styled costumes and sets and no trappings from Central Asia, which, except in stories about Jenghiz Khan, did not figure as prominently in the American popular imagination. From 1816 through 1818, *Aladdin* was one of the many theatrical offerings in Boston, New York City, and Philadelphia and was revived several times during the next several decades.[46]

A few Americans also joined the British in writing productions of *Aladdin* for the stage during the nineteenth century. In winter and spring of 1847, Thomas Comer and Silas S. Steele wrote and produced the first American adaptation, *Aladdin or the Wonderful Lamp, the Grand Chinese Spectacle,* at the Boston Museum.[47] Comer was the musical director at the Boston Museum, but he also spent much of his time acting, arranging, and composing. Steele was a local Boston playwright who wrote periodically for the museum.[48] It is uncertain how Steele and Comer's *Aladdin* differed from other versions because no libretto exists, but two music publishers, Prentis & Clark and Oliver Ditson, both located in Boston, printed many of the songs as sheet music.[49] Like other pieces of sheet music from this period, the songs from *Aladdin* relied on lyrics to denote that they were from a story set in China.

This particular production also appears to have been somewhat successful with local audiences, so much so that it was the subject of parody, in C. A. Beckett's burlesque also named *Aladdin,* as well as admiration, with composer P. J. Bishop dedicating his "Aladdin Galop" (1847) to Steele and Comer's production.[50]

The majority of Americans who performed *Aladdin,* however, were blackface minstrels, variety performers, and female burlesquers. The fact that a woman played the title character in almost every rendering since Farley's provided opportunities for a large number of female performers and for satire. In May 1857, Buckley's Serenaders, a blackface minstrel troupe, burlesqued Steele and Comer's *Aladdin,* which was described in *Porter's Spirit of the Times* as a "great expense, and in gorgeous style, a new grand burlesque extravaganza." Furthermore, although they usually blackened up their faces, for *Aladdin* they "appear[ed] in Tartaric complexions," probably a combination of yellowish greasepaint on their faces and limbs and Indian ink around their eyes for a slanting effect, a practice that would become pervasive later in the century.[51] The Worrell Sisters, Blanche and Ella Chapman and Company, Ada Harland, Lydia Thompson and Company, the Wallace Sisters, and Maggie Moore with Billy Emerson produced similar "Aladdin" skits and one-acts, from the 1840s through the 1870s.[52]

As with British productions, French operas and operettas with Chinese themes toured the United States during the nineteenth century and became the subject of revival and parody. In 1837, the English version of Daniel-François-Esprit Auber's *Le cheval de bronze* (1835), known as *The Bronze Horse,* appeared at the Bowery Theater in New York City after a successful run in London.[53] *The Bronze Horse* tells the story of a Mandarin who is magically turned into stone by one of his wives. Another wife saves him by riding on a magic bronze horse to the world of the fairy princess Stella and receiving a special bracelet. She returns to Earth with the bracelet, saves the Mandarin, and is allowed to marry the farmer whom she truly loves. Like a large number of musical productions from this period, Auber's did not borrow from eighteenth-century transcriptions of Chinese music or from the Orientalist opera tradition.[54]

Within a year of its premiere in the United States, *The Bronze Horse* began to be produced by other troupes using their own variations. Extraordinary sets and costumes were integral to these productions; lyrics and dialogue also portrayed the Chinese setting, although ultimately *The Bronze Horse* could have been set almost anywhere. In 1860, Nixon's Troupe of Equestrians from Great Britain produced the *Bronze Horse or the Spell of the Cloud King* (1860) at the Boston Theatre and at Niblo's Garden. Sets included copies of pagodas and the Great Wall, Chinese monuments with which most Americans would have been familiar. The names of characters were often gags in that they were either supposedly Chinese sounding (but usually made up of gibberish) or references to popular culture, such as Fagan, the Chinese Prime Minister, from Charles Dickens's *Oliver Twist*. Although the score for *Bronze Horse or the Spell of the Cloud King* does not exist, the music appears to have been crafted particularly for this production rather than borrowed from other musical plays or operas, a common practice during the time. These songs also contained Chinese references in their titles, such as "All Hail, Great Zamna, China Pride" and "Hark How the Bells of the Gay Pagoda," but it is unclear whether Nixon's Troupe tried to imitate Chinese music or whether they borrowed from eighteenth-century transcriptions of Chinese music.[55]

Jacques Offenbach's *Ba-Ta-Clan* (1855), retitled *Ching Chow Hi* when it appeared in London and New York City in 1865, was, like *The Bronze Horse*, another fantastic story set only liminally in China.[56] Originally, *Ba-Ta-Clan* was a one-act burlesque on French politics and the operatic works of composer Giacomo Meyerbeer. Set on an imaginary island off China's coast, it opens with the king and a group of government officials trying to quell a revolt. The characters soon realize that although they dress and sound Chinese (nonsensical Italian syllables), they are really French. The king, his officials, and the rebels, in turn, start to celebrate their Frenchness with songs from Meyerbeer's *Les Huguenots* (1836); in the end, they all decide to go home to France.[57]

American blackface minstrels and variety performers were quick to parody *Ching Chow Hi,* often combining elaborate sets and costumes with satirical political dialogue. In November 1869, George Alex Lingard and his troupe produced *Ching Chow Hi* at New York City's Theatre Comique. A reviewer described it as "musical Chinese extravaganza . . . with new scenery, full chorus, and new costumes."[58] That same year, Carcross and Dixey's Minstrels appeared in *Ching-Chung-Hi; or, Burlingame's Teacady* (1869) at the Eleventh Street Theatre in Philadelphia.[59] The reviewer described this production as a "new Chinese burlesque," which, from the title, focused on Anson Burlingame, the American diplomatic minister to China from 1861 to 1867 who had returned to the United States in 1868 as the imperial envoy for the first Chinese embassy. The Chinese, with Burlingame's assistance, negotiated a new treaty with the United States that was supposed to improve trade relations for both nations and protect the rights of Chinese immigrants, much to the anger of many supporters of anti-Chinese legislation. A year later, Kelly and Leon's Minstrels also produced a burlesque of *Ching Chow Hi,* which they periodically revived over the next eight years.[60] As in Offenbach's version, the parody by Kelly and Leon was set in China, with the troupe portraying Chinese characters who were really Americans. A reviewer noted that the scenery and costumes were "among the richest ever seen in a minstrel hall."[61]

When the Ravels, a French troupe of dancers and acrobats, arrived in the United States in 1840s, they too contributed to the number of musical productions set in China with *Kimka! or, The Misfortunes of a Ventilator* (1847). Also known as *Kim-ka; or, The Adventures of an Aeronaut,* this musical production was described as a "Chinese Pantomimic Fete," consisting of ballets, tableaus, and a battle scene, all of which were accompanied by music.[62] *Kimka* began with the actors re-creating a royal, Chinese processional with mandarins, priests, women of the royal household, flag and banner carriers, and palanquins containing the emperor, Kimka, and Lei (the emperor's daughter and Kimka's love interest). Kimka, a French balloonist, then reenters the stage, trying to fly from Paris to Beijing in a hot air balloon, but a storm forces him to land. Meanwhile, Keying and Pwan-Tin-Qua, advisers to the emperor, spot Kimka's balloon through a telescope and believe that it is a monster. (Keying was the name of the Chinese commissioner [Qiying] who controlled Canton as well as the name of a Chinese junk that was displayed in the New York City and Boston harbors in 1847.) They then sound the alarm and send guards to capture Kimka. While being chased, Kimka hides in Lei's compound, where they meet and fall in love. She pleads for Kimka's life with her father, who agrees to allow him to live if he marries Lei and shaves his head, which was probably supposed to represent the queue-wearing practice mandated during the Qing dynasty as a form of loyalty to the emperor. Kimka, however, refuses to cut his hair, and the emperor orders his execution in the "tub of punishment." The bottom of the tub, however, falls out, and Kimka, "now free, thinks that the joke has been carried far enough, and that it is more pleasant to marry a princess even if she be a Chinese one than to take a cold bath shut up in a tub."[63] The emperor agrees, and the pantomime ends with a large dance number and fireworks.

Kimka was revived and parodied several times from the 1850s through the 1870s by both dance troupes and variety performers.[64] For example, the second act of the 1873 musical play *Humpty Dumpty Abroad* lampooned *Kimka* through the physical comedy of George L. Fox. Fox's clown character, Humpty Dumpty, and his friend Pantaloon enter the stage in a hot air balloon, a few moments after the emperor of China and his entourage have arrived in a boat. They then accidentally fall out of the balloon into the water, but are saved when someone in the emperor's boat, who also happens to be fishing, reels them in on the back of a fish. While with the Chinese, Humpty and Pantaloon are entertained by a series of magic tricks and a dance called "The Fete of Pekin," before they travel on to Italy.[65] During the 1870s, numerous performers produced "Chinese Dances," "Chinese Terpsichoriosities," "Chinese Ballets," "Hong Kong Dances," and "Ching Chang Dances," also perhaps related to *Kimka.*[66]

Although composers and lyricists depicted exotic elements that appealed to American consumers, they also started to include more denigrating elements. By the 1840s, a small number of skits and songs primarily by blackface minstrels, burlesquers, and variety performers focused on cultural and political events that specifically connected the United States to China, without Europe as an intermediary. These were less celebratory and often supported more negative attitudes about China, which would later become pervasive. This is especially true of characters' names, which became caricatures of the Chinese language and sounded more like gibberish than a form of speech. By 1854, even the Ravels themselves had changed almost all the characters' names in *Kimka,* except for the title character, so that they mimicked the Chinese language or were indicators of certain traits, such as Bang-Wang-ski-hui-fon-fom-tor-touf, Has-sam-flam-dram, Ding-dong-chow-row-crac-wac, and Pretti-Bu-Bu-ru-show.[67] The most obvious examples, however, were parodies of Chinese acts by white performers. Blackface minstrels and variety performers used the instant recognition of these Chinese acts, many of which were billed as human curiosities, to create send-ups that audiences would clearly know and understand. In part, American performers tried to benefit from the celebrity and instant recognition of Chinese acts. These caricatures, however, were also tied to the growing belief in Chinese inferiority, augmented by political and economic tensions, the association of human curiosities with deviance, and, later, anxieties over Chinese immigration.

Arguably the most recognizable Chinese act during the nineteenth century was that of the Siamese Twins or Chang (Chun) and Eng (In) Bunker. Although they were born in Siam and called Siamese, their parents were mostly Chinese (their mother was half Chinese and half Malaysian) and were part of the movement of Chinese peoples throughout Southeast Asia since the fourteenth century.[68] On stage, the Bunkers did various things: they performed acrobatics and monologues, they even allowed doctors to inspect where they were attached—all of which were fair game in the American popular theater of the time. Perhaps the physicality of being attached to another person was the core humor in parodies of the Bunkers. These types of send-ups, however, were not without their dangers. In a journal kept by a member of the Julian Serenaders during their New England tour, the anonymous author wrote about a mishap involving two members of the troupe: "Concert went off in good shape barring an accident which happened to the siamese twins which prevented their performing more than the first part of their Solo."[69] Regardless of this accident, the intent of such acts was clear: for American audiences and performers there was something odd about the Bunkers that spoke not only about conjoined twins but also about race.

Americans parodied other Chinese acts during the mid-nineteenth century, although not with as much frequency as they parodied the Bunkers. After the Chinese junk named *Keying* and its crew were anchored in New York harbor near Niblo's Garden in 1847, W. K. Northall put together the *Chinese Junk Extravaganza.* This production, however, was more a criticism of

P. T. Barnum's "humbug" than a parody of the Chinese sailors and their boat.[70] The first Chinese acrobatic and magic troupe to appear in New York City in 1853 was a source of burlesque for the Woods Minstrels, another blackface minstrel troupe, who pretended to perform similar acrobatic tricks but without the use of their legs below the knees.[71] Finally, when P. T. Barnum brought Chang Yu-Shing, the Chinese Giant, to the United States in 1869, he too became a topic of comedy, most likely because he was, like the Bunkers, physically different and foreign. While touring New York and Ohio in 1870, the Arlington Minstrels created "a Chinese Giant Burlesque" that "was *short* and raised a laugh."[72]

Along the eastern seaboard of the United States, American composers and performers during the first half of the nineteenth century turned to Europe when they wanted to use China as a musical subject. Often, they republished, reworked, or simply revived European compositions and productions. There were, however, a few who wrote their own works, some of which were similar to those from Europe and others that were based on Chinese–American relations. As the century progressed, this latter development would become much more pervasive and would lead to much more derogatory stereotypes.

WESTERN AUTHORS AND MUSICIANS, the majority of whom wrote before the arrival of Chinese immigrants in the Far West, created the ideological framework from which future cultural productions in the United States would be based. Visitors to China became the authorities on Chinese cultural practices and informed readers at home about how to perceive Chinese music and theater. In contrast, European and American songwriters borrowed from chinoiserie and highlighted aspects of Chinese life that they saw as appealing. Most importantly, however, the stereotypes generated by both groups, while seemingly moving in opposite directions, pointed toward notions of difference that could be seen as either cultural or racial.

American and European writers did not describe Chinese music simply in racist terms but generated a number of signifiers to denote what they perceived to be un-musical about it. Sometimes, Chinese music was devoid of anything related to humanity—such as sounds from animals. Most implicit, however, were issues faced later and mainly by composers about whether Chinese music was similar to particular moments in Western history, related to musical traditions from Europe's margins, or existed as a culturally and racially unique phenomenon. These attitudes once again played on conceptions of Western sophistication and refinement, but they also had deeper implications that would develop by the end of the nineteenth century.

There were a few exceptions in which less racist ways of understanding the Chinese and their music appeared. These interpretations helped to undermine the more pervasive construction of Chinese music as noise and also provided the beginnings of a less racist vocabulary. More importantly, the hymn singing of Chinese converts demonstrated to Westerners that despite their supposed depravity, the Chinese could be uplifted, especially their children. This, too, had repercussions that both Chinese and Chinese Americans would later exploit.

At the same time, as Western writers were commenting on Chinese music making, American composers and performers turned to their European counterparts for inspiration, often recycling a set number of plotlines—*Aladdin, Kimka,* and *Ba-Ta-Clan*—which used China as an imaginary space for fantastical stories. Most productions represented China through magnificence, extravagance, and whimsy, with little emphasis on individual characters or hostility toward the Chinese people. Later, they also interpolated discussions of Chinese–American diplomatic relations and the appearance of Chinese human curiosities, which supported a more derisive undercurrent that was developing in the United States. It was not until 1870, however, when the effects of Chinese immigration became a subject of national debate on the stage, that there was a significant change in the musical landscape and a clear break from European traditions.

Also during this period, most composers chose not to use Chinese melodies, which were first transcribed into Western musical notation during the eighteenth century, or instrumentation. Thus, despite the exoticism found in other aspects of performance, the Chinese were undifferentiated musically from Europeans. This musical image of China confounded descriptions from writers, who portrayed the Chinese as musically unsophisticated and inferior. By the end of the nineteenth century, this too changed dramatically.

Although writers and composers described China in a set number of ways, the majority emphasized that there was something that separated "us" from "them." Ideas about Chinese cultural development and musical ability became more entrenched, particularly with the rise of "experts" who used scientific reasoning to perpetuate racism. The depiction of the Chinese musically also changed by the end of the century, with songwriters finally applying Chinese musical tokens to their compositions in order to create a more totalizing sense of difference. Chinese and Chinese Americans, however, challenged these stereotypes and undermined race-based notions of music ability and cultural development. Before these events happened, Americans turned to music as a way to express their anxieties about China, especially Chinese immigration.

CHAPTER 2

Toward Exclusion

AMERICAN POPULAR SONGS ON CHINESE IMMIGRATION, 1850–1882

THE DISCOVERY OF GOLD IN 1849 sparked a tremendous worldwide wave of migration to California that included numerous songwriters and performers. Some came as part of the Gold Rush but found music to be more profitable than mining. Others saw an opportunity among the mining camps and growing cities and came as part of professional minstrel troupes from major East Coast cities. There were a few talented individuals who wrote music in their spare time, which they later published. Chinese immigrants, attracted by many of these same opportunities, began arriving in California in substantial numbers. This historic convergence of people marked an important point of contact between Chinese immigrants, miners, and musicians, all of whom struggled to understand one another and the unique circumstances in which they found themselves. To appeal to California audiences, composers and performers tried to translate the hopes and anxieties of miners into music. They sang about the hardships faced in the gold fields, local politics, and interactions among the many people who came to California. What emerged was a music that fundamentally re-imagined the Chinese in that it departed from the tradition of at least a century of European exoticism and novelty, and treated the Chinese as an immigrant group in the United States.

Before the form evolved into a four-person minstrelsy troupe, blackface, the practice of caricaturing African Americans, had started during the 1830s with performers such as George Washington Dixon and Thomas "Daddy" Rice. Both Dixon's Zip Coon and Rice's Jim Crow were characters who contributed to stereotypes of African American men and addressed the anxieties of the emerging white working classes. Jim Crow was a happy slave who danced, sang, and enjoyed life on the plantation. By staying in his place (in the South and on a plantation), he was not a threat to anyone, especially white workers in the North. On the other hand, Zip Coon was a free black living in a northern city, a dandy who failed miserably at putting on airs and acting sophisticated. This caricature ridiculed groups up and down the social ladder, mocking powerful community elites as well as African Americans. Over the next few decades, blackface's repertoire of characters expanded in response to social and political movements—suffrage, abolition, and immigration, especially by the Germans and Irish—so that the possibility that blackface could include Chinese immigrants was in place by the 1850s.[1]

In California, with the growing numbers of Chinese during the 1850s and 1860s and the resultant tensions and conflicts, songwriters began to use these immigrants as musical subjects. Performers, influenced by blackface minstrelsy, were well aware of the lyrical and musical devices as well as those of gesture, costuming, and makeup that could be used to mark Chinese immigrants as inferior. Yellowed-up actors became the norm on the stage, limiting the theatrical opportunities for the Chinese in much the same way that blackface excluded African Americans until the 1870s. Their songs, with some exceptions, helped to define and circulate anti-Chinese sentiments throughout the Far West. Following the common practice of the day, songwriters tended to develop new lyrics for well-known popular melodies, most notably from blackface minstrelsy itself, rather than create new musical works. These melodies could easily be reworked and would be well known to audiences. Although the trajectory of attitudes was unclear during the Gold Rush, songs about the Chinese helped to codify stereotypes and expressed fears that led ultimately to exclusionary legislation.[2]

By 1870, these songs from California had circulated throughout the United States, growing from a regional phenomenon into part of a national response to Chinese immigrants. Music was not the only forum that dealt with Chinese immigration but was part of a broader spectrum of media that addressed the issue. Only a small proportion of the Chinese population lived east of the Rocky Mountains, yet they became a potent national political symbol, helping to define the boundaries of American identity and to symbolize the distinctiveness of the Far West. Savvy politicians eagerly exploited anti-Chinese sentiments to shore up support from labor organizations and Western voters. By making a scapegoat of the Chinese, they supposedly helped to resolve labor problems without legislating against factory owners and other capitalists.[3]

Anti-Chinese sentiments were also part of a broader process of creating and defining national identity and settling questions about citizenship during the nineteenth century. Like African Americans and Native Americans, the Chinese were seen by whites as unassimilable; however, unlike other groups, these immigrants were small enough in number that it was possible to imagine keeping them out and seeing those already here vanish in a generation. The qualities that made the Chinese supposedly unassimilable were used to justify the passage of laws that limited their ability to enter and settle in the United States. California's 1852 Miner's Tax began this process, establishing legal precedents in support of anti-Chinese legislation in the Far West. Other laws soon followed that affected such social practices as marriage, education, and property ownership. The lack of acceptance of the Chinese and fears about their influence on the labor market eventually led to passage of the Chinese Exclusion Act in 1882, which banned all Chinese immigrant laborers from entering the country.[4] It was not completely overturned until the passage of the Naturalization and Immigration Act of 1965, which finally allowed for a substantial number of Chinese to enter and settle in the United States.

Songs about the Chinese, first written in California and then produced and performed elsewhere, were one of the many strands that delineated national identity during the latter part of the nineteenth century. Performers and songwriters, consciously or otherwise, helped circulate particular ideas about the Chinese as an unassimilable, inferior race. These songs and performances justified discriminatory practices in legislation and daily interactions. Although the relationship between anti-Chinese legislation and music is one seen in hindsight, it demonstrates that performance was also a venue for addressing the complexity of attitudes toward race and nationality, and their circulation within American popular culture from the 1850s through the mid-1880s.

THE CREATION OF JOHN CHINAMAN

Musical performances from California of the 1850s and 1860s dealt with Chinese immigrants, commonly subsumed in the figure of John Chinaman, in a multitude of ways. This figure functioned much in the same way as did Zip Coon or Jim Crow, and he became a common image of Chinese immigrant men that played on differences such as religious practices, eating habits, and English proficiency. The largest number of songs used the John Chinaman stereotype to focus on the differences between American and Chinese men, and assumed that the latter did not belong (and that Chinese women, who were so few in number, did not matter). Despite acknowledging the efforts of some Chinese to acculturate, these songs depicted them as fundamentally foreign, thus denying them any prospect of becoming American. A few songwriters presented the Chinese as just another immigrant group participating in the Gold Rush, or mentioned them in passing and in a relatively neutral manner. These songs, like those discussed in chapter 1, used Chinese subjects to entertain or to criticize other issues in California. Only in one instance were the subjects treated positively.

A handful of songs from the 1850s depicted the Chinese as part of the worldwide mass movement of people who traveled to California to strike it rich. There is a sense in these songs that the hardships and experiences in California were universal, transcending divisions based on racial and national lines. In "California Bank Robbers" (1858), John A. Stone sang about the

California banking system robbing all sorts of people—Frenchmen, African Americans, merchants, women, and so forth.[5] Stone, otherwise known as Old Put, was a successful gold miner who later sang and performed in saloons and camps throughout the Far West with his troupe the Sierra Nevada Rangers. While using music to reflect the experiences of miners in California, Stone also relied heavily on blackface minstrelsy for inspiration.[6] This particular song was sung to the tune of "Jordan Is a Hard Road to Travel" (1853), a song attributed to the famous blackface minstrel Dan Emmett, and was consistent with Stone's practice of borrowing his melodies from well-known blackface minstrel pieces of the 1840s and 1850s. In fact, San Francisco's *Daily Herald* reported that Christy's Minstrels had performed "Jordan Is a Hard Road to Travel" in November 1854, which is perhaps when Stone had first heard this song.[7] Using a familiar air was a common way to cut publishing costs because it was more expensive to print musical notation than text; this probably also ensured that his audiences had heard the tunes before and therefore could focus instead on the lyrics. The following verse described the banking system's treatment of the blind and the Chinese:

> The blind man said to the bankers,
> "I'm poor—
> Surely, man, you don't intend to rob me!"
> The Chinaman said, as they kicked him out the door,
> "Me no shabee, John me no shabee."

Although in most of his other songs Stone treated the Chinese much more harshly, here he portrayed them as victims of banks that were willing to take advantage of the blind and the unsophisticated Chinese. What is also interesting about this verse is Stone's use of Chinese dialect, a common device used to ridicule Chinese immigrants and their inability to speak English competently. The term "shabee," however, was derived from the Spanish verb *saber* meaning "to know" or "to understand." This doubling of pidgin English with Spanish demonstrated the complex notions of difference in the Far West and the fluidity of prejudice from one despised minority to another.

Unlike any other song produced about Chinese immigrants during this period, "John Chinaman's Appeal" (1856), written and sung by Mart Taylor, openly criticized American treatment of Chinese immigrants. Taylor, who was originally from Virginia, toured the Far West from the early 1850s until his death in 1894. Unlike other songwriter/performers, he insisted that music be genteel and sentimental, a force of uplift for his mining audience. Clearly, he was not promoting European art songs and opera in the camps but rather his own musical interpretation of life in California, which was also much more inclusive.[8] The tune for "John Chinaman's Appeal" was borrowed from a blackface minstrel song "Umbrella Courtship" (1840s) and, as it turns out, was based on a popular Revolutionary War and War of 1812 tune, "Yankee Volunteer" (n.d.).[9] The lyrics of "John Chinaman's Appeal" were based on William Cowper's poem about Great Britain's involvement in the eighteenth-century slave trade—"A Negro's Complaint" (1788). In the 1840s, Free-Soilers reworked "A Negro's Complaint" into "A Negro's Appeal" (1848) and put it to music.[10] "John Chinaman's Appeal," similar to its antecedents, was in the voice of a Chinese immigrant, Gee Sing, who relays the story of his mistreatment in California.

JOHN CHINAMAN'S APPEAL

Verse 1: American, now mind my song
    If you would but hear *me* sing,
    And I will tell you of the wrong
    That happened unto "Gee Sing."
    In "fifty-two" I left my home—
    I big farewell "Hong Kong"—
    I started with Cup Gee to roam
    To the land where they use the "long tom."
Chorus: O ching hi ku tong mo ching ching,
    O ching hi ku tong *chi* do,
    Cup Gee hi ku tong mo ching ching,
    Then what could Gee or I do?
Verse 2: In forty days I reached the Bay,
    And nearly starved I was, sir.
    I cooked and ate a dog one day—
    I didn't know the laws, sir
    But soon I found my dainty meal
    Was against the city order.
    The penalty I had to feel—
    Confound the old Recorder
Verse 3: By paying up my cost and fines,
    They freed me from the locker,
    And then I started for the mines—
    I got a pick and rocker.
    I went to work in an untouched place—
    I'm sure I meant no blame, sir—
    But a white man struck me in the face
    And told me to leave his claim, sir.
Verse 4: 'Twas then I packed my tools away
    And set up in a new place,
    But there they would not let me stay—
    They didn't like the *cue* race.

And then I knew not what to do,
I could not get employ.
The Know Nothings would bid me go—
'Twas *tu nah mug ahoy.*
Verse 5: I started then for Weaverville
Where Chinamen were thriving,
But found our China agents there
In ancient feuds were driving.
So I pitched into politics,
But with the weaker party;
The Canton's with their clubs and bricks
Did drub us out "right hearty."
Verse 6: I started for Yreka then;
I thought that I would stay there,
But Found for even Chinamen
The "diggings" wouldn't pay there.
So I set up a washing shop,
But how extremely funny,
The miners all had dirty clothes,
But not a cent of money.
Verse 7: I met a big stout Indian once.
He stopped me in the trail, sir.
He drew an awful scalping knife,
And I trembled for my tails, sir.
He caught me by the hair, it's true,
In a manner quite uncivil,
But when he saw my awful cue,
He thought I was the devil.
Verse 8: Oh, now, my friends, I'm going away
From this infernal place, sir;
The balance of my days I'll stay
With the Celestial race, sir.
I'll go to raising rice and tea;
I'll be a heathen ever,
For Christians all have treated me
As men should be used never.

The laundry business was considered to be a typical occupation for Chinese immigrant men, but not because of their work experiences in their homeland. Owning a laundry was popular because it was not a form of work that American men were unwilling to perform. The fact that American miners refused to pay Gee Sing for his services was also a reflection of the contempt many had toward the Chinese and the difficulties miners faced in earning enough money to pay for their expenses. The pulling or cutting of the Chinese worker's queue and the supposed eating of domesticated animals by the Chinese frequently appeared as devices to symbolize Chinese foreignness, but here they point out the problems Chinese immigrants faced on the frontier. In the last two lines, Taylor openly condemns Americans as un-Christian in their treatment of the Chinese. Even if the Chinese were foreign or inferior, Taylor seemed to believe that Americans should not mistreat them.[11]

Aside from these examples and a handful of others, California songwriters most often used their music to emphasize supposed differences between Americans and Chinese immigrants and to promote a desire among whites that Chinese laborers leave the United States. The anonymously authored "John Chinaman" claimed that white Californians initially welcomed the Chinese but were reconsidering their opinion of them by the time this song appeared in 1855.[12]

JOHN CHINAMAN

Verse 1: John Chinaman, John Chinaman,
  But five short years ago,
  I welcomed you from Canton, John—
Verse 2: But wish I hadn't though;
  For then you honest, John,
  Not dreaming you'd make
  A citizen as useful, John,
  As any in the state.
Verse 3: I thought you'd open wide your ports
  And let our merchants in
  To barter for their crepes and teas,
  Their wares of wood and tin.
Verse 4: I thought you'd cut your queue off, John,
  And don a Yankee coat,
  And a collar high you'd raise, John,
  Around your dusky throat.
Verse 5: I imagined that the truth, John,
  You'd speak when under oath,
  But I find you'll lie and steal too—
  Yes, John, you're up to both.
Verse 6: I thought of rats and puppies, John,
  You'd eaten your last fill:
  But on such slimy pot-pies, John,
  I'm told you dinner still.

Verse 7: Oh, John, I've been deceived in you,
    And in all your thieving clan,
    For our gold is all you're after, John,
    To get it as you can.

Each stanza is an example of the ways the songwriter believed the Chinese could have become Americanized: by allowing free trade in Chinese ports, cutting off of their queues, and wearing Western clothing. The lyrics also list reasons why many began to believe that the Chinese were not only un-American but also inferior. "John Chinaman" ends with the narrator blaming Chinese greed and deceit for why the Chinese had not Americanized.

Stone's "Josh, John" (1854) goes further in questioning the desire of Chinese immigrants to assimilate.[13] Once again, the stanzas list the changes the immigrants had undergone, such as cutting their hair, giving up their traditional clothes, and living so far from all that was familiar to them. The term "Josh" in this song and its title is a double entendre in that it is not only a form of exclamation and a type of teasing or deceiving someone; it also highlights the un-Christian ways of the Chinese by playing on the word *josh* or *joss*, a nineteenth-century term used to describe Chinese religious statues.[14] The final verse summed up all that the Chinese have experienced:

You've left your national god, John,
You've left your god and your land
You've left the dress of the land of flowers,
And in leaving these, haven't taken ours;
And you've friends upon neither hand, John,
You have friends upon neither hand.

"Josh, John" placed Chinese immigrants somewhere in limbo between the United States and China, belonging to neither culture.

The supposed femininity of Chinese men and the threat of miscegenation also appeared in one song from this period. "John Chinaman's Marriage" (1868), most likely written by a San Francisco songwriter and an Irish impersonator, J. W. Conner, was written as a comical story about a woman named Cock-eyed Fan who duped a Chinese immigrant, Ching Chong. Ching Chong, after successfully finding gold, decided that he wanted to marry and settle down in San Francisco.[15] American women, however, were not interested in him, for reasons not fully explained except that he was unable to speak English well. Eventually, he meets Cock-eyed Fan, who, although not attractive, was willing to marry him. Fan's name was ambiguous as to her ethnic background, but her hair color, "carroty," and behavior were similar to those in depictions of working-class Irish immigrant women. Fan abused her husband, drank heavily, condemned the eating of rice, and eventually ran away, returning to Hangtown, the nickname for Placerville, California, which was infamous in the 1850s for a series of lynchings and general unlawfulness.[16] Ching Chong was a somewhat sympathetic character in his predicament and can be perceived as trying to become as Americanized as possible. Yet, as in several other anti-Chinese songs from the 1870s and early 1880s, Chong's inability to control his wife or money was a way to question Chinese masculinity and, by extension, their ability to become American citizens.

Songwriters and performers in California during the 1850s and 1860s were the first to exploit the John Chinaman character in song and on the stage. Blackface minstrelsy had greatly influenced these artists, and they turned to this tradition and its denigration of African Americans and European immigrants for inspiration, sometimes even borrowing songs directly from it. The John Chinaman stereotype was also similar to images found in other forms of media that exaggerated the foreignness of Chinese immigrants and highlighted the reasons why the Chinese did not belong in the United States. As with politicians, labor organizers, and missionaries, those involved in music making did not necessarily agree on the appropriate social position (if any) for the Chinese. Nevertheless, the images generated by them were a resource for performers and musicians outside the Far West who were also concerned about Chinese immigrants during the 1870s and early 1880s.

BRET HARTE'S "HEATHEN CHINEE"

Although California songs about Chinese immigrants appear to have traveled eastward as Forty-Niners and theatrical troupes returned home, it took two decades for similar songs to be produced nationally on a consistent basis. For the most part, until 1870 the only other sources of music about the Chinese available to East Coast audiences were exotic pieces from European composers or a scattering of novelty songs such as those about the appearance of human curiosities. The movement of Chinese laborers eastward after the completion of the Transcontinental Railroad in 1869 and the success of Bret Harte's poem popularly known as "Heathen Chinee" provided the impetus for songwriters and performers east of the Rocky Mountains to write skits, songs, and musical plays about Chinese immigration.[17] These productions relied heavily on stereotypical notions of race, gender, and nationality to question the place of the Chinese in the United States. Although there were a few songwriters who treated the Chinese in an ambivalent manner, the majority, like their California predecessors, used their music to highlight the un-American qualities of the Chinese. No fundamental change would come until after the mid-1880s.

Songwriters and performers who wrote post–Civil War music about the Chinese were found throughout the United States, although most lived in New York City. They enjoyed varying levels of success in blackface minstrelsy and the growing musical forms of variety, vaudeville, and musical theater. Several associated themselves with Irish immigrants and the white working classes who were strongly against Chinese immigration. There were, however, actors who were not of Irish descent, such as Tony Pastor (Italian American) and Ackland Von Boyle (German American), who performed anti-Chinese numbers. They were also aware of and catered to the large number of Irish Americans and working-class men who attended their shows.

Like California songs, these later ones were still conventional in musical form and lyrical content. Not all of the songsters from the 1870s and 1880s contained musical accompaniment or listed the tune to which a piece was performed, making musical analysis difficult. From what can be gleaned from those with musical notation, most of these songs were similar to other pieces performed in variety and minstrelsy that dealt with race and ethnicity. Songwriters after 1870 often wrote their own melodies and did not borrow tunes from earlier, well-known blackface minstrel pieces. This shift perhaps marked the realization of a potentially more diverse national audience that was not as familiar with blackface melodies, a growing acquaintance with Chinese music among both songwriters and audiences, or a decrease in the cost to print musical notation.

A few of these songwriters also used musical notation and instrumentation to solidify notions of Chinese otherness. This music was not an imitation of Chinese music but rather musical representations of difference well known to European art composers and blackface minstrels. Furthermore, although a handful of transcriptions of Chinese music were available (such as "Moo-Lee-Chwa"), popular songwriters did not attempt to incorporate them into their compositions until later in their century. The appearance of such songs was part of the evolution from California songs, which relied solely on the coupling of anti-Chinese lyrics with well-known blackface minstrelsy melodies, to songs that conveyed a sense of distinction between Americans and Chinese immigrants through particular sonic qualities.

Although Chinese immigration had become a national issue by the latter part of the 1860s, it was the publication in September 1870 and the success of Bret Harte's poem "Plain Language of Truthful James" ("Heathen Chinee") that were the catalysts for anti-Chinese songs throughout the United States. Harte intended that his poem show similarities between Americans and Chinese immigrants in the Far West as they both cheated at cards.[18] "Heathen Chinee," however, immediately created a powerful, negative image of Chinese immigrants that dominated the national consciousness. Songwriters and performers helped to perpetuate these stereotypes by performing them on the stage. At least three song versions published with musical notation appeared between 1870 and 1871. Many other songwriters also used the phrase "Heathen Chinee" or "Heathen Chinese" in their titles, but with little or no reference to Bret Harte's poem within the text.[19]

For example, three composers used Harte's "Heathen Chinee" as lyrics.[20] Henry Tucker's "Heathen Chinee" (1871) was quite simple, with only three chords. F. Boote's and Charles Towner's versions had completely different sonic qualities, using both musical notation and instrumentation to denote Chinese difference (see ill. 3). Both were written in minor keys, G and F minor respectively, which gave the lyrics a more ominous and eerie sound. Boote's "Heathen Chinee" (1870) even included diminished chords and a little syncopation, similar to devices found in Orientalist art music or black-face minstrelsy. Along with adding his own words in the form of a chorus to affirm the moral turpitude of Ah Sin, Towner, in his version of "Heathen Chinee" (1870), included orientalized sounds through the use of repeated notes in the bass clef and a recommendation that performers use a gong and a trumpet during the introduction (also note the illustration of Chinese musicians driving away American passersby at the top of the page). Towner's and Boote's versions of "Heathen Chinee," in comparison to other songs from the 1870s and 1880s with accompaniment, were exceptional. Although the lyrics shared some of the stereotypes found in other songs, the accompaniment pointed to musical shifts in the depiction of Chinese topics by using orientalized sounds.

In 1870, Bret Harte's "Heathen Chinee" helped bring debates about Chinese immigration into the national spotlight. Musical versions of "Heathen Chinee" were also among the first attempts to relate Chinese immigrants with the "Orientalist" music tradition. Throughout the next decade, performers and songwriters again and again turned to "Heathen Chinee" along with earlier songs and productions from California for inspiration.

YELLOWFACE

Unlike the majority of songs about Chinese immigration produced in California before 1870, in which the singer portrayed a character who was understood to be both white and of American stock, most pieces sung after 1870 included Chinese impersonations, known in the twentieth century as yellowface. Like blackface, yellowface became a way for performers to comment—in this case on Chinese immigrant inferiority—by inscribing stereotypes onto the performer's body.[21] These actors usually wore a navy blue or black tunic with loose fitting pants, attire that was common among laborers from southern China and known as a *shan ku* (or in Cantonese, *sam fu*). This image of Chinese immigrants as lower class was a shift from earlier depictions of the Chinese as educated, sophisticated "Mandarins" (although some were shown to be greedy, conniving, and feminine) who wore brightly colored and embroidered silk robes. Queues and makeup to sallow the skin and slant the eyes were also popular. Although European and American performers had produced Chinese characters since the late seventeenth century as part

THE HEATHEN CHINEE.

OVERTURE.

Words by BRET HARTE.

Music by CHARLES TOWNER.

Ill. 3. Charles Towner and Bret Harte's "The Heathen Chinee" (1870). Courtesy of the Lester S. Levy Collection of Sheet Music, Special Collections, Johns Hopkins University.

of the older counterdiscourse that used China as a fantasy world and alternative to Western life, this practice was virtually gone by the 1870s.

The most common device for distinguishing between Chinese and Americans on the stage was a combination of pidgin English and gibberish. Americans in California and abroad in China often commented on the accent of Chinese English-speakers. Martha Noyes Williams recalled that the Chinese spoke in "English baby-talk."[22] Dialect was not new to the American stage but was similarly found in the impersonations of African Americans, Irish and German immigrants, and other stock characters, such as the Yankee and the Southern Gentleman. At times, certain dialects were indistinguishable. The chorus of Frank Curtis's "The Artful Chinee" (1870s) was similar to that in the blackface minstrelsy song "Ching a Ring Chaw; or, Sambo's 'Dress to He' Bred'rin" (ca. 1833), which Eric Lott in *Love and Theft* points out was an exaggerated West Indian dialect.[23]

THE ARTFUL CHINEE

Chingaring chi, and chingaring chee,
Chingaring chi for the young Chinee.

CHING A RING CHAW

Chinger ringer, ring ching, ching
Ho ah, Dinah ding kom darkee,
Chinger ringer, ring ching chaw,
Ho ah ding cum darkey.

Pidgin English in "The Artful Chinee" was supposed to distinguish the Chinese, but by borrowing from "Ching a Ring Chaw," the author lumped them together with African Americans. In general, the use of dialects marked a group of people as unassimilated, or as unassimilable, and therefore they did not speak English properly. Nonsensical gibberish, which was common in blackface minstrelsy and in nursery songs for children, was another device used to demonstrate the inferiority of Chinese immigrants and their inability to speak English coherently.

In spite of songs like "The Artful Chinee," which conflated signifiers of racial inferiority, performers usually tried to distinguish Chinese dialect. Americans living in California sometimes commented on the distinctive ways in which Chinese immigrants spoke English. George McKinley Murrell, a gold prospector in El Dorado, California, noted in an 1851 letter to his sister Eliza that the Chinese mispronounced certain letters in English. "There are several letters of the English Alphabet that they [the Chinese] cannot pronounce at all. Among them the letter R is conspicuous which they invariably pronounce L."[24] Almost two decades later, Ackland Von Boyle in "What!

Never?" (1879) told fellow performers about the particulars of Chinese dialect. "The Chinese in attempting to speak english 'hardly ever' fail to use 'L' for 'R.' "[25] John "Chinee" Leach's "Chun Wow Low" (1882) included the same devices put forth by Von Boyle and even added nonsensical words to make it similar to what many Americans believed Chinese sounded like.[26]

> Chun wow low, eatum chow, chow,
> Chinaman a walla good likum bow wow;
> Litta Dog, litta cat, litta mouse, litta lat.
> Alla wella good for to makum me fat.

The prevalence of "bow," "wow," and "chow," although making little or no sense, associated the Chinese with dogs and eating, both of which were called "chow" in the 1870s. "Chow" also alluded to the common belief that Chinese immigrants ate dogs (as well as cats, mice, and rats).[27]

A few instances of yellowface impersonation can be found before 1870. Charley Backus's Chinese laundryman skit, produced first in California in 1854 and then in New York City, seems to be the first American impersonation of a Chinese immigrant.[28] The melodrama *Fast Folks; or, The Early Days of California* (1858), first produced in San Francisco and then three years later in Philadelphia, included a small part for a Chinese immigrant character, Gee Ho. Besides providing a comic element, Gee Ho recalled the decision of *People v. Hall* (1854), which forbade Chinese immigrants from testifying in court because they were not able to become citizens. In *Fast Folks,* Gee Ho identifies the person who "salt[ed] the claim," but others in the courtroom challenge his statement because of his nation of origin.[29]

It was not until 1870, however, that a number of plays included roles based on Chinese immigrants. As in *Fast Folks,* these were small, comedic parts, but for some actors, most notably Charles T. Parsloe Jr., such roles became the hallmark of their careers. Most of these plays were set in California or the Far West, an indication that Chinese characters were still integral to the portrayal of that region to the rest of the nation. Starting with James C. McCloskey's *Across the Continent; or, Scenes from New York Life on the Pacific R.R.* (1870), there were at least thirteen plays with small Chinese immigrant roles from 1870 through 1882. Several of these were quite successful and toured the United States for several years, especially *Danites; or, The Heart of the Sierras* (1878), *The Chinese Question* (1878), *My Partner* (1879), and *Gentleman from Nevada* (1880).[30]

Variety and minstrel performers also produced Chinese caricatures after the success of Bret Harte's "Heathen Chinee." Theater columns noted several performers who staged Chinese skits or songs during the 1870s and early 1880s. Edward Harrigan and Josh Hart, accomplished actors in variety and musical theater, produced a "Heathen Chinee" skit in Chicago at the West

Side Opera House; Annie Yeamans, who eventually performed with Harrigan and Hart, was also listed as one of the few women to give a "Chinese Performance." Lydia Thompson and Company (who had also burlesqued "Aladdin") reenacted "The Great Heathen Chinee Card Game" (1871) at the Boston Theatre with Harry Beckett and Willie Edouin. The skit "Chinese Invasion" (1874), with Maggie Moore and J. C. Williamson, was a precursor to their roles in *The Chinese Question* (1878). "Chinese Shoemaker" (1874) at the Metropolitan Theater in New York City addressed the importation of Chinese laborers to work in a shoe factory in North Adams, Massachusetts, in 1872. Finally, Joseph Murphy, an Irish character actor, left the cast of *Kerry Gow* (1876) for a week in July 1879 and delved into Chinese impersonation at the California Theater in San Francisco (see ill. 4).[31]

Two actors, John "Chinee" Leach and Ackland Von Boyle, tried to make careers out of performing Chinese impersonations on the variety stage. Their success was somewhat limited, although Leach had the much longer career of the two. Von Boyle first appeared in variety in 1879, and followed up by portraying similar characters in the play *Our Coming Candidate* (1878) and the one-act *Our Coming Citizen* (1879) (see ill. 5). A year after his debut, he disappeared

Ill. 4. Backus Minstrels playbill, California Theater, San Francisco. Courtesy of the Harvard Theatre Collection, Houghton Library.

ACLAND VON BOYLE.

Ill. 5. Portrait of Ackland Von Boyle from the *New York Dramatic Mirror*, January 31, 1880. Courtesy of the Library of Congress.

from variety altogether, only to reappear as a lecturer on comedy at New York area churches and church-affiliated organizations from 1880 through 1885.[32]

Leach first appeared as a Chinese impersonator in the fall of 1876 in San Francisco. Later, in 1878, he toured the United States in such skits as "Chinese and Irish Specialties" (1878), "Ireland-vs.-China; or, Ching Wang's Laundry" (1879), "The Chinese Must Go" (1879), "Trouble in a Chinese Washhouse" (1880), and "Sam Lee's Washhouse" (1880). After the passage of the Chinese Exclusion Act, Leach continued his Chinese caricatures in skits such as "Modernized Chinaman" (1883), "The Everyday Chinaman" (1884), and "The Chinese Wash-House" (1884), and revivals of several plays and musicals, including *One Hundred Wives* (1880), *Pearl of Pekin* (1888), and *Our Flat* (1889). Leach continued touring into the twentieth century, telling funny stories to audiences in combination with ethnic impersonations; he also appeared in two silent films—an unknown role in *Dorian's Divorce* (1916) and Wing Lee in *My Partner* (1916), which was a remake of the 1879 play.[33]

Variety and the legitimate stage allowed several actors and actresses to travel throughout the country performing Chinese immigrant caricatures for audiences, many of whom had limited contact or had never seen someone from China before. Critics and actors constantly emphasized the authenticity of these performances, which did not necessarily mean that the impersonations were true to life but that actors had a certain amount of authority to represent the Chinese. The constant concern with what was realistic about these performances, however, underlined the anxiety about believability. Reviewers, who probably knew no alternative, frequently commented on Leach's and Von Boyle's realistic portrayals. What was especially important to Von Boyle's performances was his makeup. Newspaper quotes from an advertisement for his act noted that "Mr. Von Boyle's looks and actions are those of the veritable John [Chinaman]." Another such quote from the *Brooklyn Times* stated, "Mr. Von Boyle must be complimented on his make-up. He is by far the best stage Chinaman we have seen."[34] Leach received similar praise for his authenticity, even from those who had contact with Chinese immigrants. Several critics stated that his skill was tied to his study of Cantonese and his experiences among Chinese immigrants in San Francisco. In the article "Leach as Chinaman," an unnamed journalist noted that Leach had grown up in San Francisco, where he "studied the Chinese language" and "acquired their characteristics and peculiarities of speech and manner," making him "unquestionably the best impersonator of a Chinaman on the American stage."[35] Praise for Leach was not universal. A critic from the *Columbus Citizen* in Ohio complained that Leach's caricature was unlike any "Chink ever seen in this vicinity." Nevertheless, he was still "a hit with the audience."[36]

During the late 1870s, several reviewers believed that Leach's impersonations endorsed exclusionary legislation. In his skits, Leach addressed the debate surrounding Chinese immigration specifically. One critic for the *San Francisco Call* wrote that Leach presented the "Kearney Question" in a "good natured" fashion.[37] Ironically, Leach had actually addressed Chinese exclusion through the eyes of a Chinese immigrant man. The subversive possibilities of mixing a discussion on exclusion with Chinese impersonation, however, eluded this reviewer and most likely Leach's audiences. Perhaps, as noted in the *Territorial Enterprise* of Virginia City, Nevada, this was because at the end of the act, Leach's Chinese character was beaten up.[38] A writer in Boston, while admitting his lack of contact with Chinese immigrants, stated that Leach's performance converted the whole audience to support legislative restrictions. "If the Chinese are but half so bad as John C. Leach's imitations of them proved to be, then every Howard [Athenaeum] patron is a confirmed Kearneyite."[39] The terms "Kearney Question" and "Kearneyite" came from the name of a San Francisco labor organizer, Denis Kearney, who applied political pressure on local, state, and federal governments during the 1870s and 1880s to protect white working-class jobs from competing Chinese immigrant labor and to prevent Chinese laborers from entering the United States.

During the second half of the nineteenth century, yellowface developed as a specific response to contact with Chinese immigrants. It was related to blackface in that both used similar devices to parody African Americans and immigrant groups. Chinese characters had appeared on the stage during previous centuries, but they had not necessarily been seen as authentic, and, for the most part, they had had a far less insidious intent than characterizations of Chinese immigrants by the 1870s. Beginning with caricatures of Chinese immigrants as early as 1854, yellowface impersonations were a crucial way of circulating ideas of difference and inferiority, all of which supported anti-Chinese attitudes.

"PECULIAR" CULTURAL PRACTICES AND CHINESE EXCLUSION

Yellowface impersonations and songs about Chinese immigrants worked in several different ways to demonstrate how and why the Chinese did not fit into American life. Many performers asserted that their "abnormal" cultural practices marked the Chinese as inferior and not as appealingly exotic. The foibles of many Chinese immigrants as they tried to negotiate living in the United States were also frequently the subject of parody. Their inability to speak English well and to perform what most Americans saw as more sophisticated and appealing music represented their failure to become American. Finally, what were seen as their moral failings, through such activities as gambling and cheating, confirmed that Chinese immigrants were a threat to American society and progress. Although there were touches of sympathy toward the Chinese as victims, the sum of these themes was that the Chinese were inferior to whites and did not belong in the United States.

Although Chinese restaurants became increasingly popular, songwriters and performers had nothing good to say about Chinese food in the 1870s and 1880s. In this respect, they continued a line of criticism found in earlier California songs, while also fitting into a much broader pattern of using eating and drinking habits as a way to depict a group's supposed inferiority, whether by minstrelsy's image of the watermelon-loving darky or the drunken Irishman.[40] Variety songs depicted Chinese immigrants as eating a combination of domesticated animals and vermin—namely, dogs, cats, rats, and mice. Jason Johnson of Hooley's Minstrels sang his own version of "Heathen Chinee" (1873) that laid out what were supposedly Chinese eating habits.

> Verse 2: Lady she am vellie good, makie plenty chow chow,
> She live way up top side house
> Take a little pussey cat and a little bow-wow.
> Boil em in a pot, slew wit a little mouse.
> Verse 3: Some say pig meat makie goodie chow chow

No muchie largie too muchie small,
Up sky, down sky, down come chow chow
Down come a pussy cat, Bow wow and all.

The eating of cats and dogs, as Robert G. Lee argues in *Orientals,* pointed to
the inhumanity and savagery of the Chinese. The types of animals that were
mentioned also indicated certain attitudes about Chinese masculinity, namely,
that Chinese men were cowardly and idle. Domesticated animals, which were
supposed to be friendly and obedient, and vermin, which were abundant in
cities, were easily caught.[41] The eating of vermin, especially those in American
cities, also fueled concerns about cleanliness and hygiene. In contrast, African
Americans found themselves at the other extreme: they were perceived as savage and violent because they caught wild animals such as opossums and rac-
coons. This image reinforced the need to restrict them as well.

Variety performers also used Chinese music making to mark difference,
thus confirming anti-Chinese attitudes that had been generated in European
and American writings since at least the eighteenth century. These songs
criticized the unpleasantness of Chinese traditions and questioned whether
Chinese immigrants would be able to learn American music. "Nigger-vs.-
Chinese" (1870), which was sung in a black dialect, criticized Chinese immigrants for being unable to play American musical instruments: "Dey cannot
learn to play the fiddle, / Or pick the ole Banjo, / Or stave de head ob de
jamborine, / dey are so mighty slow."[42] In many ways, "Nigger-vs.-Chinese"
was ironic, considering that the narrator refers to musical instruments tied to
African American musical traditions and to blackface minstrelsy as integral to
American music, in contrast to many music elites who saw Europe as the root
of American culture. Three years later, "The Chinese Shoemaker" (1873) tells
the story of the arrival of Chinese laborers in North Adams, Massachusetts,
where they were used as scabs in local shoe factories. The last verse describes
a Chinese shoemaker who tried to serenade his American wife with a song
from his homeland. His neighbors, however, did not appreciate the shoemaker's endeavor and killed him. Afterward, they cut off his queue and sold it,
an act similar to portrayals of scalpings by savage Indians.[43]

A handful of minstrelsy and variety performers played Chinese musical
instruments on the stage not to educate audiences about Chinese music but
rather to define it as "noise." Chinese immigrants and American visitors to
China had brought musical instruments to the United States since at least the
1820s. Musical instrument dealers also sold these products because of their
potential use in American bands and orchestras and as curiosities.[44] White
minstrels and variety actors performed what critics and playbills called a "Chinese fiddle," probably some kind of *huqin,* a family of string instruments com-

monly described by Americans and Europeans as a violin or a fiddle and criticized for the high-pitched sounds it generated. One of the first records of an American performing on a Chinese instrument was that of R. Bishop Buckley of Buckley's Serenaders in New York City in 1853. Along with playing the banjo and singing with the rest of the troupe, Buckley played a "Chinese Fiddle Solo, never attempted by any other performer."[45] By the 1870s, several actors and actresses played the "Chinese fiddle." In 1870, Johnny Thompson at the Theatre Comique in New York City included a Chinese fiddle solo in the skit "A Day after the Fair." Annie Yeamans gave her own rendition of Chinese fiddle playing at the Theatre Comique in Cincinnati, Ohio. James H. Budworth, an African American and German impersonator, was also a versatile musician who played the banjo and what was described as the Chinese and Japanese fiddles. Even John "Chinee" Leach "personated a Chinaman in speech and song, playing the accompaniment on a real Chinese fiddle" at a San Francisco Elks lodge.[46]

Anti-Chinese songwriters often focused on questions of masculinity, an indirect way of addressing issues of work and citizenship, which catered to an audience consisting mostly of white working-class men. Although citizenship restrictions based on race had, in theory, been removed after the Civil War, gender still determined who could participate in political life during the latter part of the nineteenth century. Unnatural or comic contact with women, who sometimes were Chinese but usually were Americans or Irish immigrants, was one way to question Chinese masculinity and Chinese immigrant men's capability of becoming citizens. Many of these men competed with women in the workforce, especially Irish immigrant women. Furthermore, because few women emigrated from China, intimate relationships between Chinese men and non-Chinese women developed, despite antimiscegenation laws and threats of violence. Those Chinese women who did travel to the United States during this period were often the wives and daughters of merchants (not of laborers), or they were prostitutes who had been sold, kidnapped, or lured away from their families.[47]

Irish women (and sometimes men) clashed with Chinese men in the work place as well as over sex and marriage. A common site of conflict in anti-Chinese songs was the laundry, a place that also symbolized the supposed effeminacy of Chinese men as they performed what American as well as Chinese culture considered women's work.[48] Because Chinese laundries were often in competition with those run by Irish immigrant women, this conflict was a venue to question Chinese masculinity and to draw attention to the tensions between Chinese and Irish workers. The song "Since the Chinese Ruint the Thrade" (1871) describes the problems an Irish washerwoman faced because of Chinese competition.[49]

SINCE THE CHINESE RUINT THE THRADE

Verse 1: From me shanty down on Sixth Street,
    It's meself have jist kim down;
    I've lived there this eighteen year
    It's in path they call Cork Town.
    I'm on the way to the City Hall
    To get a little aid;
    It's meself that has to ax it now
    Since the Chinese ruint the thrade.
Chorus: For I kin wash an' iron a shirt,
    An' I kin scrub a flure;
    An' I kin starch a collar as stiff
    As any Chineseman, I'm shure;
    But ther dhirty, pigtailed haythens,
    An' ther prices they are paid
    Have brought me to the state you
    See—
    They've ontirely ruint ther thrade.
Verse 2: I'm a widdy woman, I'd have ye know:
    Poor Mike was kilt at wark.
    He got a fall from the City Hall,
    For he was a mason's clark.
    An' me daughter Ellen is gone this year
    Wid a Frinch bally troupe, ther jade,
    So I find it hard to get along
    Since the Chinese ruint ther thrade.
Verse 3: It makes me wild, whin I'm on the street,
    To see those haythens' signs:
    Ah Sung, Ah Sing, Sam Lee, Ah Wing,
    An'ther ilegant sprid on ther lines.
    If iver I get me hands on Ah Sing,
    I'll make him Ah Sing indade—
    On me clothesline I'll pin the leather skin
    Of the haythen that ruint the thrade.

Irish women, unlike Chinese men, were often perceived to be brutish and aggressive because they worked outside the home and because they were Irish. Yet the conditions under which many Irish immigrant women worked cannot be taken lightly, nor can their worries about competition, because they too had few options.[50] Throughout "Since the Chinese Ruint the Thrade," the speaker lists some of the problems many washerwoman faced—price competition, the death of husbands, and the disappearance of daughters (perhaps, as in this song, to prostitution—"jade" was a slang term for prostitute). The negative and crude descriptions used by so many composers and performers, many of whom identified themselves as Irish or Irish American, worked on multiple levels: they promoted the removal of Chinese immigrants, aligned Irishness with whiteness, and acknowledged the problems many working women faced, while still playing on the lack of femininity among these women.

As in Conner's "John Chinaman's Marriage," unions between Chinese immigrant men and European immigrant or American women were frequently the subject of songs on the variety and minstrel stage. In these songs, happy marriages, or even successful courtships, of Chinese immigrant men ended in tragedy, even when they involved Chinese immigrant women. Both men and women attacked Chinese immigrant men, wives or lovers ran off with white men, and immigrant men died from unexpected circumstances if they had anything close to a successful relationship. The inability of the Chinese to control their wives and to fight off attacks located these men in what Robert G. Lee has called a "third sex," an androgynous position somewhere between masculinity and femininity.[51] This position of being neither woman nor man, a position also held by other groups such as Irish women, had serious political implications and supported the logic of exclusion.

Stories of romance and love involving Chinese immigrant men sometimes involved emasculating acts. After working somewhere east of California, "Big Long John" (1873) decided to go to San Francisco to see "his sweetheart, Chum Chum Fee," but his trip ends when a Native American cuts off his queue.[52]

> Now when he awoke he felt so bad,
> That he hollered with all his might,
> Put his hand to his head and it made him so sick,
> That he died that very same night.
> He was found next day about 12N,
> By the captain of a Hong Kong crew;
> He wrote to his sweetheart, Chum Chum Fee,
> That he died from loss of his cue.

The queue, which was long and braided, confirmed his femininity because of its similarity to some American women's hairstyles; the word itself could also be a pun on the slang term *pool cue*. Native American men were also depicted with long hair, but it signified their closeness to nature and their unkempt state. Although the act of cutting off a queue could be used to denote becoming American, this act emasculated Big Long John so that he was ashamed to visit his lover and, instead, died in despair. Further, a Native American man committing this act reconfirmed not only John's femininity but also the primitiveness and inferiority of both groups. By portraying Chinese men as "less than manly," the songwriter Luke Schoolcraft (who also performed this piece) tied normal masculinity to the characteristics of being white and American.

Although Chinese men were portrayed as effeminate, they were also presented as desiring white women. Sexual relations across racial lines did occur, although in 1880, California became the first state to pass an antimiscegenation law forbidding marriages between whites and Chinese immigrants. At least one song described Chinese–Irish unions, but this subject may have been a touchy one, given the rising status of the Irish and the fact that they were an important part of working-class audiences.[53] In "Ah-Sin, Chinee Song" (1877), the title of which comes from Harte's "Heathen Chinee" and a play Harte released in 1876 also called *Ah Sin*, an Irish woman leaves her Chinese husband for an American man.[54]

> My name Ah Sin, come from China,
> Me like Irish gal, she like me;
> Me from Hong Kong, Melican man come 'long,
> Stealy Irish gal from poor Chinee!

As the song continues, Ah Sin is hit by his drunken wife and later is kicked down the stairs by her lover. Even when Ah Sin goes to the police, he—not the perpetrators of violence against him—is arrested.[55]

In at least one instance, a song described a relationship between an African American woman and a Chinese immigrant man. "Ah Ling's True Love" (1877) tells the story of a Chinese man pursuing a married, African American woman named Susie Green.[56] Ah Ling finally convinces Green to leave her husband and to sail away with him, but in the final lines of the song, their ship is lost at sea. Ah Ling and Green's relationship pointed to the multifaceted process of Chinese racialization by conflating the inferiority of Chinese immigrants with African Americans. Later in the century, connections between African Americans and Chinese immigrants would increase as Chinese stereotypes took new forms and as African Americans decided to caricature the Chinese in order to define their own American qualities.

The death of the Chinese immigrant men in "Ah Ling's True Love" and "The Chinese Shoemaker" is similar to the storyline in other songs that used violence, like sexuality, to fulfill white fantasies by demonstrating Chinese inferiority. The contrast with musical portrayals of other racial and ethnic groups is telling. During the 1870s and 1880s, there were references to Italian immigrants carrying stilettos and African Americans, razors. These allusions highlighted the potentially violent nature of these two groups, especially in their behavior toward native-born whites. On the stage, at least, these groups were not the subjects of brutal acts but the possible perpetrators, a characterization that justified controlling these populations and committing violence against them.

Violence against Chinese immigrants also fulfilled white fantasies, and all sorts of people committed violence against the Chinese. Unlike Italian immigrants and African Americans, the Chinese were seen as more feminine and therefore were the recipients of violence, not potential offenders. While confirming Chinese effeminacy, these songs and skits allowed audiences to experience their most base desires vicariously yet maintain a sense of manliness. A reviewer in the Nevada *Territorial Enterprise* noted that John "Chinee" Leach's impersonations were "a happy interlude" for audiences, who "rejoice[d] when at last he [wa]s beaten half to death."[57] The song "Sang Lee" (1878) relates the story of the title character, who owned a laundry and reportedly worked very hard. The local grocery man, however, sold him soap that did not clean well, leading one of Lee's clients to beat him to death.[58] On one level, Sang Lee was a sympathetic and tragic character, but on another level, his violent death fulfilled other psychological needs of white audiences in that it addressed the anxieties many white men had about the racial diversity of the Far West, which many wanted to make as white as possible. As with white Southerners who feared African American men in the post–Civil War period, whites in other parts of the country were concerned with the possible pollution of the Caucasian race through interracial contact, especially sex and marriage.

Anti-Chinese songs, including depictions of violence, had a particular resonance with Irish performers and audiences. This dynamic is particularly intriguing in the enormously popular stage works of Edward Harrigan and David Braham, which also revealed the rising prestige of the Irish as well as the power of Irish composers, performers, and audiences. In their productions, Harrigan and Braham constructed an elaborate hierarchy of the Lower East Side in which they encouraged Irish pride in relation to other immigrant and racial groups. This hierarchy was most likely very popular with their audiences, who were at least partially made up of Irish immigrants or Irish Americans.[59] In their musical plays, sexual relations between Irish and Chinese were completely avoided; instead, Chinese men married Italian women, whom Harrigan saw as a newer and more foreign group of immigrants. Periodically, however, they used their productions to look at the conflicts between Chinese and Irish laundries. In *Mulligan's Silver Wedding* (1881), Honora Dublin complains openly about Hog Eye, a Chinese laundryman, who competes with Dublin's laundry business:

You're not half a man. You're a nagur, you eat your dinner with drumsticks. You're a monkey, you have a tail growing out of your head. . . . You're a mongrel Asiatic. . . . Why don't you have whiskers on your face like a man you baboon you. . . . the likes of you coming to a free country and walking around in your petticoats and calling yourself a man. Bah,

ye omadoon you. . . . It's the rotten pipe you smoke. The neighbors are
moving out of Mulligan Alley from the fume of it.[60]

Dublin's monologue reflects the convergence within popular culture of older,
anti-Chinese attitudes and new forms of scientific racism that began in the
nineteenth century. Her use of animalistic and feminine terms to describe
Hog Eye demonstrates the differences she saw between herself and her com-
petitor. Her statement is not only about competition but also about her fear
of the degradation of whiteness and American identity. Although at first
equating Chinese immigrants with African Americans, with whom the Irish
also competed in New York City, Dublin decided that the Chinese were even
further down the evolutionary scale by virtue of their racial inferiority and
their inability to become American.

Although some composers and performers in California who sang about
the Chinese in the 1850s and 1860s identified themselves as Irish or Irish
American, they did not directly address the conflicts between these two
groups on the stage. This issue, however, did appear during the 1870s and
1880s, when the "Chinese Question" became a national subject of debate
among labor unions, many of which had large numbers of Irish members.
Many men of Irish ancestry were also members of the Democratic Party,
which supported limits on Chinese immigration. With ambivalence about the
social position of the Irish still persisting, anti-Chinese songs were a means to
contrast Chinese racial inferiority with Irish "whiteness." Further, because
Chinese immigrants frequently competed with Irish unskilled laborers or
worked as scabs in semi-skilled industries, composers and performers were
able to aid their fellow Irish Americans in their fight against labor competition. In these instances, Chinese immigrants were often peripheral, because
the focus of these productions and songs was the confirmation and acceptance
of the Irish as white and American.

Variety performer, songwriter, and producer Tony Pastor, himself an Italian American, smugly sang about labor competition in his version of "John
Chinaman" (1871).[61]

Now Coolie labor is the cry,
"Pat" must give place to Pagan "John,"
Whom *Christian* bosses, rich and sly,
Have anxiously the heart set on.
For he's nice, cheap Chinaman;
A meek, submissive Chinaman,
Who ne'r "turns Turk," or "strikes" his work
For more pay, like the Irishman.

Here, although Pastor noted that the Chinese in the eyes of capitalists were good workers, they were un-American and unmanly because, unlike the Irish, they were not part of organized labor. This was also one of the few moments in music where factory owners and businessmen were accused of using the Chinese to depress wages and avoid strikes. The italicization of the word "Christian" told the singer to stress this word when sung, emphasizing not that the bosses were Christian but that they were un-Christian in the treatment of their fellow white men. The use of the term "Christian" also obscured the differences between Irish Catholics and the large number of Protestants in the United States, who often condemned Catholics as Papists.

In at least one instance, Irish characters appealed to both their fellow immigrants and African Americans in response to the threat of Chinese immigration. While campaigning for the position of coroner, Peter McSorley, in Harrigan and Braham's *McSorley's Inflation* (1882), tried to befriend both the Irish and African American voters by ridiculing the Chinese. He asserted during one of his speeches that "the Chinaman. Ah, he's the scum of a barbarization that would put his lepress hands upon the anglo-saxon circassion and drive us into the whirlpool of the Pacific Ocean."[62] This scene was unusual in that most of Harrigan and Braham's musical plays were about conflicts between Irish immigrants and African Americans. In this instance, Harrigan and Braham brought these groups together because of their relationship to American identity and their dislike for the Chinese (they could also vote, which Chinese immigrants could not do). Although African Americans were considered inferior, they were uniquely American; although the Irish population still consisted of a large number of immigrants, they were perceived to be more like "white" folks and could eventually claim American identity through assimilation and acculturation. None of these things was perceived as possible for Chinese immigrants.

Other songwriters and performers portrayed Irish American politicians in New York City who used anti-Chinese sentiment to shore up votes. These characters were clear about their opinion of the Chinese, and in order to help their constituents, they advocated excluding and even removing Chinese immigrants from the United States. These songs also showed that the Irish were not only involved in labor organizations but also in the political process by electing one of their own into positions of state and local power. "When McCormack Rules the State" (1880) and Pat Rooney's "Is That Mr. Rielly?" (1882) were cast as political platform speeches by Irish Americans from New York City's Bowery. Both songs promise to remove, or even kill, Chinese immigrants to win votes.[63]

Irish immigrants and Irish Americans were more involved than their Chinese counterparts in mainstream politics, labor, and music and theater, so they had multiple venues in which to vocalize their concerns about job competition, racial purity, and American identity. Chinese immigrants, especially because they could not become citizens, did not have as much access to public spaces in which they could encourage understanding of their minority group and stop the passage of restrictions.[64] In a certain sense, songs about the conflicts between the Chinese and Irish were just as much a commentary on the role of the Irish in the United States as they were depictions of interethnic struggles. At the same time, Irish characterizations demonstrated problems surrounding whether racial inferiority limited the Chinese's ability to become American.

BEGINNING IN THE 1850s, contact with Chinese immigrants reconfigured images of the Chinese on the stage and in music. Songwriters and performers no longer turned to Europe, but to experiences in the United States, particularly in the Far West. Americans in California were the first to address in music their anxieties about Chinese immigration; with the help of Bret Harte's "Heathen Chinee," anti-Chinese songs appeared in theaters and songsters throughout the country. With a few exceptions, these songs reinforced ideas of inferiority and questioned whether the Chinese were able to assimilate into American life.

To support the marginalization of Chinese immigrants, American songwriters employed certain lyrical devices that portrayed this group as deviant and often focused on issues of gender, citizenship, and violence. A few songs also turned to "Oriental" musical devices, which would later dominate the musical images of the Chinese in the twentieth century. Performers contributed to the representation of the Chinese immigrant on the stage through the use of yellowface—a combination of dialect, costuming, and makeup similar to blackface—in order to give a more total characterization than previously had been seen. Furthermore, the majority of American audiences had limited opportunities to observe real Chinese persons, often relying instead on impersonators, who touted their performances as authentic.

By the 1870s and 1880s, songs about and impersonations of Chinese immigrants proliferated throughout the United States. These productions used notions of difference to separate the Chinese from Americans to such an extent that the Chinese appeared unassimilable and needed to be restricted from entering the country. Conceptions of their deviance and inferiority left little room for their acceptance into American society and culture. Instead, they were seen as innately foreign, which was legitimated through the passage of anti-Chinese legislation starting in the 1850s and culminated in 1882 with the Chinese Exclusion Act.

CHAPTER 3

Chinese and Chinese Immigrant Performers on the American Stage, 1830s–1920s

ALTHOUGH PUSHED TO THE MARGINS of the music and theater industries, Chinese and Chinese immigrant performers were present on the American stage throughout the nineteenth and early twentieth centuries. American entrepreneurs who hoped to find commercially lucrative novelty acts introduced Chinese performers as human curiosities; Chinese agents also organized troupes to tour the United States, although with somewhat different motives and results. These acts traveled throughout the country, including cities and towns of the hinterland outside both New York City and San Francisco, and disseminated Chinese culture, sometimes for American audiences but also for Chinese immigrant communities. Most importantly, it was through these performances that white audiences observed Chinese music and theater practices on their own terms, and Chinese immigrants preserved and maintained contact with their cultural heritage. These performances also influenced how whites portrayed the Chinese, especially by the turn of the century, and expanded the types of spaces in which people of Chinese ancestry could represent themselves.

The rise of Chinese immigration by the 1850s created a need for Chinese cultural institutions in the United States. Starting in California, new venues for Chinese music and theater sprang up with the growth of enclaves in the Far West and in cities along the eastern seaboard. Many immigrants performed at the amateur level in their leisure time and for community celebrations or festivals. Chinese businessmen in the United States and China also financially backed visiting troupes and built permanent spaces for entertainment, such as restaurants, brothels, gambling halls, and theaters. These venues were extensions of traditions with which Chinese immigrants were well acquainted and helped them reconnect with their homeland. Outsiders also frequented these spaces out of curiosity.

Although Chinese performances had to face American preconceptions about music and theater, these acts also left room for audiences to formulate a variety of opinions, and perhaps even countered the mainstream discourse that Chinese musical and theatrical traditions were inferior.[1] By this period, a few acts played to beliefs in Chinese virtuosity in certain areas, especially juggling and magic. Others, such as human curiosities and, later, entertainers at world expositions, were seen by whites as examples of Chinese inferiority and exoticism. Critics and theater managers also influenced attitudes through their descriptions of acts and their reviews, as, for example, equating Chinese music and theater with noise or earlier stages of European human development.

In some cases, Chinese acts helped to expose songwriters and dramatists to new concepts of performance from which they could borrow. These imitations were often in the form of parody and ridicule, as in yellowface, but not always. Melodic structures, instrumentation, and staging could potentially be integrated into productions containing Chinese characters, or productions could be set in China to create a more exotic effect. More importantly, Chinese musical and theatrical practices influenced the performing arts in the United States more broadly, helping to break from the Western traditions that many artists believed by the end of the nineteenth century were too restrictive and commercialized.

During the nineteenth and early twentieth centuries, Americans did not completely control the production of Chinese images on the American stage and in music. Chinese performers, although a small minority, found spaces, such as dime museums, Chinese immigrant businesses, and world expositions, in which to entertain and educate audiences.[2] They also helped foster innovation in Western musical and theatrical practices. Outside the realm of the stage, Chinese performers influenced how Americans perceived race, nation, and culture, and where they stood in debates over how, and if, the Chinese belonged in the United States.

HUMAN CURIOSITIES

By the late 1820s, entertainment entrepreneurs were bringing Chinese performers, both individuals and groups, to the United States. Following the success of popular museums that had appeared earlier in the decade, impresarios tried to create acts that were amusing, educational, and ultimately lucrative in order to bring in as many people as possible, including semi-literate and illiterate audiences. Organizers often displayed human curiosities in museums or, if it was a large group, in theaters that accommodated the size of the act and its audience. In rural areas, entrepreneurs used whatever public hall or space was available.[3]

Chinese human curiosities appeared in a combination of what Robert Bogdan calls the exotic and aggrandized modes. Using the exotic mode, managers and showmen displayed non-Western people in ways that fed off the audience's notions of exoticism and primitiveness. With Asian subjects, this included exaggerated and stereotypical acting, exotic backdrops, costumes, and stage properties. Entrepreneurs also displayed non-Westerners who had physical defects in ways that highlighted both their deformities and the peculiarities of their homeland. In the aggrandized mode of display, performers often appeared normal on the surface but had amazing physical or mental talents. People with disabilities were also exhibited in this way, showing that, despite physical or mental difficulties, they were able to live relatively normal lives or do extraordinary things. Those exhibited in this fashion wore elaborate costumes and often possessed military or royal titles, such as General and Princess. Doctors also examined these performers in front of audiences to validate their capabilities and abnormalities.[4] These aspects of display emphasized the grandeur and exotic elements that Americans found appealing; however, inferiority was also reinforced through these performances, many of which featured social and cultural practices, including music.

Not all Chinese human displays during the nineteenth century involved music—Chang and Eng Bunker, or the Siamese Twins, did not sing or perform on musical instruments—but many did. Starting in 1834, Afong Moy, also called the Chinese Lady, performed Chinese songs for American audiences for the first time. Other displays that included music soon followed: Peters' Chinese Museum (1844–1850); the *Keying*, a Chinese junk (1847); Barnum's Chinese Family (1850–1853); and the Chinese Artistes (1852–1854).[5] All of these acts visited major American cities and towns, many of which did not have a sizable Chinese immigrant community. Thus, except for yellowface performances by white actors, these acts were for many Americans their only contact with the Chinese and represented a potential counternarrative to more racist attitudes.

Perhaps inspired by the success of Captain Abel Coffin, who first displayed the Siamese Twins in 1829, Captain Benjamin T. Obear of Beverly, Massachusetts, brought a Chinese woman, listed as Auphinoy on his passenger list, and her male servant to be displayed for American audiences in the fall of 1834.[6] A year earlier, the firms F. & N. G. Carnes, Gracie, Prime & Co., and Henry William Delafield organized ten ships, with Captain Obear commanding the *Washington* (formerly known as the *Howard*), to sail to China to import inexpensive Chinese objects—watercolors on rice paper, fans, medicines, and tea—to the United States.[7] At first, Obear temporarily exhibited Auphinoy, popularly known as Afong Moy, the Chinese Lady, and her attendant (Acong or Atung) for New York audiences in October 1834 near his ship, and then at a private residence at 8 Park Place. From advertisements and reviews, Moy was reportedly between fourteen and nineteen years old and had left her parents to travel to the United States because they were unable to take care of her. The money she earned was supposed to help her parents (whether Afong Moy or her parents saw any of her earnings is unclear). Other articles noted that she was supposed to be in the United States for only two years before returning home to Canton.[8] There was little information given about her attendant Acong/Atung.

In many ways, Afong Moy's act, which traveled throughout the United States, reemphasized what Americans saw as the differences between themselves and the Chinese, and by extension, the latter's inferiority. The stage or room in which audiences were allowed to observe her was decorated as a "Chinese Saloon" and contained Chinese export goods that Obear probably had brought from China. There were paper lanterns, gold and red satin damask draped on the walls and around windows, paintings of Chinese "Deities, Beauties, and Chinese Characters," and what was commonly known as Chinese Chippendale furniture. Her clothes, as observed by a correspondent for the *Sun* of Philadelphia, were "an outward mantle of blue silk, sumptuously embroidered, and yellow silk pantalettes," probably a *shan ku*. She sat in a "cushioned chair on a platform" and answered questions translated by her attendant, which allowed audiences to hear what a Chinese dialect sounded like.[9] What made her act especially novel were her bound feet, which she displayed on a platform or stage so that audiences could have a good view of them as she walked. For some audiences, she even removed her bandages.[10] Foot binding had been frequently addressed in travel writings and newspapers as another manifestation of Chinese cruelty, especially toward women, and cultural decline. To a certain extent, Afong Moy's bound feet were, like the physical peculiarity of Chang and Eng Bunker, a physical abnormality exploited to bring in audiences. Yet because foot binding was part of Chinese culture, this type of aberrance helped to reinforce assumptions that Chinese inferiority was based not on something innate but on their customs, which could be changed.

Beginning with her engagement in New Haven, Connecticut, advertisements for Afong Moy stated that she was singing a "Chinese Song" for audiences (see ill. 6).[11] It is unclear whether she had been singing in her performances before this time, but, as stated in advertisements, her singing gave observers "an idea of the [Chinese] Language and Cadence." Playbills, advertisements, and reviews, unfortunately, did not give song titles or explicit descriptions. It is also unclear how her singing was received in each city. A journalist in Pensacola, Florida, wrote: "This little lady sings, but not prettily," a comment that fit with already popular attitudes about Chinese music.[12]

Although she supposedly left for China on the *Mary Ballard* in 1837, Afong Moy reappeared on stage ten years later in New York City and Boston, using chopsticks, explaining Chinese social practices, walking on her bound feet, and singing. Writers for the *New York Commercial Advertiser* questioned whether Afong Moy (whom other writers called Lady Tshing-ka-ko-ka) was even Chinese because she seemed so Americanized, probably a reference to

FOR ONE WEEK ONLY,
(Owing to other engagements.)

Unprecedented Attraction,

In the large HALL of the

NORTH AMERICAN HOTEL,
Corner of Bienville and Levee streets,

Commencing Monday, March 28, and to close, positively, on Saturday, April 2d.

Exhibition to commence each evening at 8 o'clock

Tickets ONE DOLLAR, children half price.

THE CHINESE LADY,
AFONG MOY,

Lately exhibited in Mobile, Providence, Boston, Salem, Philadelphia, Baltimore, Washington, Richmond, Norfolk, Charleston, New York and New Haven, will have the honor of appearing before the Company in a splendid

CHINESE SALOON,

fitted up with rich Canton

Satin Dam- ask Chinese

Paintings. Lanterns,

and Cu- riosities.

AFONG MOY is a native of Canton city, about sixteen years of age, mild and engaging in her manners; addresses the visitors in English and Chinese, and occasionally WALKS BEFORE THE COMPANY, so as to afford an opportunity of observing her

ASTONISHING LITTLE FEET!

For which the Chinese Ladies are so remarkable. Afong's feet is FOUR INCHES and an eighth in length, being about the size of an infant's of one year old. She will be richly dressed in

The CHINESE Costume.

And in order to give the audience an idea of the Language and Cadence of her country, she will sing

A CHINESE SONG.

AFONG MOY is at present under the care of the Lady of the conductor of the exhibition, and is making rapid progress in acquiring the English language. Various Chinese curiosities will be shown and explained to the Company, and every pains taken to satisfy the curious, as to the manners and customs of these singular people

She was brought to this country by Captain Obear, of the ship Washington, under a heavy guarantee to return her to her parents in two years and is now on her way to New York for that purpose, to embark for Canton in the 'Mary Ballard' just arrived from China. The conductor of the exhibition, consequently, can remain but a very short time in each city going up the river, by the way of Pittsburg, and confidently hopes, the same liberal patronage shown in other cities, will not be withheld in this, after travelling so many thousand miles to solicit the favor.

☞ A small quantity of beautiful Chinese Paintings, on rice paper, for sale.

Ill. 6. Broadside for Afong Moy, North American Hotel, New Orleans, Louisiana. Courtesy of the American Antiquarian Society.

her ability to speak English and to discuss the differences between the United States and China. "But is the lady Chinese! Though we have almost intimated a contrary opinion in the foregoing remarks, we still honestly think that she is—if she was born in China of Chinese parents. All depends upon that." Her singing was one of the aspects of her act that affirmed her Chinese identity and its inferiority. The critic noted that she sang "a succession of sound, (we use the singular number advisedly) which she calls singing—She affects impromptu songs also, the sentiments of which are doubtless quite as poetical as the language is intelligible."[13] In September 1847, she reportedly left Boston for a European tour.[14]

The *Keying,* which arrived in New York's harbor in 1847, the same summer that Afong Moy returned to the stage, was a floating museum of Chinese life. Named after the Chinese commissioner Qiying and captained by Charles A. Kellett from Australia, the junk included a Chinese crew (at least twenty-six to forty Chinese sailors) and objects. Critics commented that the ship was "China in miniature," privileging direct contact with people and objects, and was as educational as traveling to or reading extensively about China. A reporter from the *New York Herald* noted that "she is, indeed, a novelty, and one hour's stay on board of her will give a better insight into Chinese manners and customs, than can be learned in a library of books." Other newspapers recorded similar views.[15]

Among the crew's many activities were dancing, singing, and music making. When they arrived in New York City, for instance, the crew fired three guns and two members played gongs. They also conducted a festival during the last week of July, which audiences were allowed to attend. As reported in the *New York Herald,* the celebration included "dancing, singing &c., &c., and the music of gongs, reeds and other instruments of native use and manufacture." The journalist noted that the music "will no doubt sound very strange to persons who never heard such music before." Audiences, of course, did not see the festival as a special celebration for the crew members but as an entertainment, which they, along with the press, wanted reenacted on a daily basis.[16] When finally sailing out of New York harbor in October, the crew sang a "farewell song" that coincided with a series of gestures. They continued "until they were out of sight and hearing."[17]

Although audiences enjoyed observing the sailors, it finally came out that Kellett had forced his Chinese crew to be part of the *Keying* exhibit. The Chinese crew had been hired in China for a voyage to Java or Singapore, at which time they were supposedly promised that they could leave or stay aboard for the next eight months and receive a salary of $8 a month. Kellett and his European crewmen, however, had forced the Chinese sailors to stay aboard and travel on to the United States. After a few rounds of allegations and denials between Kellett and the Chinese sailors, twenty-six crewmembers filed a libel suit against the *Keying,* which they won. They received their back wages and tickets back to Canton.[18]

P. T. Barnum's Chinese Family, which first appeared in spring 1850, also gave American audiences contact with Chinese music making. Earlier that year, Barnum had purchased John R. Peters Jr.'s Chinese Museum and rehired his two Chinese guides, T'sow-Chaoong and Le-Kaw-Hing, whom he re-named Aleet-Mong and Soo-Chune, respectively.[19] To make his act more exciting, Barnum added two women (a "Chinese Lady" with bound feet named Pwan-Ye-Koo and her "servant" Lum-Akum), Soo-Chune's daughter, Amoon, and son, Mun Chung, to make the Chinese Family. Like Afong Moy, the Family was one of the few opportunities Americans had to see "real" Chinese people on stage and to ask them questions through their interpreter, T'sow-Chaoong/Aleet-Mong.[20]

Among their various activities, the Chinese Family sang and played musical instruments together. Once an hour, the family sang for audiences with Le-Kaw-Hing/Soo-Chune on the *erh hu* and Pwan-Ye-Koo on the *pipa.* Le-Kaw-Hing/Soo-Chune, who had been called Professor of Music while working for Peters (which probably meant that he was a professional musician and not a pro-fessor), also performed on several musical instruments from Peters's collection and sang.[21] Sometimes, Pwan-Ye-Koo sang solo as well, which was also dis-cussed in the press. A critic for the *Boston Post* wrote that Pwan-Ye-Koo's "songs are very unique things, and her performances on the Chinese lute is truly inter-esting, beating time as she does with her feet, 2½ inches long."[22] Unlike other reviews and travel narratives, this commentary did not complain overtly about the quality of her music, making it an anomaly among American and European writings. The critic, however, was more interested in her feet, which P. T. Bar-num used to present Pwan-Ye-Koo as a "Chinese Lady" (much like Afong Moy) and to bring in audiences, than in her music ability.[23]

That summer Barnum advertised in New York City's local newspapers that the Chinese Family was traveling to Great Britain for the 1851 Crystal Palace Exhibition and to meet Queen Victoria. This, however, was only par-tially true. By May 1851, the Chinese Family was located in a building near Albert-gate in Knightsbridge, not far from the London Crystal Palace Exhibi-tion. They went without T'sow-Chaoong/Aleet-Mong, who was replaced by Oong (Charles) Ar-Showe, an employee at Redding's Tea Store in Boston.[24] Music was still integral to their display in Great Britain. Both the *Critic,* a journal dedicated to the promotion of the Crystal Palace, and the *London Times* stated that Pwan-Ye-Koo was "said to be a perfect vocalist, according to the Chinese notion of vocalism" and that Le-Kaw-Hing/Soo-Chune was "a musical professor of the first rank."[25]

The most provocative commentary on the Chinese Family came from French composer, conductor, and music critic Hector Berlioz, who had traveled to London to be a judge of musical instrument manufacturing at the exposition and correspondent for the *Journal des Débats*. Although he spent most of his time at the exposition, Berlioz also visited the Chinese Family to make his own determination as to whether Chinese scales were similar to those used in the West (he had read contradictory descriptions). After listening to the Chinese Family, Berlioz concluded that Chinese music used four tones that were similar to those in the West, a claim that reduced the exoticism of Chinese music while also making it appear less complex than Western music.[26]

Berlioz's discussion of the Chinese Family focused not only on theoretical questions; he also described and critiqued their performance. When Berlioz entered the salon, the Chinese Family was sitting "motionless on a little stage." First, Le-Kaw-Hing/Soo-Chune sang a song containing ten to twelve verses while he played the *erh hu* and Pwan-Ye-Koo the *pipa*. Then Pwan-Ye-Koo sang while Le-Kaw-Hing/Soo-Chune accompanied her with a transverse flute known as a *dizi*. Overall, Berlioz disliked this performance. He reported that the musical instruments, which he described in terms of European mandolins and flutes, were poorly constructed. Le-Kaw-Hing/Soo-Chune's singing was "nasal, guttural, groaning, hideous, such as I may compare, without much exaggeration, to the sounds uttered by a dog, when, after sleeping a long time, he yawns while stretching himself." In contrast, Berlioz admitted that Pwan-Ye-Koo sang comparatively well, but still he framed her performance in racial and class terms. He described her as "a child, who . . . amuses itself in strumming on the keys of a piano," "a provincial cook-maid singing 'Pierre, mon ami Pierre,' whilst washing her dishes," or "the Esmeraldas of our cafes."[27] Berlioz, however, qualified his negative statements about Pwan-Ye-Koo and argued that because she was not of "the highest order," despite Barnum's description of her as a "Lady," she was not representative of Chinese female musicianship among the elite. For Berlioz, it was only women of Chinese aristocratic and wealthy families who were able to study music extensively, much like their European counterparts, yet they would never be allowed to travel abroad or to perform for money in front of an audience. He even complained that he could not see her bound feet fully, so they were probably "good-sized plebeian" ones, which she hid under her dress. Here, Berlioz seemed to maintain the belief that in China there were skilled musicians in the Western sense. Yet like so many other writers during the mid-nineteenth century, he found this performance to be mediocre in comparison to that produced in Europe, especially by art music composers such as himself.[28]

Two years after the appearance of Barnum's Chinese Family in New York City, another captain, Captain L. Coffin, with the help of an American entrepreneur, Dr. John H. Gihon, brought a troupe of sixteen performers, called the Chinese Artistes, to San Francisco. Also known as the Chinese Magicians, Chinese Jugglers, or "À la Chinois," they were one of the first Chinese acts to premiere in San Francisco, and they performed for an audience made up of Chinese, Latin American, and European immigrants and Americans who had traveled to California for the Gold Rush. Although the troupe did not fill a whole evening's program, the Chinese Artistes were a huge success. The critic for San Francisco's *Daily Herald* gushed that they were "novel," "extraordinary," and "remarkable."[29] Since at least the eighteenth century, Europeans and, later, Americans commented positively on Chinese magic, juggling, and acrobatics and often compared them to traditions found in the West. It was only a matter of time before entrepreneurs would introduce these acts to American audiences in hopes of bringing in huge crowds.[30]

Much like the French pantomime *Kimka*, the Chinese Artistes began with an elaborate procession, with Chin Gan, a Chinese dwarf, in a sedan chair at the front.[31] They then performed a wide variety of acts: chopstick use, illusions and sleight of hand tricks, somersaults, plate spinning on bamboo sticks, knife throwing, ball and cup juggling, fire eating, stilt walking, manipulation of large balls with their feet, and a mock decapitation. The most controversial trick was the impalement, a knife-throwing number that is still popular today, with one person throwing knives across the stage at another who is standing against a board.[32] In Memphis, Tennessee, a local critic felt that "the impalement itself is worth twice the entrance money." He also recommended seeing the knife throwing in general, which "was one of the most remarkable exhibitions we ever witnessed."[33] Other newspaper writers condemned the impalement stunt because it was so dangerous. The *New York Times,* which catered to a more refined theater-going crowd, wrote that this number was "revolting." "Notwithstanding the announcement that no injury can possibly be done to the impaled, we noticed last evening that many left the Theatre without seeing it. It is hard to realize that the performance can be safely carried through."[34] The impalement still received a great deal of exposure in advertisements and reviews as one of the most amazing routines ever seen, playing on the titillating aspect of this number and allowing people to dismiss such depictions as vulgar.

All stunts included musical accompaniment by a small band of up to nine instrumentalists and sometimes vocals. Ching Moon played several examples of Chinese music for audiences as a solo number. Unfortunately, it is unclear what instruments he used except for a gong; American writers also described Chin Gan as playing a fiddle, probably some kind of huqin. Although relaying little information about what was actually played and the types of instruments, most critics emphasized the displeasure audiences felt during these musical interludes. In New Orleans, a local critic admitted that he and the audiences "were scarcely prepared" to listen to Chinese music, although he apparently had read that they "knew but little of the harmony of sounds, but we did not suppose them so entirely deficient as this exhibition demonstrates."[35] The critic for the *Spirit of the Times* noted that "their music is one of the most amusing features of the performance; there are two gongs, four stringed instruments, and several vocalists." He continued, complaining, "and yet it is a sort of 'Dumb Orchestra,' which would be 'drowned' by the magnificent Alboni, saving the gongs."[36] By calling the musicians "amusing" and "dumb," the anonymous writer was openly critical of their act and ability; however, in an interesting twist, the noisiness of Chinese music, which was often connected to volume, did not appear in this review. These performers, except for when they played the gong, could easily be overwhelmed by the singing of Marietta Alboni, one of the many operatic singing sensations from Europe who toured the United States during the early 1850s.[37]

In the mid-nineteenth century, Chinese human curiosities gave people in the United States their first experiences with musical and theatrical traditions from China. These acts traveled throughout the country, visiting towns and cities that were not direct participants in the China trade and did not have a Chinese immigrant community. Organizers often combined markers of Chinese inferiority with the more appealing aspects of exoticism and skill of the performers, sending audiences mixed messages about how to perceive these performers specifically and the Chinese generally. Of these acts, acrobats, jugglers, and magicians were especially popular and appeared on the American stage throughout the 1850s and 1860s, only to be eclipsed by the arrival of Japanese performers in 1867. Nevertheless, the display of Chinese men and women as human curiosities continued throughout the century at venues such as dime museums, variety houses, and circuses.

CHINESE IMMIGRANTS AND MUSIC IN PUBLIC AND PRIVATE SPACES

As with other immigrant groups, the Chinese brought their own entertainment traditions—not necessarily for commercial purposes but as a way to stay in touch with their culture. Many who came played musical instruments and sang in their free time in the mines or in the growing towns and cities of the Far West. Ronald Riddle, who has written extensively on Chinese music in San Francisco, noted that after work, many laborers played instruments and sang in the backrooms of Chinese-owned shops.[38] Musicians were employed by Chinese businesses to entertain, or for community celebrations and festivals. These venues also provided a mechanism for incorporating Chinese music into Western traditions. For Chinese immigrants, however, music making reconnected them with their homeland and was a way to express their feelings about life in the United States.

Chinese immigrants incorporated music into entertainment as well as civic and religious rituals, which whites frequently observed. Businesses, homes, festivals, temples, and frontier camps were all locations for music making. Marlon K. Hom illustrates in *Songs of Gold Mountain* that some immigrants and their loved ones who were left behind produced *Gamsaan Go* (in Mandarin, *Jin Shan Ge*), or "Gold Mountain songs," songs by men and women on both sides of the Pacific that explored the immigrant experience. Song subjects included the desire to find gold or work, encounters with anti-Chinese discrimination, and general experiences of living in a foreign country.[39]

Chinese musicians and singers appeared in brothels, gambling halls, and restaurants, all of which were centers of sociability. In his memoir on life in nineteenth-century California, Charles Warren Stoddard described his experience as a youth in an unnamed Chinatown restaurant in San Francisco. The restaurant was tiered, with the top floor boasting the most expensive menu as well as musical accompaniment by a small band.[40] In another restaurant owned by Yune Fong, an American tourist in 1878 noted that although musicians were not playing, there were musical instruments hung along the walls.[41] Miriam Squier, wife of magazine publisher Frank Leslie, wrote about a Chinese restaurant she visited in San Francisco that had an alcove for musicians to sit and play, although they were not there when she ate dinner.[42]

Some of the few Chinese women living in the United States during the nineteenth and early twentieth centuries performed and sang in places of leisure. L. Vernon Briggs described the arrival of several Chinese women to San Francisco from Hong Kong in 1881. He noted that these women, who lived primarily in Tai Ping Shan, also known as Exceeding Peace Hill, in San Francisco, were trained musicians and vocalists and that many had performed on flower boats (a euphemism for prostitution) in China.[43] The *San Francisco Chronicle* (ca. 1876) published an illustration of a reception in Chinatown that included both male and female musicians. The description noted that a wealthy Chinese merchant had given this dinner at a local restaurant for his friends, and it had included "music, singing, recitations, and a sumptuous bill of fare for the attractions." Two women sang for the merchant's guests and kept time on a small kettledrum; the men played percussion and stringed instruments.[44]

In his memoir *Father and Glorious Descendent,* Pardee Lowe recounted seeing female performers at a banquet he attended in San Francisco with his father, sometime in the early twentieth century before the fall of the Qing dynasty in 1912. These banquets, usually intended to celebrate community events, weddings, and births, were held in large restaurants. At one such banquet, a group of seven musicians, five of whom were women, played instruments and sang songs from operas. Several women, whom he called singsong girls (also a euphemism for prostitutes), sat at every table in the restaurant. Lowe's mother did not attend this particular banquet.[45]

Other establishments, such as gambling halls, also had musicians. These enterprises were located throughout the Far West and in Chinese sections of major cities such as Boston, New York City, Philadelphia, and Chicago. In 1855, the *Annals of San Francisco* reported that several Chinese gambling establishments had small bands consisting of five or six musicians and sometimes a singer.[46] During the late 1860s, musical performances late into the night in a gambling hall above the first Chinese theater on Jackson Street in San Francisco prompted frequent complaints by neighbors. The police finally raided the building in December 1869, and the *Alta California* reported that five musicians escaped capture.[47]

Social settings aside, Chinese immigrants maintained their musical traditions at religious and civic events. Weddings, funerals, festivals, and general worship were all activities that required musical accompaniment. Although Chinese immigrants sent a large number of their dead home to be buried, some had funerals in the United States. These services included chanting by a local priest or a group of mourners and a processional to the gravesite led by musicians. A reporter, Colonel Albert Evans, described in his reminiscences, *À la California,* the funeral procession of a man named Ah Sam in San Francisco during the early 1870s. It included official mourners who, besides crying and wailing, sang.[48] During the funeral of Lee Yu Doo in New York City, a band, consisting of a *jinghu* (a type of huqin), suona, and gongs, played as mourners lined up by twos for the processional.[49] The *New York Times* also described the funeral of Ying Hing, which reportedly included the playing of drums, gongs, and cymbals at the gravesite.[50]

As in funerals, weddings included a processional with a small band of musicians. When Chu Fong, perhaps the manager of the Doyers Street Theater in New York City, married Lum San Toy in 1893, someone beat a gong outside Chu's home to scare away evil spirits. Before the ceremony, a band, consisting of cymbals, a suona, and jinghu, also played. Ironically, Chu then had an American band play a march for the processional.[51]

Among Chinese immigrants who converted to Christianity, music making along with English skills were important not only for conversion and worship but also for bridging the gap between Chinese and American culture. Protestant missionaries, many of whom had also worked in China, set up schools and churches in the Far West and in major cities in the East, where immigrants could learn to sing hymns and play the piano or organ. Eventually, many immigrant churches organized their own choirs and hired an accompanist from their community, who was to perform for services, holidays, and special events, among other duties. Through their participation in Western religious music, these converts, like their counterparts in their homeland, challenged notions of racial inferiority that pervaded Americans' perceptions of Chinese musical ability.[52]

Several American missionaries wrote about the musical skills of immigrants in their congregations. Episcopal missionary and minister Otis Gibson described a service at M. C. Briggs's Methodist mission on Jackson Street in San Francisco. Although some did not participate, many converts sang hymns in Cantonese, accompanied by an organ. Gibson remarked that although he did not understand the words, two of the hymns were to the tunes "Nettleton" and "Jesus Loves Me."[53] In his travel narrative on religion in California, Presbyterian minister Charles Augustus Stoddard described attending the fortieth anniversary celebration of the Presbyterian Chinese Mission School in San Francisco, founded in 1853. The evening program included "recitations, songs, and original addresses by Louis Fon, Tang Ting, Lee Ling, Gen Yan, Quon Woon, Pon Sam, and other members of the school." A Mrs. Cheung Wong accompanied and directed the choir and soloists.[54]

Chinese participation in Christianity was not limited to singing Western hymns in Cantonese or English. Immigrants also incorporated their own traditions and created something new. During the fourth anniversary of the Methodist Episcopal School at a Chinese theater in San Francisco in 1877, Chinese and a few Japanese converts sang hymns and played instruments for the audience. One performer, Hok Hun (also known as Hok Bun or Hok Kan), performed something of his own creation for the event. "The musician first played his tune on the flute, and then sang to an organ accompaniment by George Howe," reported a journalist for the *Alta California*. "The tune seemed quite 'peculiar' to the ear of an 'outside barbarian,' but it was exceedingly well executed, and the feeling with which it was sung and the gracefulness of the few, evidently involuntary, gestures was charming, and it won a hearty encore." He also noted that whereas most Americans "were only accustomed to the nasal twangs and bagpipe notes of the ordinary Chinamen," these converts "demonstrated clearly the fact that with proper training, this race possesses voices of melody and power." For this reporter, although the Chinese were supposedly limited in their music ability, these converts opened up the possibility of doubt on two fronts—Hok Hun's solo (and its countering of notions of Chinese music as noise) and their hymn singing.[55]

In addition to being a significant part of worship at Christian missions, music was an important aspect of worship and prayer at Chinese shrines, known to Europeans and Americans as "joss houses." Shrines were built in every town and city with a significant Chinese immigrant population, although American writers seemed unable to distinguish between Buddhist, Daoist, or Confucian practices. During prayer, priests assisted worshippers by playing gongs, drums, or a *muyu* (a fish-shaped wooden block used to keep time). The suona, *sanxian* (a long-necked lute), huqin, and *qing* (sonorous stones) were added during special ceremonies and festivals. Many times priests read from important religious texts, displayed sacred symbols, burned incense and paper prayers, and chanted, all accompanied by music. While visiting San Francisco in 1889, Mary H. Wills described a large band in a temple that played for several hours. She listed the instruments used as "horns, anvils, cymbals, and indescribable instruments," names that clearly alluded to Wills's attitude about what she heard. Like other writers, Wills saw Chinese practices as beyond her conceptualization of music.[56]

The most noted Chinese celebration was New Year's, held sometime in January or February, depending on the lunar calendar. After five days of cleaning and decorating, men and women stayed up all night eating, singing, playing mahjong, or just talking as they waited for the New Year to arrive. Newspapers noted that small bands performed during the final day of New Year's. In 1870, Belleville, New Jersey, was home to a large number of Chinese immigrant men who had been hired to work at Hervey's Laundry, a large-scale commercial laundry just over the Hudson River from Manhattan. Because of this critical mass of immigrants, Belleville was also the location of the only shrine in the New York and New Jersey area until 1885. During New Year's, many immigrants traveled from throughout the region to celebrate the holiday at this shrine. Similar celebrations were held in communities with sizable Chinese immigrant populations throughout the United States.[57]

During the 1850s and 1860s and before American nativism became a repressive force in the Far West, Chinese musicians participated in American civic events.[58] Miska Hauser, a Hungarian concert violinist who toured the United States during the 1850s, described a Fourth of July celebration in San Francisco in 1853. Among the marchers were reportedly four hundred Chinese immigrants, some on horseback and in carriages but the majority on foot. Of the three carriages that were part of this group, the first carried four of the most important Chinese men in San Francisco and the other two held musicians. "The second carried four musicians, comically dressed, plus Chinese drums, cymbals, and other instruments. In the third carriage was a string and percussion orchestra." The *Daily Herald* in San Francisco reported the following year that a group of Chinese immigrants marched again in the parade. Three men led the group on horseback, followed by a covered wagon filled with seven or eight musicians, a group of marchers on foot, and finally another group of musicians.[59]

Like other immigrants, the Chinese brought their traditions with them to the United States. Music was important for religious and civic purposes as well as for entertainment and leisure. These performances also provided white audiences with a much wider array of "real" Chinese performers and a repertoire of somewhat conflicting symbols regarding Chinese culture. Yet although Americans heard Chinese music during celebrations or at certain Chinese-owned businesses, most chose to focus on one particular institution: the theater.

CHINESE THEATERS

Europeans and Americans were very clear about their dislike for what they saw and heard of the Chinese operatic tradition. Although elaborate costumes, martial arts, and acrobatics fascinated writers, the majority believed that Chinese operas were completely contrary to their notions of music and theater. Thus, most would-be impresarios were quick to realize that although on a certain level these troupes were novel, it was difficult to make them appealing to American audiences. The failure of the Tong Hook Tong Dramatic Company in 1853 confirmed this belief.

Chinese businessmen started sponsoring operatic troupes in the 1850s to perform for immigrant audiences in the United States. There were several different theatrical traditions in China during the nineteenth century from which to choose, but because most immigrants were from Guangdong Province, most opera troupes that came to America were also from this region. Cantonese opera emerged during the middle of the nineteenth century along the Pearl River Delta, near the cities of Canton and Hong Kong, and reached its "golden age" by the late 1910s. This opera form was similar to others in China, especially the Beijing tradition from which the Cantonese is partially derived. As with Beijing, Cantonese used preexisting tune types; stylized movements; plots based on folktales, legends, myths, and historical stories; acrobatics; martial arts; simple sets and stage properties; and elaborate and symbolic costumes and makeup. There were also differences. Cantonese operas included folk stories from Guangdong Province, larger orchestras (up to twelve musicians as opposed to two or three), and by the 1910s and 1920s, local dialect, which made plots and dialogue much more accessible to Cantonese-speaking audiences. Other operatic traditions existed in Guangdong Province, but these catered mostly to government officials and wealthy merchants who enjoyed more elite productions that were tied to court life. Immigrants, the majority of whom were not of these classes, watched and enjoyed the more popular Cantonese version.[60]

The Tong Hook Tong Dramatic Company (also called the Tung Hook Tong or Tong Hooktung) arrived in San Francisco from Canton sometime in early October 1852 with 123 actors, musicians, and stagehands. The troupe was located at the American Theatre and performed selections from several operas. For its premiere, it opened with *"The Eight Genii" Offering Their Congratulations to the High Ruler Yuk Hwang, on His Birthday* also known as *A Birthday Greeting from the Eight Immortals* (*Bat Sin Ho Sau/Ba Sian He Shou*), which Nancy Yunhwa Rao in her study of New York's Chinese theater in the 1920s and 1930s notes was a common playlet given on special occasions. *Soo Tsin Made High Minister by the Six States* or *The Six Countries Invest a Chancellor* (*Liu Guo Da Feng Xiang*) was also produced that night, which introduced the whole cast.[61] During their last few days in San Francisco, they also put together a separate acrobatic and tumbling routine, perhaps because of the success of the Chinese Artistes, who had performed a similar program at the American earlier that month.[62]

Although houses were reported full, some reviewers were unsure how to judge the Tong Hook Tong. A critic from the *San Francisco Daily Herald* admitted that he did not know what to write because he was not acquainted with Chinese culture and language. He noted that the Chinese had "a most unique conception of dramatic entertainment" but that the audience seemed to "enjoy the declamation of their own tragedians with quite as much satisfaction as we would listen to the polished readings of a [Charles] Kemble or a [William Charles] Macready." Kemble and Macready were well-known British actors who toured the United States during the antebellum period performing Shakespeare. Although creating this link emphasized the popularity of the Tong Hook Tong among Chinese immigrants (and ignored other audience members), it also played to the association of Chinese opera with Shakespearean drama and the similarity of Chinese culture with that of England of the sixteenth century. This reviewer also complimented the attractiveness of the actresses and the company's costumes. "The females attached to the company are altogether the best specimens we have yet been favored with; and the dresses and paraphernalia are certainly very rich and gorgeous."[63] Although he could have been alluding to the femininity of Chinese men, he may well have been unaware that he was watching men playing women.

Because of their success with California audiences and the enticements of American entrepreneur George W. Beach, part of the Tong Hook Tong troupe left California for New York City. Yet, as John Kuo Wei Tchen, Ronald Riddle, and Arthur Bonner have already described, Beach backed out of their contract when the troupe arrived and left the company deep in debt to the steamship company that had brought it to New York. To make matters worse, its performances were not as profitable as it had hoped. Although the Tong Hook Tong received praise for its costumes, stage fighting, and acrobatics, it was seen as too foreign for New York audiences. The *Spirit of the Times* stated that "the Tong-Hook Tongs are great in other things than Opera; their military movements, their leapings and jumpings, and somersaultings, are well worth seeing—*once*."[64] Only when its eight acrobats performed at Burton's Theater in August did it experience full houses. The critic from the *New York Evening Post* believed that its tumbling exceeded anything else he had seen and noted that audiences enjoyed the troupe's hair trick (two acrobats held a pole on their shoulders with another putting his hair over it and using it to pull himself off the floor). In fact, on August 18, William Evans Burton, owner of the Burton Theater, raised admission for the whole house to 50 cents a person—and it was still packed.[65]

After its failure to win the hearts of audiences in the East, the Tong Hook Tong finally decided to leave either for California, where it had already seen success, or for China. Sympathetic to its situation, several actors and managers in New York City and Philadelphia gave benefit performances for the Tong Hook Tong, but they were unable to raise enough money to pay the troupe's debts and its passage. That fall, the commissioner of foreign emigration reportedly received an offer from G. G. Dennis, Esq., an agent for the Boston-based Hoogly Company, and a Captain Bratt from Warren, Rhode Island, to take the troupe to Hong Kong for $100 per person. Neither the ship nor Dennis appeared. Later, a Mr. Bayley also offered to take the actors to Cuba to work on a plantation where they would earn $4 a month. The Tong Hook Tong refused.[66] With no money to pay for passage home or to California and no one willing to book them, some went to the workhouse on Blackwell's Island or lived off of public charities on Ward's Island. Others became tobacco rollers, and one was a servant at the Five Points Mission.

Fortunately, by 1854 those remaining in New York City were finally given passage to wherever they desired through the work of the Chinese Relief Committee and especially Edward W. Syle, an Episcopalian missionary who had worked on and off in Shanghai from the 1840s through the 1860s and had been an ardent believer in the musical ability of his converts. Twenty-four went to California, although one died en route from an unknown fever. Six stayed in New York City to work, and four others decided to stay east to pursue their education. Six traveled on to Shanghai, which perhaps was their homeport or was a good location for unemployed performers to find work. Only four returned to Canton.[67]

Despite the catastrophe that surrounded the Tong Hook Tong, operatic troupes catering primarily to immigrant communities arrived periodically in the United States during the 1850s and 1860s. Their port of entry was San Francisco, which was also the center of Chinese cultural life and a place where organizers could easily rent theaters or other buildings in which troupes could perform. In 1855, for example, a fifty-person troupe appeared in San Francisco at the newly created Shanghai Theater on Dupont Street, which was managed by two immigrants, Chan Akin and Lee A-Kroon. Later that year, the Shanghai hosted performances from the Grand Musical Opera of Guangdong, which starred Leang Shang (Leang Chang). In December 1856, a Chinese troupe with fifteen actors appeared at the Adelphi Theater, previously the home of the French-language theater in San Francisco, and then traveled to the interior of the state before returning to the Adelphi for New Year's.[68]

Because the immigrant population during the 1850s and 1860s was in large part spread throughout the gold fields, several Cantonese companies trekked to the mining camps and interior cities of California, where their potential audiences lived and worked. Sacramento, which had its own theater, hosted several companies. In May 1855, a troupe managed by Leong Ahghue (who was also its interpreter) performed at the Sacramento Theater.[69] Small towns in the foothills of the Sierra Nevadas, such as Placerville and Oroville, were not easily accessible, but troupes still traveled to them. To facilitate the trip, they often limited the number of costumes, trappings, and musical instruments they brought with them; some carried materials to construct a makeshift outdoor theater for communities that did not have a theater or a building large enough to function as one.[70]

In a few instances, whites hired Chinese operatic troupes for non-Chinese audiences, but not without alterations to the program. Thomas Maguire, the San Franciscan theater mogul, sponsored Chinese productions at his Opera House in May 1860. To appeal to white audiences, however, he reworked each selection, removing objectionable parts such as birthing scenes, which reportedly horrified audiences who had seen the Tong Hook Tong in 1852, and ending the program with acrobatics and juggling. The play-bill also highlighted the lavishness of their costumes and gave synopses of the plotlines. To add to the hype, Maguire reported in the press that the five lead-ing actors were on their way to Paris to perform for Louis Napoleon. It is unclear whether they eventually traveled to France or if this was a ploy to attract audiences, a practice most successfully employed by P. T. Barnum.[71]

As part of the increasing segregation of the San Francisco Chinese com-munity in the 1860s, theatrical troupes performed with less frequency at American-owned theaters and for mixed audiences. Chinese businessmen finally found it more beneficial to themselves and the burgeoning "China-town" to build and manage their own theaters that catered to the specific needs of their community. In this way they always had a space for theatrical and musical performances or a meeting spot for large groups of people. The rise of anti-Chinese attitudes, violence, and legislation also encouraged the construction of separate theatrical spaces. By the mid-1860s, two semi-permanent Chinese theaters appeared on Dupont and Jackson streets; in 1868, there were two permanent structures.[72] The Royal Chinese or Hing Chuen Yuen Theater, also called the Prosperous Complete Origin Theater, opened on January 27, 1868, with a troupe that previously had appeared at a white-owned theater in San Francisco during the fall of 1867. This building was the first permanent Chinese theater since the arrival of the Tong Hook Tong, who had brought materials from China to build a theater (and which later became a processing center for Chinese immigrants). A few months later, the Orien-tal Academy of Music opened to house the Yun Sing Ping Company recently arrived from China.[73]

In the face of growing anti-Chinese attitudes and violence, these theaters flourished, with new buildings springing up in San Francisco's China-town throughout the 1870s and 1880s.[74] The Hing Chuen Yuen Theater, for instance, was simple on the outside, without any of the architectural flourishes found on most contemporary American theaters. Inside, there was a dress circle and gallery made up of benches, and there were even sections set off for Americans and for Chinese women, which led to protests by several immigrant men who wanted to maintain the theater as male-only.[75] As in permanent theatrical structures in China during the nineteenth century, the stage was a platform with a space in the back for musicians and two doors on each end for performers to enter and exit. There was no proscenium, wings, or flies.[76] Chinese theaters were also popular with American residents and the growing number of tourists from the East who were curious about Chinese culture. For Chinese immigrants, however, especially men who had no families in the United States, these theaters were places to socialize and to maintain contact with an art form that was deeply a part of their heritage.[77]

By the 1880s and 1890s, semi-permanent and permanent Chinese theaters were found in cities outside of California in which immigrants had established sizable communities. Portland, Oregon, hosted several touring troupes that traveled north from San Francisco and had a Chinese theater periodically during the late nineteenth and early twentieth centuries. From 1896 through 1898, Liberty Hall in Astoria, Oregon, was converted into a Chinese theater. Seattle witnessed its first Chinese theatrical performances in 1876. From 1883 through 1885, there was a Chinese theater at Second and Alder streets; seven years later, the Chou Shi (Wong Lung) Company performed at the Seattle Theater. In Los Angeles, theatrical performances were mentioned in the 1880s. By 1893 there was a permanent theater structure in Chinatown, but it was not open continuously. The Boston chapter of the American Folk-Lore Society and a group of local Chinese immigrants sponsored a troupe to perform in the basement of the Harrison Avenue Hotel in 1891. The audience was a mixture of Chinese and Americans—Oliver Wendell Holmes, William Dean Howells, and other community leaders attended. Six years later, a man named Li Toy briefly managed a Chinese theater at 20 Beach Street.[78]

In New York City, a Cantonese opera troupe did not perform again until 1889, over thirty-five years after the fiasco surrounding the Tong Hook Tong. By this time, New York's Chinatown was home to one of the largest Chinese immigrant communities in the country and was the social and cultural center for immigrants living and working throughout the city and its suburbs. Immigrants from all over came to see the Swin Tien Lok (Soon Han Lok) Dramatic Company (also known as Royal Company of Hong Kong), which had traveled from California to perform at the Windsor Theatre that year. Organizers refused to allow Chinese women into the audience, but up to two hundred Americans did attend (it is unclear if American women were permitted). Like Maguire in San Francisco, managers handed out programs in English to make the performance accessible to an English-speaking audience.[79] The appearance of the Swin Tien Lok, however, by no means meant that New York's Chinatown had a permanent theater and company. From 1890 through 1893, troupes came and went, appearing in mainstream theaters and performing for both heterogeneous and immigrant audiences. Finally, local businessman Chu Fong opened the first Chinese-owned theater on Doyers Street in Chinatown, formerly the location of the Chinese Mission Sunday School, in spring 1893. Chu's Chinese Concert Company sponsored troupes not only from California but also from Havana, Cuba, which had a sizable immigrant community and maintained its own theater.[80] Unfortunately, because Chu often held performances on Sunday, which conflicted with New York's blue laws, police officers periodically closed down the Doyers Street Theater and revoked his license.[81] By 1897, Chu had closed the theater permanently, reportedly because of the lack of patrons and conflicts with local gambling hall owners.[82]

During the nineteenth century, Chinese theaters in the United States went through a series of stylistic changes tied mostly to the role of women on the stage and in the audience. Theaters in China had traditionally banned women from the stage, and instead, men or young boys played female parts. In some major Chinese cities there were all-female troupes, which mainly were affiliated with teahouses and brothels; coed troupes did not appear in China until the late 1910s and 1920s. In the United States, women were able to gain access to the stage as early as the 1880s, despite their small numbers. Perhaps Chinese theater owners and managers were influenced by the European and American theatrical tradition in which women had been allowed to portray female roles since the eighteenth century; by the mid-nineteenth century, some were even portraying men in burlesque.[83] It is also possible that because some of the young women who came from China were trained musicians and vocalists, they were hired to fill in when a troupe did not have enough actors.

Ronald Riddle reports that as early as 1878, a San Francisco playbill listed both "Male and Female Artists" at a Chinese theater. Alfred Trumble's analysis of Chinese immigrant life in The "Heathen Chinee" commented that Chinese theaters in San Francisco were modernizing now that they allowed women into their productions. By the 1890s, a Mrs. Ah Moy starred at Chinese theaters in San Francisco with two other women—Mucy Kwai and Nuey Toeung.[84] New York City also had Chinese actresses beginning in the 1890s. Helen F. Clark in the Century noted that although women were not listed in advertisements or playbills, they performed small parts and were either the wives or daughters of other cast members.[85] By 1896, Chu Fong brought Yut Gum (also called Ah Kone), "the Bernhardt of the Celestial Realm," from California for $1,650 for ten months, plus board and other

LIFE-SIZE HEAD OF CHINA'S GREATEST ACTRESS.

Ill. 7. Portrait of Yut Gum from the *New York World,* June 21, 1896. Courtesy of the Library of Congress.

expenses (see ill. 7). She, along with her husband, had been living in the United States for nine years, and they spent much of their time performing in San Francisco and Portland. Yut stayed in New York City until the Doyers Street Theater closed in 1897.[86]

The appearance of Chinese and American women in the audience also broke from the traditional practice of nineteenth-century China. Of course, this development created tension within the immigrant community, many of whose members were concerned about women in public spaces, especially theaters. In 1868, members of the Tong Wing Company of Washermen protested outside of the Hing Chuen Yuen Theater because it not only allowed women into the theater but also had created a women-only section in the dress circle. Although women enjoyed going to the theater, they were well aware of the danger of commingling with the other sex. Alice Sue Fun recalled going to the theater with her mother during the early part of the twentieth century. Fun's mother rarely left the house except to go to the theater, and when she went, she always brought the children so that she was not alone in public.[87]

Despite the spread of Chinese theaters and troupes throughout the United States, these institutions began to fade by the 1890s. The passage of the Chinese Exclusion Act in 1882 and its subsequent renewal cut into their prospective audience base. Many immigrants who temporarily returned to China chose not to travel to the United States or were refused entrance. This also deterred many Chinese and American entrepreneurs from bringing in new troupes.[88] The legal definition of an actor and how it related to Chinese exclusion policies caused problems for theaters too. In January 1883, the federal court in Portland, Oregon, faced the first legal question relating to actors and exclusion. The presiding judge in the case decided that because actors' work was not of a physical nature and thus they were not in competition with white laborers, they would be allowed to enter the country.[89] In 1898, however, U.S. attorney general John W. Griggs reinterpreted U.S. immigration law. Instead of allowing anyone who was not a laborer to immigrate, his interpretation specifically outlined who was able to enter: teachers, students, merchants, diplomats, and tourists. Actors were not included in this list and therefore were excluded. Although there were some Chinese actors in the United States before 1898, there were apparently not enough to sustain existing theaters. Ironically, at about the same time, organizers of world expositions were granted special permission to bring in entertainers. They, however, faced strict restrictions on how long actors could stay and on the number of possible Chinese participants entering the United States.[90]

Because of these changes, Chinese theaters throughout the country started to decline. Although in 1892 San Francisco boasted of having as many as six theaters, by 1900 there were only two. The 1906 San Francisco Earthquake exacerbated this situation, destroying all of Chinatown and its remaining two theaters. Performances still occurred during the 1900s and 1910s in semi-permanent structures and in available buildings. Actors also continued to perform for community festivals, benefits, and banquets.[91]

The New York Chinese community faced similar problems. After Chu Fong closed the Doyers Street Theater in 1897, Chin Yu (Chung Yu), a local restaurateur, ran the theater through 1900, followed by Charlie Gong. As in the 1890s, police still frequented the theater not only to make sure no blue laws were broken but also to watch for men who were involved in what was popularly called the tong wars. Finally, after five men, including one actor, were killed during two separate performances, the Doyers Street Theater was closed in 1910. The local Rescue Society bought the building and converted it into the Chinatown Midnight Mission.[92]

New opportunities emerged at the beginning of the twentieth century in vaudeville and mainstream American theaters that allowed Chinese performers more contact with non-Chinese audiences. Ronald Riddle notes that Chinese actress Mar Yit Or performed with a Cantonese opera troupe at the Oriental Theater in San Francisco in 1909. Beginning in the fall of 1916, the Fong Choy Company, consisting of five women and six men, performed what reviewers called a "Chinese operetta." After performing at the Great North-ern Hippodrome in Chicago, the troupe visited Indiana and Minnesota before heading West through Canada and then returning to the United States at Tacoma, Washington. As late as 1932, a troupe called the Gale Quadruplets appeared at the Boston Opera House to "tell you about the Chinese Drama."[93]

Coinciding with what has been called the "golden age" of Cantonese opera, Chinese theaters witnessed a revitalization in American cities by the 1920s. This was partially tied to changes in China, including the acceptance of women as performers and the introduction of Western theatrical technologies. The Immigration Bureau also altered its policy toward Chinese actors and actresses who performed in Cantonese operas. Starting around 1924, per-formers were able to obtain six-month to one-year renewable bonds for $1,000 each, which were supposed to guarantee that they worked only at a specified theater and then left the country after three consecutive years. They were not allowed to reenter the United States for six months, but after that time, performers could reapply for bonds and return. Federal requirements for entry also mandated that actors be over the age of sixteen and without a con-tagious disease, and that at no time would they request public charity.[94]

These changes encouraged the reestablishment of Chinese theaters in San Francisco, Los Angeles, Portland, New York City, Boston, and Chicago, so that although the theaters were constantly under the scrutiny of immigration inspectors, they thrived throughout the decade. By the 1930s, however, social and cultural shifts in the United States—the Great Depression, talkies, and finally, Chinese American interest in American popular culture—forced the theaters to close once again.[95]

Thus, Chinese theaters in the United States went through cycles of devel-opment, innovation, and collapse. Shifts in the immigrant community, the passage of anti-Chinese legislation, and developments in popular culture influenced the success of these troupes and theaters. Furthermore, in response to their situation in the United States, Chinese immigrants broke from tradi-tions in their homeland, especially those relating to women and, later, stage design, and created something that was more "Chinese American." Many Americans also visited these theaters, primarily in San Francisco and New York City, and periodically American impresarios hosted troupes for non-Chinese audiences. Although most reviews and travel narratives supported the construction of Chinese music as unmusical, these theatrical spaces were sites where Americans could be exposed to non-Western traditions and potentially reevaluate their understandings of music. Most importantly, although the

Chinese Exclusion Act helped shut off the flow of "real" Chinese music, it created the false impression—reflected by its absence in most music histories of the period—that there had not been much of it.

WORLD EXPOSITIONS

With the Columbian Exposition in Chicago in 1893, Chinese entertainers for the first time appeared in what at the fair was called the Chinese Village. It contained several buildings, including a theater, and was located along the main thoroughfare of the amusement zone. Separated from other sections in the fair, the amusement zone was where sightseers went to be entertained and to shop. This section, unlike the main exposition buildings, was not seen as having any educational value or valorized as the future of civilization. Instead, much like human curiosities, the Chinese Village reconfirmed notions of Chinese inferiority and highlighted the more exotic elements of Chinese culture. Nonetheless, world expositions in the United States from the Columbian Exposition on were another place where Chinese immigrants tried to promote intercultural understanding and where Americans could learn about alternative forms of music and performance.

Because Chinese immigrants had some say in how the Chinese Village was organized and presented, it operated differently compared with the earlier human curiosities and displays. Organizers, the majority of whom were merchants, hoped that a venue such as an exposition would enable them to expose a large number of Americans to their heritage. More generally, they also believed that these exhibits could generate positive attitudes about the Chinese by emphasizing the greatness of their civilization and, by extension, its similarities to that of the West. To do this, promoters tried to find ways to make Americans rethink their preconceptions of Chinese culture by highlighting acts known to be popular with American audiences, such as magic acts, acrobatics, and juggling, and eliminating those that were not as well liked. They also erected ornate buildings, sold popular Chinese export goods, and handed out informational booklets.[96]

Since the late 1830s, museums in the United States had displayed objects as a way to disseminate information about China, including its music and theater traditions. For a small fee, those looking for entertainment as well as scholars interested in a deeper understanding of China could walk through these collections. By the 1820s and 1830s, the Peabody Museum, created by the East India Marine Society of Salem, Massachusetts, included Chinese musical instruments.[97] Nathan Dunn (1838) and John R. Peters Jr. (1844) also created traveling Chinese museums that appeared in several major cities along the eastern seaboard from the late 1830s through 1850. Both included several glass cases containing costumes, musical instruments, models of community celebrations, and figurines. Peters also hired Le-Kaw-Hing as a "Professor of Music," who later became Soo-Chune in Barnum's Chinese Family.[98]

It was Chinese immigrants who led the way in using expositions to question anti-Chinese attitudes in the United States. In 1892, the Chinese government refused to participate in the Columbian Exposition after the passage of the Geary Act (1892), which renewed the exclusion of Chinese immigrant laborers first passed in 1882 and required all immigrants to register with the federal government. Despite China's boycott, a group of merchants felt that a Chinese presence at the Chicago fair was an important way to fight negative attitudes. These merchants, known as the Wah Mee (also called Chinese-America) Exposition Company, applied to install a series of exhibits—a joss house (which functioned as a museum), bazaar, restaurant, and theater—that collectively became known as the Chinese Village on the Midway Plaisance.[99] The Wah Mee Company also produced brochures and programs in English that listed the snacks and drinks visitors could purchase and briefly described the displays installed in the joss house and the history of Chinese drama. One program, for example, stated that these operas were "exact reproductions of life occurrences, some of them having taken place 2400 years ago." This comment upheld the idea that China was a great and ancient civilization, which appealed to audiences interested both in the past and in places supposedly unaffected by modern life. It also confirmed the belief that China was unchanging and had not experienced "progress"—through either biological or social/cultural forces—as the West had.[100]

To add to the appeal of the Chinese Village, the Wah Mee Company brought in artisans and performers from outside the United States. Although not all were laborers, still they were required to have permits and proof that they were traveling to the Columbian Exposition. Seven actors from Havana, after a brief stint at the Doyers Street Theater in New York City, traveled on to Chicago; another 200 artisans and performers arrived from China via San Francisco.[101] Unfortunately, to complicate matters, 215 supposed actors arrived in Tacoma, Washington, in April 1893, but inspectors discovered that their papers were forged and sent them home.[102] As a result of this event, Americans began to fear the Chinese would use expositions to circumvent the law—bringing men and women into the country as actors and artisans, only to have them disappear into immigrant enclaves.

Once they got to the Chicago exposition, performers faced a rigorous schedule of entertaining the continuously coming and going audiences. From nine o'clock in the morning until ten o'clock at night, with short breaks in between, performers put up a mixture of operatic numbers, tumbling, juggling, and magic. Jugglers and acrobats also performed on the main thoroughfare of the Midway Plaisance. Operatic pieces were modified to fit American tastes—perhaps shortened into action-packed vignettes. In *The Adventures of Uncle Jeremiah and Family at the Great Fair*, Charles Stevens McClellan observed that the theater was "to occidental taste which all but oriental enthusiasts will appreciate." It appears that McClellan had attended a Cantonese opera performance elsewhere and realized the modifications were purposely made for white audiences.[103]

The main organizers of the Columbian Exposition, however, compromised the educational purposes put forth by Chinese immigrants in several ways. The exposition's promoters relegated the Chinese Village to the amusement section along the Midway Plaisance, away from Western musical and theatrical venues in the White City, and hired an American showman, Colonel H. Sling, to oversee the Chinese section. Thus the Chinese cultural displays were lumped together with other non-Western and folk displays that were intended to amuse and not necessarily to inform or to teach more positive attitudes. The physical separation of the Chinese Village from the main exhibition buildings also revealed the fair organizers' condescension toward countries like China. In their view, Chinese opera was simply one of many attractions intended to entertain tourists. It was not equated with what was perceived to be more civilized and progressive forms of culture.[104]

Except for the Pan-American Exhibition in Buffalo, New York, other fairs after the Columbian likewise included a Chinese Village with a theater as part of the amusement zone. The 1894 California Mid-Winter International Exposition in San Francisco and the 1895 Cotton States and International Exposition in Atlanta had Chinese theaters and brought in performers from China. In 1899, the National Export Exposition in Philadelphia also included "a Midway Plaisance, equal if not superior to the famous World's Fair Midway at Chicago, and comprising a Chinese Village, a Chinese Theatre, acrobats, and customs." The Women's Exhibition at Madison Square Garden in 1902 displayed women from non-Western countries with their children. Many of them sang and performed on musical instruments. Finally, the Alaska-Yukon-Pacific Exposition in Seattle in 1910, the Panama California Exposition in San Diego in 1915, and the Sesqui-Centennial in Philadelphia in 1926 listed Chinese theaters in their amusement zones.[105]

In 1898, a group of Chinese merchants, some of whom were involved with the Columbian Exposition, again organized a Chinese Village for the Trans-Mississippi and International Exposition in Omaha, Nebraska. This time, however, they brought Chinese men and women from northern China, especially from around Shanghai, Tianjin, and Beijing, because they believed white audiences would see these performers differently than those from the south, a cultural group with whom Americans were already acquainted through immigration and who they perceived negatively. The most famous Chinese entertainer at the Trans-Mississippi Exposition, Ching Ling Foo (Chee Ling

Qua),was an important, innovative magician at the turn of the century who popularized the image of the Asian magician. After his appearance at the fair and later in vaudeville, the demand for Chinese magicians increased, and managers and agents petitioned the federal government for permission to bring in these types of performers. Several European and American magicians also began to perform in yellowface, such as William Ellsworth Robinson under the stage name Chung Ling Soo, a name chosen specifically to confuse audiences with the "real" thing—Ching Ling Foo.[106]

The Chinese government sent its first official exhibition to the Louisiana Purchase Exposition in St. Louis in 1904, in hopes of improving its image. In many ways, this exhibition was similar to displays from the earlier part of the nineteenth century that used descriptive catalogs and labels in combination with objects and models. The Chinese Pavilion, a miniature reproduction of Prince Pu Lun's summer palace in Beijing, contained manufactured goods, agricultural products, and natural resources. It also included a Grand Entertainment Hall, but it is unclear if any performances were given in this space or if it was used to house display cases. With Chinese government participation, exposition organizers now treated Chinese cultural contributions differently in that Chinese objects, including musical instruments, were displayed away from the amusement zone and in educational venues. Aside from the Chinese Pavilion, organizers displayed more than twenty musical instruments, mostly string instruments, in the Palace of Arts as part of the official exhibit from the city of Tianjin. The placement of these instruments, although still exotic and novel, aligned them more with other displays purported to be representative of progress and Western civilization.[107]

The Chinese government, however, was not involved with putting together an entertainment concession that included music and theater. Instead, a group of Philadelphia Chinese merchants, the Yeo Ging Company, created another Chinese Village for the Pike, the amusement section of the Louisiana Purchase Exposition. Wong Yu Sun of Chicago, Captain Fred L. Esola of San Francisco, and a Mr. Budd of Boston managed the Chinese Village, which included a theater, joss house, teahouse, restaurant, and bazaar. Actors and musicians were again permitted through an act of Congress to enter the United States from China. Yet because Americans were so concerned that Chinese workers would try to immigrate illegally, everyone was fingerprinted and tagged.[108]

At the Panama-Pacific International Exposition at San Francisco in 1915, the local Chinese American community worked with the newly founded Chinese Republic to put together an official exhibit and another Chinese Village for an area of the exposition called the Amusement Zone. Chinese and Chinese Americans hoped that because a republican government had replaced the Qing dynasty in 1912, Americans would look more favorably on their exhibits and, by extension, their people. As with the Louisiana Purchase Exposition, Chinese and Chinese American promoters had nine separate displays installed as part of various educational exhibits as well as another Chinese Pavilion. The Chinese Village included a scaled-down version of the Forbidden City in Beijing, a traditional Chinese home, and a theater.[109]

Chinese and Chinese American organizers were able to exercise a certain level of control over images of the Chinese at the fair. When theater executive Sid Grauman, who would later open Grauman's Chinese Theater in Los Angeles in 1927, established a Zone venue called Underground Chinatown to highlight the evils of the Chinese immigrant community in San Francisco (especially opium use), local Chinese Americans and the Chinese consul protested and finally had American fair officials close the exhibit. This victory was short-lived. Later, organizers opened Underground Slumming as part of the Chinese Village.[110]

Starting with the Columbian Exposition in 1893, world fairs allowed Chinese immigrants and, later, Chinese government officials some room to package their performing arts traditions on their own terms. In the end, these groups hoped to alleviate anti-Chinese attitudes and to develop more positive relations between China and the United States. Still, they faced obstacles that had the potential to undermine their work—generally negative preconceptions about Chinese music and theatrical traditions, the location of Chinese theaters in amusement zones, and commentators who ridiculed their exhibits. They were well aware of what American audiences preferred, and they emphasized these aspects in performances and reading material. Among the things non-Chinese audiences did not favor—although it could not be entirely avoided—was music.

THE OPPORTUNITY FOR AMERICANS to watch Chinese performers in the nineteenth and early twentieth centuries was extensive, but for many observers these performances only helped reconfirm their conceptions of Chinese inferiority and the reasons the Chinese should not be allowed to settle in the United States. Like many who visited China, Americans at home supported attitudes that framed Chinese music and theatrical practices as representative of an inferior evolutionary state. Thus, by the 1870s, Chinese traditions disappeared from many mainstream stages and were restricted to immigrant communities or, with few exceptions, dime museums, circuses, and fairs. There were also moments when audiences and critics praised what they saw on the stage, particularly costuming, acrobatics, and magic. An even smaller but growing number of American and European artists, who were set on breaking from the rigid theories and practices that dominated their culture, believed that Chinese culture offered new ways to reinvigorate Western civilization.

For Chinese immigrants, music and drama were significant, but for different reasons. The performing arts helped Chinese immigrants reconnect with their homeland and heritage and escape the rigors of everyday life. Music and drama also were important ways to expose Americans to Chinese culture and to encourage understanding, especially through the use of handouts, lecturers/translators, and more positively viewed Chinese traditions such as acrobatics and magic. Those who studied Western music in missions either in China or the United States also helped raise questions about the stereotype of the Chinese as an "unmusical" race. The combination of these forces demonstrated the visibility of Chinese immigrants as musicians and actors, and their influence more broadly on constructions of race and culture, despite their erasure from the literature on music and theater in the United States.

CHAPTER 4

The Sounds of Chinese Otherness and American Popular Music, 1880s–1920s

BY THE 1880s, with the number of opportunities for Americans to hear Chinese music, American songwriters began to incorporate Chinese-inspired sounds into their music. To some extent this development was a continuation of the racist discourse that saw the Chinese as foreign and inferior, with the American composer, through the use of musical notation and instrumentation, becoming just another mechanism in the marginalizing of a group of people. Yet the borrowing of Chinese musical traditions allowed songwriters to expand their understanding of music and break down the rules of music composition that many found restricting. Some composers believed that, as with other traditions from the non-Western world, Chinese culture contained remedies for what they saw as the West's cultural stagnation. Although still tied to debates on the progress of Western civilization, Chinese music for these musicians had become a source of inspiration and innovation, and it impacted the development of American music in ways that have not been widely acknowledged.

At this time, much of the source material for Chinese music came from missionaries, civil servants, traders, and music experts, all of whom worked in Chinese communities at home and abroad. As accurate as they tried to be, these writers were not only Euro-centric in almost every aspect of their work, but they framed their findings as authoritative texts on "authentic" Chinese music. Thus, their actions were located somewhere between ethnomusicology, which emerged in the post–World War II era and emphasized cultural sensitivity, and comparative musicology, the late nineteenth-century precursor to ethnomusicology that compared Western and non-Western traditions in ways that reaffirmed racist attitudes. In spite of the prevailing belief that Chinese music was noise and therefore beyond notational description, these visitors attempted to bridge this gap and published analyses and examples of Chinese music for American and European readers. What was perhaps unforeseen was how these texts would also become a resource for American popular songwriters.

Beginning in the 1880s, a noticeable shift occurred in American music that paralleled a shift in American attitudes on race and the practice of seeing Asia as monolithic. Up to this time, only a few songwriters had incorporated Orientalist sounds, as Charles Towner had in "Heathen Chinee." By the 1880s, American songwriters began to follow the European practice of using sound to mark the Chinese as Other. Since the eighteenth century, European composers had used certain aural cues to demarcate the "Orient"—especially the Ottoman Empire, a major source of intercultural contact and anxiety—from Europe. By the following century, Americans too had turned to sound to define the American "race" through music. By the use of certain melodies and instrumentation, composers and music experts hoped to find a way to embody an American identity separate from a European one without losing a sense of whiteness. To do this, musicians relied on their training in Western music (both art and popular), which they combined with transcriptions and writings on folk traditions. Interestingly, the music of certain groups (Appalachian whites, Native Americans, and African Americans) was seen as unique to the United States and was appropriated by composers to help fashion an American sound. Chinese music, however, helped shape the definition of what it meant to be American in other ways—by acting as a foil.

To create a Chinese sound, American songwriters turned to another set of sonic devices that were associated with non-Western and non-art music—blackface minstrelsy and African American musical traditions. As musical representations of difference, African American signifiers were well known to American art and popular composers since at least the 1830s, when the first blackface minstrels appeared. By combining African American traditions with European Orientalism and transcriptions of Chinese music, they again played to notions of difference and inferiority and expanded on the conflation of the non-Western world.[1] Ironically, in contrast to the popular perception of Chinese music as noise, American songwriters created a sonic middle ground that was somewhere between art music and unorganized sound.

There were also a few songwriters who turned to non-Western musical traditions for reasons that did not necessarily reinforce American racism. These musicians were frustrated by Victorian values and the commercialization of the arts and so looked to China in their quest for alternative forms of expression. These individuals, called antimodernists by T. J. Jackson Lears, specifically examined cultures and societies that they believed were more primitive and less evolved in order to reinvigorate their own.[2] Ultimately, they produced new ideas about music and performance, which although still tied to attitudes about race and civilization, created alternative attitudes toward Chinese culture and opportunities for Chinese and Chinese Americans.

By writing down Chinese "noise" in Western musical notation and incorporating Chinese instruments in ways that appealed to audiences, American musicians created connections between China and the West that the vocabulary surrounding noise had obscured. Beginning in the 1880s, the embodiment of Chinese music in popular culture countered the belief that Chinese music was beyond the scope of Western listeners. As with songs from earlier in the century, race was central—whether through the explicit perpetuation of Chinese difference by means of sound or through the use of "primitive" traditions to reinvigorate Western ones.

TRANSCRIPTIONS OF CHINESE MUSIC

Over the course of the nineteenth century, scholars working with music expanded on seventeenth- and eighteenth-century ideas of observation and experimentation through the creation of new systems of analysis. At the same time, they implemented new technologies for classifying, collecting, and preserving social practices and cultural productions. Conducting research on Chinese music, however, was difficult. Few music experts traveled to China or were in personal contact with Chinese musicians living in Europe and the United States. Many missionaries, civil servants, and merchants, however, lived and worked extensively with the Chinese and were also interested in studying their culture. These impromptu scholars were more concerned with promoting cultural understanding and uplift than with scientific rigor, but they provided European and American experts with information they could then use to affirm their own beliefs about cultural development and race.[3] By the end of the nineteenth century, these works became an important resource for songwriters and eventually found their way into American popular song.

A central tenet in ethnomusicology today is that the cultural bias of the listener/observer affects any analysis and recording of music from another culture. This belief, however, sharply contrasts with that of nineteenth-century European and American writers, who saw their work as much more absolute in its depiction of music traditions from the non-Western world. Although unacknowledged at the time, their transcriptions were riddled with problems and inconsistencies. Until the invention of the phonographic cylinder, all music recordings relied on the imperfect ability of the listener to recall what was played. Unless the musical piece was repeated *exactly* the same way several times (which did not fit Chinese music practices and their allowance for improvisation), this was incredibly difficult. There were also dissimilarities between the notes on the page and the actual pitches they represented, that is, the pitches often had no equivalence on the Western tempered scale. Furthermore, preconceived notions about race and culture (including the construction of noise and music) affected recordings and subsequent analyses by these writers.

Using this raw data, music experts and amateurs tried to find a common thread between Chinese and Western musical traditions. Simultaneously, however, they delineated what constituted civilized culture. Through scientific methods (as they understood them), these writers created a musical hierarchy, which placed Western art music on top. Their work also validated racist attitudes by demonstrating to their own satisfaction that non-Westerners were culturally less developed and could not understand more complex ideas. Although this seemingly confirmed the superiority of their own culture, it also provided information for others to interpret in a different manner.

A small number of Jesuit missionaries during the eighteenth century produced some of the earliest European works on Chinese music. Following the words and deeds of their order's founder, Francis Xavier, they believed that the best way to convert was to explain Christianity in ways that related to Chinese life. Jesuit missionaries spent much of their time studying Chinese language and culture, and for some this study developed into admiration. A few of these missionaries also analyzed and published what they had learned, and their work became the basis of Western knowledge about Chinese musical and theatrical traditions and an early source of musical expression.[4] Later in the 1790s, members of the first British embassy, although more concerned with diplomatic and trade relations than intercultural understanding, wrote down "Moo-Lee-Chwa" and "The Peyho Boatmen."

French Jesuits Joseph-Henri-Marie de Prémare and Joseph-Marie Amiot were among the most influential writers on Chinese music and theater. They had lived in China for many years, studied Chinese tracts, and sent analyses, transcriptions of melodies, and translations back to France, where they were finally published. Both argued that the Chinese had derived and perfected their system of music scientifically during ancient times and that it was a system similar to the one created by the ancient Greeks, which had become the basis of modern Western music. They also noted, however, that these ideas had been lost or disregarded over time, which led to the present-day degraded state of music in China. In particular, Prémare translated the lyrics of a Chinese opera—*Chao Shih Ku Erh*, or *The Orphan of the House of Chao*—into French, which Voltaire, Arthur Murphy, and a number of other composers and playwrights rewrote for European audiences during the eighteenth century.[5]

By the 1830s, American and British Protestant missionaries living abroad had established societies and intellectual journals specifically for sharing knowledge about China. American traders brought these publications back to the United States for those interested in Chinese civilization and current events, and local newspapers frequently printed excerpts from them. In 1830, British missionary Robert Morrison (the first Protestant missionary to proselytize in China) of the London Missionary Society founded the Christian Union and later the Society for the Diffusion of Useful Knowledge. Two years later, Bostonian Dr. Elijah C. Bridgman took a printing press to China to ease the dissemination of biblical tracts for the American branch of the Episcopalian Missionary Board. With this press and the financial support of Morrison's Christian Union, Bridgman began to publish and edit a monthly journal, the *Chinese Repository*, in 1832. Several other societies were established during the nineteenth century, many of which published journals and comprehensive works on Chinese civilization.[6]

In 1839, the *Chinese Repository* published one of the first analyses of Chinese musical instruments since Amiot and, like its predecessor, opened up the possibility of deeper understanding and appreciation. G. Tradescant Lay, who in *The Chinese as They Are* had described the mediocrity of Chinese opera, catalogued the various types of Chinese musical instruments, and examined Chinese musical practices and theories.[7] In this article, Lay used many of the same images that previous travelers had employed to support Chinese inferiority. He argued that although the Chinese had scientifically reasoned their musical theories, they were behind those of the West. It is interesting that Lay found Chinese melodies similar to those of the Scots, which may reveal other prejudices at work or a familiarity with writers who had made similar points. Unlike other authors, however, Lay observed that harmony did exist in Chinese music, but only in a very limited sense. Furthermore, he argued that the development of harmony had been restricted primarily because the Chinese musical notation system was so complicated that it took several months to learn even the simplest of songs. Here he implied that Chinese musicians worked with a more complicated system of notation and that with something simpler such as that used in the West, they could easily read and write more sophisticated music. In the end, he regarded his comments not as a condemnation but as a demonstration of his own curiosity and the value of studying non-Western cultures, which Europeans and Americans could eventually find enjoyable with some familiarity.[8]

A similar group of American and British missionaries in Shanghai wrote about Chinese music for the *Journal of the North-China Branch of the Royal Asiatic Society*. Founded in 1859, this journal consisted of papers originally given by members of the Shanghai Literary and Scientific Society, which later became a branch of the Royal Asiatic Society. In its first edition, Edward W. Syle, who had written on the ability of Chinese converts to learn hymns and had helped members of the stranded Tong Hook Tong Company return home, analyzed Chinese musical notation. Reportedly, Syle had studied with a local teacher who exposed him to Chinese notation and played several melodies for him on a type of flute, melodies Syle eventually learned to play on the melodeon. As a result of his studies, he lectured and later published his analysis on the inefficiency of Chinese musical notation in comparison to that invented in the West.[9] As part of his analysis, he published a transcription of a melody he called "Siau Chok," which was seen as an important example of Chinese music and would later appear in several world music histories.[10]

Thanks to the work of such an international group of amateurs, much more information about Chinese music and theater became generally available over the course of the nineteenth century, as did more systematic analyses. In 1884, J. A. Van Aalst published *Chinese Music* through the Statistical Department of the Inspectorate General of Customs in Shanghai, an international institution established in the 1850s to regulate trade between China and Western nations. Little is known about Van Aalst, who reportedly was a German national who worked for this office. His eighty-four-page pamphlet, excerpts of which appeared in the *New York Times*, was one of the few attempts to analyze Chinese traditions on a large scale in the nineteenth century. Along with Amiot and Prémare, Van Aalst became a major resource on Chinese music for contemporary and future musicians and music experts. The *New York Times* in January 1886 noted that *Chinese Music* was a model for other ethnographic works, specifically those about Native Americans.[11]

From his introductory comments, Van Aalst's purpose seems to be unusually culturally sensitive. He disagreed with missionaries, diplomats, and other visitors (dilettantes in his estimation) who portrayed the Chinese as a "strange people, with a peculiar language, institutions, customs, and manners." Furthermore, those who framed Chinese music as "detestable, noisy, monotonous" were "erroneous."[12] Only someone with his expertise could systematically analyze and represent what was "real" Chinese music.

Ultimately, Van Aalst found that "real" Chinese music was as inferior as other writers had claimed, yet because of his musical expertise, he believed he could explain why there was this difference between Chinese and Western music. He conceded that ritual and sacred music were "passably sweet" and that a few theatrical songs were "pretty" or contained "beauty of language."[13] Nevertheless, for Van Aalst, Chinese music had at least four specific defects:

(1) The intervals of the Chinese scale not being *tempered,* some of the notes sound to foreign ears utterly false and discordant; (2) the instruments not being constructed with the rigorous precision which characterizes our European instruments, there is no exact justness of intonation, and the Chinese must content themselves with an *a peu pres*; (3) the melodies being always in unison, always in the same key, always equally loud and unchangeable in movement, they cannot fail to appear wearisome and monotonous in comparison with our complicated melodies; and (4) Chinese melodies are never definitely major nor minor; they are constantly floating between the two, and the natural result is that they lack the vigour, the majesty, the sprightliness, the animation of our major mode; the plaintive sadness, the tender, lamentations of our minor mode;

and the charming effects resulting from the alternations of the two modes.[14]

This list reflects Van Aalst's musical bias, which only helped reaffirm his readers' anti-Chinese attitudes. Harmony, temperament, modes, and consistent instrument construction epitomized in Van Aalst's mind Western musical sophistication and refinement. Without these ideas and practices, Van Aalst believed that Chinese music lacked expressiveness and depth.

By the 1880s and 1890s, studies and lectures soon started to appear in the United States based on the work of the growing number of experts at home. Herbert E. Krehbiel, music critic for the *New York Tribune* and *New York Times* and key advocate for the establishment of an American music, lectured and wrote about China, which he saw as a window to previous periods of Western musical development.[15] Unlike other writers, Krehbiel did not do fieldwork in China, but instead relied on previous research and worked with Chinese musicians in New York's Chinatown. He even learned to play the qin, reportedly giving "quite a tune."[16]

Working with American composer Henry Holden Huss, Krehbiel harmonized several transcriptions of Chinese music and gave them lyrics in English. Krehbiel and Huss put together these changes not only to make them palatable for American audiences but also to create examples for what they proposed some day would be a Chinese school of music. Music that was going to represent the Chinese nation, however, still had to fit Western ideals, especially its harmonic structure. The melodies that he reworked—Barrow's version of "Moo-Lee-Chwa," Van Aalst's "A Wedding March," "A Funeral March," "Guiding March," and "Wang Ta Niang" ("Madame Wang")—were only one step removed, if that, from the ways in which popular songwriters evoked China. For example, Krehbiel and Huss made a series of major alterations to Barrow's "Moo-Lee-Chwa," although Barrow had argued in *Travels in China* that his version was more authentic than Kambra and Scott's 1796 published version. Krehbiel and Huss, however, rewrote the lyrics, harmonized the melody, added a musical introduction, and transposed it to a lower key, all of which, paradoxically, made it closer to Kambra and Scott's "Moo-Lee-Chwa." Similar changes were made to the other songs.[17]

A high point in the professionalization of music transcription and analysis occurred with Thomas Edison's invention of the phonograph in 1877 and Alexander J. Ellis's development of the system of cents in 1885. The phonograph was useful because it was much more sensitive to variations in pitch that were otherwise lost in Western musical notation. Furthermore, phonographic cylinders preserved music for future generations and allowed listeners to hear the same tune repeatedly without worrying about any deviation or improvisation on the part of the musician. While studying with Asian and African musicians (including Chinese) at the 1884 International Health Exhibition in London, Alexander J. Ellis devised a way to divide each semitone of the Western tempered scale into one hundred parts. Through this system, he hoped that every possible tone anyone performed on any instrument or vocally could be written down.[18] Thanks to Ellis and Edison, those interested in recording Chinese music could get a more accurate understanding of what they heard.

American music experts quickly turned to these devices. In 1891, Benjamin Ives Gilman used the phonograph and cents to conduct field research with Chinese musicians and to analyze their performances. Trained at Johns Hopkins University in the Department of Philosophy during the 1880s, Gilman worked with Jesse Walter Fewkes, who was the first person to use the phonograph for ethnographic purposes while working with the Passamaquoddy of Maine in 1890. Later that year, Fewkes approached Gilman about transcribing his recordings of Zuni and Hopi music, which they then published in 1891.[19] Also in 1891, Gilman recorded a group of Chinese immigrant musicians living and working in New York's Chinatown. Unlike previous authors who studied Chinese musical notation, instrument construction, and Western transcriptions, Gilman used the phonographic cylinder to record Chinese musicians, whose compositions he then copied down in Western musical notation, placing a line over particular notes to indicate that the pitch was actually somewhere between that note and a semitone higher.[20] Unfortunately, only his writings still exist.

Gilman was emblematic of the scholars of his time. Although his intent was to clarify the differences and similarities between Chinese and Western musical practices, he revealed more about the prejudices that were circulating throughout the United States and Europe. Sometimes he affirmed universalistic notions of music and made connections between these two traditions. First, he argued that the Chinese had theorized and used the diatonic scale (other theorists, including Van Aalst, had argued that the Chinese rarely wrote songs based on the diatonic scale). Gilman's performers, however, slightly lowered the semitones that were critical to the construction of a diatonic scale and created something that he believed was similar to Celtic or Arabic music. This practice, Gilman contended, was tied to the introduction of Mongolian scales from the fourteenth century, which eventually led to the abandonment of semitones. Theories on human stages of development, however, also crept into his analysis. Gilman associated Chinese performances and theories with Western European ones from before the seventeenth century, which had led to temperament and harmonic movement. Like so many others, Gilman still endorsed a hierarchical view of civilization based on race.

During the nineteenth and early twentieth centuries, a diverse group of scholars and amateurs wrote critical analyses of Chinese music that influenced American attitudes and perceptions. By merely deciding to treat what they heard as music, they dealt a critical blow to the construction of Chinese music as noise and to questions surrounding the musical ability of the Chinese. But their work did much more. Like that of Amiot and Prémare, some of their writing demonstrated similarities between Chinese and Western traditions and promoted intercultural understanding. These authors, however, still turned to evolutionary theories about race and placed the Chinese on a lower level of development. Whether this lower stage reflected a lack of progress by the Chinese or a decline from a previous state of superiority, no one agreed. Beyond the scope of these writers was the fact that the information they gathered would be used by popular songwriters looking for new ways to express themselves and to embody the Chinese as musical subjects.

MUSICAL REPRESENTATIONS

By the mid-1880s, the information generated by music amateurs and experts, the partial containment of anti-Chinese attitudes through legislation, and popular and scientific ideas on race converged and informed American music in new ways. Increasing numbers of Chinese songs were being published in the United States using Western musical notation, which allowed songwriters access to something other than descriptions of Chinese music as noise. Both Orientalist operas from Europe and co-opted African American music were also readily available sources from which whites could borrow. By turning to this wealth of material, some composers used this repertoire of sounds to convey Chinese foreignness and inferiority, often combining information about Chinese music with musical tokens relating to the "Orient" and African Americans. Frustrated by the state of the performing arts in the United States, a few also turned to material written by Americans and Europeans about Chinese music as well as to one-on-one contacts with immigrant musicians living in the Chinatowns of New York and San Francisco. In addition to supporting associations between Shakespeare and Chinese traditions made by previous writers, these artists identified Chinese practices as precursors of Richard Wagner's concept of "total art," the complete integration of stagecraft, costumes, makeup, music, dialogue, and acting. As with other writers and musicians, however, they believed that Chinese traditions lacked the theoretical underpinnings found in Wagner's operas and thus needed Western cultural guidance.

In general, songwriters, in combining Chinese transcriptions, African American music, and Orientalist operas, used a set number of devices to denote musical Otherness.[21] To a certain extent, these signifiers had been in use since the late eighteenth century as part of the construction of the "Orient," but many were new and related to phenomena particular to the United States. First, syncopation and dissonance found in Orientalist operas and African American music appeared in many Tin Pan Alley songs. Composers also used sounds that were not found on a twelve-note, tempered scale to depict Chinese subjects. Finally, American songwriters added Chinese musical instruments, repetitive and droning rhythms, and pentatonicisms from transcriptions of "real" Chinese music (the latter two were also found in Orientalist operas) to their repertoire. In the end, these specific devices allowed songwriters to express racial differences and to find new modes of expression.

Many American songwriters applied musical devices that were mentioned in eighteenth- and nineteenth-century analyses of Chinese music. Although there was no unanimity, some authors wrote that the Chinese used the pentatonic scale. Others noted that the third in the Chinese scale was lower than that used in the West and sounded more like the minor scale. In 1839, G. Tradescant Lay stated that Chinese musicians had a limited sense of harmony and that many instruments were tuned in intervals a fourth or a fifth apart. Descriptions and drawings of particular musical instruments, especially gongs and cymbals, were also available; these instruments were also for sale in the United States for a good part of the nineteenth century.[22] All such efforts to delineate Chinese musical practices in familiar Western terms by writers had obscured the deep differences in music traditions and, rather unexpectedly, also gave musicians the tools to incorporate what was commonly held to be Chinese into their own songwriting.

Research on Chinese music conducted by professionals and amateurs influenced popular songwriters in other ways as well. In a search for authenticity, a few argued that there was usable music underneath what most Westerners heard as noise. A journalist for the *New York Tribune*, perhaps Krehbiel himself, wrote that composers only needed "to find the kernel of melody inside the shell and husk of noise" in order to find Chinese music, which they could then translate into Western musical notation.[23] The actual motifs employed by songwriters, however, were often part of a more stereotypical repertoire.

In a few instances, American songwriters chose simply to harmonize European or American recordings of Chinese music, much like Krehbiel and Huss had done. Songs from Francis Powers's *The First Born* in 1897 are good examples. This play, which told the story of the kidnapping and death of a pipe bowl mender's son in San Francisco's Chinatown, was one of the first attempts at portraying Chinese immigrants in a relatively realistic manner.[24] It is also one of the earliest examples of American songwriters turning to Chinese musical traditions for inspiration, and not for ridicule or parody. As part of Powers's depiction of Chinese immigrants, he hired two songwriters, Lee Johnson and William Furst, to compose Chinese-sounding music to be played periodically throughout the production. Johnson was a San Francisco resident and composer of many popular songs, including "coon" songs. By 1897, Furst was the general musical director for Charles Frohman, who owned several theaters around New York City. Later, he would go on to write incidental music for the works of playwright and producer David Belasco, including *Madame Butterfly* (1900) and *The Darling of the Gods* (1903), both of which were set in Japan.

For *The First Born,* Johnson wrote several songs reportedly based on Chinese melodies. "Chinese Highbinder Patrol" (1879), which a critic for the *New York Tribune* described as "authentic," has an eerie sound, augmented by what American audiences saw as a combination of musical devices associated with the "Orient": grace notes, parallel fourths and fifths, a minor key, repeated sixteenth notes, and pentatonicisms (see ill. 8).[25] It also has a set of four sixteenth notes in measures 18 and 25 that are similar to a melody transcribed and published in *Chinese Music* by J. A. Van Aalst called "Ballad" (see ill. 9). Reviewers noted that the noisiness of Johnson's music was similar to that of the Chinese. "With the clash and crash of huge cymbals, the squeak and squeal of Chinese instruments and the queer rhythm of the oriental music," the second act of *The First Born* began, wrote one such critic.[26] For the rest of his songs, Johnson could have easily visited Chinatown for inspiration or simply borrowed from the Orientalist or "coon" song tradition, with which he was already familiar.

Unlike Johnson, Furst admitted that the songs he wrote for *The First Born* were based on melodies he had heard in San Francisco's Chinatown. He titled these songs "Death Wail," "Joss Hymn," and "Feast of the Frost." All three were described as pentatonic.[27] Of all his songs for *The First Born,* however, the ballad sung by Loey Tsing (a prostitute first played by May Buckley) was the most noted in the press. Her untitled solo was also based on Van Aalst's "Ballad" (see ills. 9 and 10), and although Furst's is in a different key, which made it an all-black-note pentatonic melody, it is exactly the same as the melody of "Ballad." The *New York Tribune* stated that Furst's key change was a way to appease American audiences, who might perceive Van Aalst's version to be too high pitched and shrill.[28]

Furst helped break ground again in 1912 by writing the music for the play *The Yellow Jacket.* Set in China, Henry Benrimo and George Hazelton's *The Yellow Jacket* was another first in that it incorporated theatrical traditions from China into an American production that was not a form of parody.[29] Theater critic Sheldon Cheney, who saw most theater produced before World War I as unimaginative and in decline, wrote that *The Yellow Jacket* was "one of those fine flashes of genius that sometimes suddenly illumine the dark periods of an art."[30] In response to what they saw as major problems in theatrical realism, Hazelton and Benrimo combined several operas translated from Chinese and borrowed from Chinese opera's more episodic storyline, stylized action, and symbolic costumes, sets, and makeup to create something novel and inspiring to both audiences and fellow playwrights.

Ill. 8. Introduction from Lee Johnson's "Chinese Highbinder Patrol" (1897). Courtesy of the Daniel K. E. Ching Collection, Chinese Historical Society of America.

Ill. 9. William Furst's "A Chinese Ballad" (1897), published in the *New York Tribune.* Courtesy of the Library of Congress.

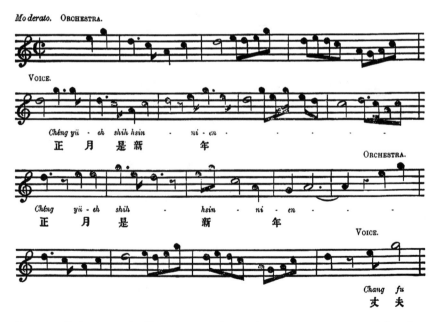

Ill. 10. "Ballad," transcribed by J. A. Van Aalst in *Chinese Music.* Courtesy of the Library of Congress.

Ironically, although Benrimo and Hazelton tried to emulate Chinese theatrical practices, they avoided one critical aspect: having the performers sing all their lines. Indeed, there was an orchestra that sat in an alcove at the back of the stage, but the actors, with one exception, did not sing. Reasons for this were not clear except for the cast's inability to learn to sing their lines and at the same time study other aspects of Chinese performance. Benrimo and Hazelton might have also been concerned that audiences would find *The Yellow Jacket* less appealing if they had to listen to "Chinese" music throughout the production. As one reviewer noted: "To make the story understandable to an American audience English is spoken and the Oriental music has been blended with a flavor Occidental. Its character is said to be retained."[31]

The one song that was integrated into the storyline of *The Yellow Jacket* was a siren's call sung by four prostitutes. As he had in *The First Born,* Furst turned again to Van Aalst's *Chinese Music,* in particular his transcription of "Yen-Hua-Liu-Hsiang" ("The Haunts of Pleasure"), also known as "Shih-Wu T'o Hua" ("The Fifteen Bunches of Flowers"). Van Aalst's "Yen-Hua-Liu-Hsiang," however, was the lamentation of a young woman whose parents had sold her into prostitution, and not a song of seduction. To complicate matters, over a decade earlier George Carter Stent, a British missionary also living in Shanghai, published "Yen-Hua-Liu-Hsiang" with a completely different melodic line. To explain these differences, Van Aalst wrote that although he agreed with Stent's analysis and translation of the lyrics, he felt compelled to take "the liberty to replace the music which he [Stent] has given by the *real* and *correct* tunes."[32] This statement was part of Van Aalst's condemnation of missionaries, even those such as Stent who spent time studying Chinese music. It also points to the inability of Westerners, including Van Aalst, to write down what they heard or to understand the extent of the improvisational nature of music in China, which allowed singers to put the same words to very different tunes. Furst, however, did not seem to doubt Van Aalst.

Aside from "Yen-Hua-Liu-Hsiang," the music in *The Yellow Jacket* was incidental, found only during the opening and closing of the production, scene changes, and action sequences, all of which were played on a mishmash of Chinese and American instruments. Even in these sections, Furst borrowed from Van Aalst. In three separate scenes, Furst incorporated Van Aalst's "Wang Ta Niang" ("Madame Wang") as a leitmotif to embody the hero Wu Hoo Git's enduring love for the virtuous Moy Fay Loy. Again, the translated lyrics told a somewhat different story. "Wang Ta Niang" is a story of a young girl who asks her neighbor to arrange a marriage for her with her lover, a young student, and not a celebration of female virtue as in *The Yellow Jacket*.[33] For the rest of the score, he reportedly relied on Orientalist traditions and his personal studies of Chinese theaters in San Francisco.

Unlike music from *The First Born* and *The Yellow Jacket,* the majority of songs with Chinese themes were only peripherally similar to those described or written down by Westerners who had observed Chinese musicians. These melodies contained certain aural cues that were tied to the conceptualization of China and, more broadly, the Orient. Piano and organ music written for silent films were some of the most explicit examples. By the late 1900s, a handful of music publishers and filmmakers began to produce collections of "mood" music. These "moods" were not only associated with emotions but also with national and racial types.[34] In 1913, songwriter and violinist J. S. Zamecnik, who had studied violin with Antonín Dvořák, compiled a collection of music to be played during silent films, including his own "Chinese Music," for publisher Sam Fox in Cleveland, Ohio.[35] Zamecnik's "Chinese Music" was somewhat similar to earlier transcriptions, such as "Air No. 1" by John Barrow, which was pentatonic and contained two sets of four sixteenth notes followed by a quarter note on the fifth interval of the scale (see ills. 11 and 12).[36] ("Chinese Music" is slightly different, with two sets of four sixteenth notes followed by two eighth notes.) These same devices were found in numerous popular songs about the Chinese during this period, such as William P. Brayton's "The Mandarin" (1906) and Frank Davis and Win Brookhouse's "All Aboard for Chinatown" (1915).[37]

Popular songwriters worked with excerpts from transcriptions of Chinese melodies and overlaid them with Western harmonic structures much like those found in silent film music. Often, these composers chose to use parallel fourths, fifths, octaves, and minor thirds, which had been mentioned in European and American discussions of Chinese music. The most famous example was William Jerome and Jean Schwartz's "Chinatown, My Chinatown" (1910), a replacement for another very unpopular song, "Apache Chinese" (1910), in the musical revue Up and Down Broadway (see ill. 13).[38] In "Chinatown, My Chinatown," Jerome and Schwartz used Chinese musical tokens in the introduction and verses that were similar to motifs found in Zamecnik's "Chinese Music." Even Billboard magazine recognized its potential because of its "sweetly plaintive melody with dreamy lyrics" and recommended that all who performed should "get it."[39] By 1915, Billboard also reported that several vaudevillians were performing "Chinatown, My Chinatown" and that many of them were Chinese Americans who sang it in both English and Cantonese.[40] "Chinatown, My Chinatown" even became popular with jazz musicians, who made at least twenty-five recordings of it between 1928 and 1941.[41]

The tune popularly known as "Chopsticks" (1877) also represented the intensification between Orientalist musical devices and Chinese themes. One of the earliest versions was Euphemia Allen's (alias Arthur de Lulli) "The Celebrated Chop Waltz" (1877). That same year, Alexander Borodin published "The Coteletten Polka" (1877) (coteletten is from the French word côte-lette, meaning "cutlet" or "chop"), based on a melody his daughter had played on

CHINESE MUSIC

Ill. 11. J. S. Zamecnik's "Chinese Music" (1913). Courtesy of the Daniel K. E. Ching Collection, Chinese Historical Society of America.

Ill. 12. "Chinese Popular Air No. 1" (1805), transcribed by John Barrow in *Travels in China*. Courtesy of the Newberry Library.

Ill. 13. William Jerome and Jean Schwartz's "Chinatown, My Chinatown" (1910). Courtesy of the Sam DeVincent Collection of Illustrated American Sheet Music, Archives Center, National Museum of American History, Behring Center, Smithsonian Institution.

Ill. 13. *(continued)*

Chinatown my Chinatown 3

Ill. 13. (*continued*)

the piano. In 1878 and 1879, Alexander Borodin, César Cui, Anatol Konstinovich Lyadov, Nikolay Andreyevich Rimsky-Korsakov, and Franz Liszt wrote twenty-four variations of Borodin's tune in the collection *Paraphrases* (1878).[42]

Neither "The Celebrated Chop Waltz" nor "The Coteletten Polka," however, had anything to do with China, or with the East Asian eating instrument. Instead, it was an exercise for young children, using their index fingers, which imitated the act of chopping. Nevertheless, because some of the intervals were similar to those mentioned in writings about Chinese music and found in Orientalist operas, American publishers were using the phrase "Chop Sticks" in place of the original title by 1879. Other songwriters who wrote variations also used the phrase "Chop Sticks," as in George F. Morris's "The Chop Sticks Galop" (1879) and Archie Gottler and Abe Frankl's "Ragging the Chopsticks" (1919). The association of "Chop Sticks" with China was usually confirmed by the illustration on the cover, which, paradoxically, did not necessarily include actual chopsticks. The sheet music cover for "The Chop Sticks Galop" included a Chinese man serenading a woman on a *sanxian*. She is looking out the window of a pagoda-like building decorated with paper lanterns. Not all adaptations were associated with China, however. "Ragging the Chopsticks" was supposed to be "a reminder of your childhood days at the Piano" and had no references on the cover or in the lyrics to China. In another version of "Chop Sticks" (ca. 1902), written by "De Zulli" (a reference to Allan's pseudonym De Lulli), the sheet music cover depicts a Japanese woman in a kimono holding a fan. Perhaps the illustrator chose to follow the Japanese vogue at the turn of the century, once again exemplifying the interchangeability of representations of China and Japan.[43]

Like "Chopsticks," the dance piece "Chinese Serenade" (1880) by Hermann Fliege was another enduring source of inspiration for American songwriters who wished to incorporate Chinese motifs. Born in Stendal, Germany, in 1829, Fliege was a music director in Berlin and later in St. Petersburg. An anonymous reviewer in Boston's *Musical Herald* wrote that Fliege's use of Oriental devices was similar to those found in F. Alexander's "Turkish Patrol" (1880), another dance composition with Asian flourishes. Ironically, despite his comments about Turkish elements, this same critic believed that these sounds "represent[ed] the feelings of Celestials" and also "possibly" supported "the views of Denis Kearney," one of the most vocal proponents of Chinese exclusion policies in California during the 1870s and early 1880s.[44]

"Chinese Serenade" appeared to have been quite popular with American publishers in the 1880s. Several companies reproduced it, including C. H. Ditson and Company in New York City, John Church in Cincinnati, George Willig and Company in Baltimore, and White, Smith, and Company in

Boston. The July 1882 issue of the *Musical Herald* contained a version of this song.[45] Newspapers also reported several marching bands performing "Chinese Serenade." Both Gilmore's Band at Manhattan Beach in 1882 and the Boston Ideal Club in 1893 played it during their concerts. The Boston Ideal Club included "original Chinese Effects," a reference to the inclusion of either "real" Chinese instruments or an elaboration of the "Oriental" signifiers already found in "Chinese Serenade."[46] In the early twentieth century, "Chinese Serenade" was in the *Album of Photo-Play Music* to be performed during Chinese scenes in silent films.[47]

A critical development that increased the number of musical signifiers for Chinese otherness was the frequent use of musical signifiers associated with African Americans. Although these devices could be used to distinguish between African Americans and the Chinese, their power in signifying a racial Other also allowed for the lumping together of these two groups in contrast to whites. Syncopated rhythms, unfamiliar instrumentation, chromaticisms, and atonal or "bent" notes were associated with both Chinese and African Americans. There was, however, something contradictory about commingling these two groups together through sound. By combining Chinese subjects with African American traditions, songwriters not only created something new but also deflated the foreignness embodied in many representations of the Chinese. By the beginning of the twentieth century, white songwriters were writing ragtime pieces and "coon" songs with Chinese tokens. W. C. Powell's "Ragtime Laundry" (1901) and George W. Meyer's "The Chinatown Rag" (1910) were similar in form to the classic piano rags made famous by Scott Joplin (for example, AABBACCDD, with each letter representing a strain made up of sixteen bars). These pieces also included devices that could be conceived of as "Oriental" or even "Chinese": intervals a fourth and an octave apart, dissonances, grace notes, syncopation, and pentatonic embellishments.[48] Not all white composers, however, used Chinese-inspired sounds with rags. "Chop Suey Rag" (1915), for example, was similar to other piano rags, but it did not include Chinese musical tokens.[49] The blues were also popular among white songwriters, but such songs fit the blues tradition in name only.[50]

A few African American composers incorporated Orientalist devices into music. This practice was somewhat similar to that of African American actors who portrayed Chinese immigrants on the stage and, in some cases, sung these songs. The mixing of African American music with Orientalist devices by African Americans enabled them to experiment with modes of expression. It also, however, added to the confusion about American identity and race. W. C. Handy, popularly known as the father of the blues, published Fred D. Moore and Oscar Gardner's "Chinese Blues" (1915) in *A Treasury of the Blues* and incorporated this song into the 1915 musical revue *Broadway Rastus*.

Although "Chinese Blues" is similar to other blues pieces that dealt with hardship and love, the chorus is written in the voice of a Chinese man and the verses in the voice of a narrator.[51] By the 1920s, several jazz bands recorded "Chinese Blues" as an instrumental piece.

African American songwriters also combined ragtime, most noted for its syncopated rhythms, with Chinese material. Although written more than ten years after the popularity of ragtime had peaked, "Up and Down in China" (1926) by African American songwriter and bandleader William Robison embodied the syncopated rhythm and chromatic movement found in piano ragtime.[52] Structurally, however, "Up and Down in China," with its strains of varying lengths, contrasted with Scott Joplin's classic ragtime. It was also part of the "Orientalist" tradition (see ill. 14).

A wide variety of sounds emerged by the end of the nineteenth century in songs about Chinese and Chinese immigrants. African American traditions, Orientalist operas, Chinese instruments, and transcriptions of Chinese melodies were all important sources for American popular songwriters. This development allowed composers to produce a more totalizing image of the Chinese as foreign and inferior through sounds associated with the non-Western world. Also tied to race was the development through which other songwriters used China to reinvigorate the performing arts in the United States by returning the arts to a more primitive state—similar to what many believed existed in China. Ironically, the mixing of Chinese/Orientalist and African American traditions created the possibility for the Chinese to be associated with traditions some saw as quintessentially American.

BEGINNING IN THE 1830s, a small number of missionaries, merchants, diplomats, and scholars began to take Chinese music seriously rather than regarding it as noise. They had various interests in China, but something united them—the mission of deepening the common understanding of Chinese culture. Some recirculated older stereotypes of Chinese inferiority, which they helped to reinforce through empirical methods and the authoritative conclusions that these methods yielded. Even here, however, new understandings and affinities emerged. The information and recordings they produced became the basis of Western knowledge of Chinese music and theater and, rather unexpectedly, a resource for popular songwriters.

Although interested in profits, popular songwriters turned to the information and recordings generated by those working with the Chinese in the United States and China. They also borrowed from Orientalist opera and African American traditions, two forms of Othering also in use during the nineteenth and early twentieth centuries. This was something new among composers, who previously, with a few exceptions, wrote Western-style melodies for songs with Chinese subjects. By the 1880s, the racialization of

UP AND DOWN IN CHINA

WILLARD ROBISON

Ill. 14. Willard Robison's "Up and Down in China" (1926), from *Six Studies in Modern Syncopation for Piano*. Courtesy of Northwestern University Music Library.

Ill. 14. (*continued*)

Ill. 14. (continued)

the Chinese, which was found most commonly through visual images and the written word, became more complete with the inclusion of sound in this project. Beliefs in racial inferiority, however, also supported songwriters who thought Americans needed to return to their primitive selves in order to avoid the decline of Western civilization, which many saw was tied to the commercialization and rigidity of the arts.

After the passage of the Chinese Exclusion Act, a similar reevaluation of lyrics, characters, and performers added to these new and at times contradictory images.

CHAPTER 5

From Aversion to Fascination

New Lyrics and Voices, 1880s–1920s

AT THE END OF THE NINETEENTH CENTURY, the musical expression of American popular music changed in ways other than notation and instrumentation. By the mid-1880s, lyricists and performers had begun to produce an assortment of songs, skits, and musicals with Chinese themes, which were combined with emerging Chinese musical motifs. This development was tied in part to the consolidation of the American music industry into Tin Pan Alley, the name given to several streets in New York City that were the center of music publishing in the United States from the 1890s through World War II. New sites and modes of consumption increased the distribution of music and enabled songwriters to reach a wider, more diverse audience. The phonograph, piano rolls, vaudeville, musical comedy, and sheet music catered not only to white working-class men, as had been the case with earlier songs about Chinese immigration, but also to the middle classes and especially to women. These changes in the makeup of audiences led popular songwriters to produce a more varied view of the Chinese in the United States and abroad.[1]

Shifting attitudes toward the Chinese also influenced the ways in which they were portrayed at the turn of the century. Legislation had mitigated some of the open hostility surrounding Chinese immigration, and for some Americans, what was once unconditional hatred became a form of fascination. By the end of the nineteenth century, both China and Chinatowns were popular tourist destinations for whites who were looking for a more bucolic (albeit exotic) world that contrasted with their own increasingly urban and industrial one. Sympathetic views continued to emerge with China's transition to a republic in 1912. Older anxieties continued throughout this period, however. Anti-immigrant fears of unrestricted groups—merchants, students, ministers, and those of the working classes who remained in the United States—persisted and led to further restrictions and violence. New scientific attitudes toward race based on Social Darwinism and the application of empirical methods to social and cultural relationships also helped maintained anti-Chinese attitudes. The allure of Chinese culture had its limits.[2]

As part of these changes, Tin Pan Alley songwriters broke away from the depiction of the solitary Chinese immigrant man on the frontier and located Chinese subjects in two disparate places—China and Chinatowns. These places became sites where exoticism satisfied non-Chinese fantasies and ignored the realities of those who lived and worked there. By the 1870s, national economic interest began to focus on China as a vast market for American products and, concurrently, as a source of curiosity for visitors. China trade was no longer about bringing Chinese goods to the United States but about exporting American products to China. Tourists saw China as a country filled with ancient treasures and quaint people untouched by modernity. Chinatown, on the other hand, had a different image. Like a menagerie, it was a place where whites could observe and even experience Chinese life without traveling abroad. Some Chinese immigrants took advantage of the growing interest in China and helped transform what had once been seen as slums into tourist destinations. This phenomenon opened up the community and created new connections between whites and Chinese immigrants, but it sent other messages as well. Chinese restaurants and bazaars (as well as theaters, temples, and opium dens) were popular places for white tourists to spend their time and money, and these institutions had the potential to help diminish hostility toward Chinese immigrants. These businesses, however, also played to American conceptions of exoticism and reinforced the view that Chinese immigrants were outsiders and potential sources of vice. Ultimately, as artificial as these Chinatowns were, they became the backdrop for how most Americans viewed the Chinese in America.[3]

Post-1880 musical productions containing Chinese subjects served as a forum to develop notions of gender and race in new, contradictory ways. Questions surrounding Chinese masculinity persisted, mostly conveyed through performance styles and sheet music covers, while white women in yellowface and songs depicting Chinese women increased dramatically. Portrayals of Chinese women in popular music, as in nineteenth- and twentieth-century art music, served as models of femininity, simultaneously functioning as a criticism of feminism for being "unnatural" and as justification for the sexual desires of white men. A handful of more daring American popular songwriters, however, deviated from this paradigm and allowed their music to be more undefined about the threat of miscegenation and, more broadly, race. In contrast, white women on the stage helped to reinforce the Othering of the Chinese by yellowing up and playing to the extremes of femininity, in much the same way that since the 1850s, white men had treated Chinese immigrant men as sexually abnormal. By becoming "Chinese," however, these white actresses had found an acceptable way to express their sexuality, a practice associated with the New Woman and her break with the Victorian mores that had denied respectable white women access to public spaces and their desires.[4]

The racialization of the Chinese by whites moved in yet another intriguing direction after 1880; now portrayals of the Chinese seemed to change from focusing on their conflicts with Irish immigrants and toward comparing them with African Americans.[5] Songs containing Chinese and African American subjects helped reconfirm the racial inferiority of both groups, with one striking difference: in comparison to the Chinese, African Americans were presented as American, which opened the door slightly for African American inclusion. African American songwriters and performers also inherited Chinese stereotypes in much the same way that they had come into blackface ones. Yet because of the positioning of the Chinese as alien, the deployment of the Chinese/African American motif by African Americans reaffirmed the association of African American traditions with American identity and elevated African Americans' social position in much the same way that that of the Irish before them had been elevated.

Coinciding with changes in the music industry and attitudes toward the Chinese, aural and visual messages by American songwriters and performers continued to circulate and reaffirm the racialization of the Chinese and their containment both inside and outside the United States. Despite the persistence of these stereotypes, there was a qualitative shift and diversification in the representation of the Chinese (as well as a dramatic increase in the number of songs and productions) that, at times, were quite ambivalent. Race and gender were integral as before, but they appeared in new ways and were reproduced by new groups of performers. Anxieties over modern life were also contrasted with the picturesque and, by extension, the primitiveness of China and Chinatowns. Songwriters, working with notation and instrumentation, produced an interpretation of Chinese life in lyrics and performance that served racist ends by creating a more unified picture of Chinese difference and inferiority. In the meantime, exoticism made a limited range of social, economic, and cultural opportunities available for Chinese Americans, even on the stage.

YELLOWFACE AND ITS CODIFICATION

By the latter part of the nineteenth century, the practice of white actors in yellowface expanded and was codified into visual stereotypes that persist even to today.[6] Representations of the Chinese, particularly immigrants, were still tied to notions of their foreignness and inferiority, but they also contained elements of exoticism from earlier in the nineteenth century and were influenced by the increasing amount of goods and information from China. Performers relied on a set number of costumes, wigs, properties, and scenery to create Chinese characters on the stage. Furthermore, with the introduction of new makeup technologies, they tried to make their characters look more realistic. The emphasis placed on authenticity, however, was also a result of the direct challenge represented by the increasing numbers of nonwhite performers on the stage. American audiences by the end of the nineteenth century also had had more contact with Chinese immigrants in general and with an increasing number of Chinese and Chinese American performers whose acts challenged the practice of yellowface.[7]

By the 1890s, costumes diversified beyond the proverbial blue baggy pants and jacket worn in past decades and became much more elaborate, with brightly colored silks and satins that included embroidery, sequins, pompoms, mirrors, and braiding. Clothes worn by Chinese merchants, government officials, royalty, and actors appeared on the stage. Men and women also sported a number of different hats, headpieces, and jewelry.[8] Actors and actresses mixed American and Chinese costumes and created completely new fashions on the stage, some of which influenced or were influenced by the fashion industry and its use of the "Orient" for inspiration.[9]

The discontinuance of the queue under the Republic of China also had an effect on American performers and their portrayals of the Chinese. Although some Chinese immigrants had cut their hair during the nineteenth century, large numbers of Chinese men cropped their hair short in the 1910s, which American actors in yellowface reflected in the kinds of wigs they wore. Queues, however, did not vanish from the stage, especially in productions that were set during the Qing dynasty, contained Manchurian characters, or were revivals of nineteenth-century plays whose Chinese immigrant characters had worn queues in the original production. Philip Ostermayer's *Catalogue of Theatrical and Society Hair Goods* listed a shorthaired Chinese wig called "Coolie" and another with a queue known as "Chinese." These wig names had nothing to do with the hairstyles worn by particular groups of Chinese men but were probably seen as interchangeable terms.[10] During the Qing dynasty, all men were required by law to wear queues, including laborers, whom Americans improperly called coolies. *Coolie* was the term applied to Chinese laborers who were signed to long-term contracts, many times unwillingly, to work on large plantations in South America and the Caribbean. Americans in the nineteenth century employed this term in a derogatory way to refer to Chinese immigrant workers in the United States because it implied that they were "un-free" and, by extension, "un-American."[11] Theatrical catalogs included long moustaches and goatees for older male characters and a bald cap or a small ring of hair for philosophers and priests, similar to depictions of men in Chinese art that were popular at the time. Traditional female characters wore wigs consisting of two long, black braids, sometimes wound on the side of the head with a decorative ornament.[12] The 1939 script and production manual for *The Yellow Jacket* (1912), produced by Samuel French, Inc., a New York and London publishing firm that rents plays and musicals to professional and amateur theatrical companies, included illustrations of the hairstyles of each Chinese female character in the production (see ill. 15).[13]

MOY FAH LOY

CHEE MOO   CHOW WAN

DUE JUNG FAH   TSO   FOUR GIRLS

Ill. 15. Female hairstyles from the libretto of *The Yellow Jacket*. Courtesy of the Library of Congress.

Stage makeup played an important part in creating a new array of Chinese characters. Earlier performers, although playing on racial stereotypes, wore comparatively simple makeup. Actors hid their eyebrows by gluing them down with joining paste and covering them with greasepaint. They also covered all exposed skin, including arms, hands, and necks, with greasepaint—the 1877 theatrical makeup guide *How to "Make-Up"* recommended a combination of the tones called Mongolian and Dutch Pink.[14] Because performers and theatrical goods manufacturers believed that the Chinese had large noses and lacked facial hair, actors were prescribed to paint around their nostrils in a darker color and add a dark shadow or an eyebrow below the nose to create a wispy mustache for male characters. The most important aspect were the eyes, the defining factor in making up a Chinese face. Eyes were to be outlined in Indian ink, with the bottom line extending out beyond the eye to create a slanting effect.

Early twentieth-century makeup techniques were much more intricate and complex in order to create "authentic" representations and to allow for a wider variety of Chinese characters. By at least the 1880s, the production of greasepaint had become specialized so that most guides recommended the use of No. 16, otherwise known as "Chinese."[15] Only one guide from 1928 argued that Chinese No. 16 was the incorrect greasepaint shade for Chinese characters and recommended the use of a color not based on a specific nation of origin, Olive No. 13.[16] Sex also affected greasepaint recommendations. Traditional female characters were to be paler, with the reasons given being their lack of time outdoors and their use of lightening powders. Modern Chinese women were to be somewhat tan to indicate that they spent more time in the sun. Noses were to be broadened and flattened by highlighting the nostrils and shading the top, or, thanks to new theatrical technologies, they could be completely reshaped through prosthetics. Drawing a line about three-fourths of an inch beyond the eye and adding a highlighter on the lid were techniques used to slant the eyes. In more elaborate characterizations, systems of tape and putty were implemented to slant the eye, a method used predominately in the movie industry.[17] Lips were to be full and painted with a deep red color. "Sing Song Girls," a common name given to female performers who also worked as prostitutes in China and the United States, needed "small cupid's bow lips . . . in a bright color."[18] For the sinister Fu Manchu and Dragon Lady characters, actors and actresses wore long fingernails or metal sheaths that were four to five inches in length.[19] These characters represented the extremes of American fears about the Chinese, particularly fears of interracial sex and procreation, but they were also part of the expansion of character types at the turn of the century. The great villain Fu Manchu, who first appeared in the novels of English writer Sax Rohmer in the 1910s, was a character in dramatic performances and films well into the post–World War II era.[20] Fu Manchu's female counterpart, the Dragon Lady, was first played in film by Anna May Wong as Princess Ling Moy in *Daughter of the Dragon* (1931), a role that shaped the rest of Wong's career.

Costumes and makeup were not the only ways in which actors and actresses tried to denote Chineseness; directors and set designers used props and backdrops to help set the "Oriental" mood. The curtain for *The Yellow Jacket,* for instance, was made "of denim" and "the design painted in gold bronze" with broken lines to hint that it was embroidered (see ill. 16). The border at the bottom alternated the "characters of the turtle—which with the Chinese stands for happiness."[21] As in earlier, more exotic productions, Chinese stylized objects and export goods, such as porcelains, furniture, and fans, also appeared. The revue *Around the World* at the New York Hippodrome in 1926 included a number set in China. The backdrop for this scene was black, but Chinese hangings and lanterns were suspended from above.[22] At times, designers combined motifs from several Asian nations to create a scene as foreign and novel as possible. A review of *The Daughter of Heaven* (1912) remarked that the sets were similar to those used for the production *The Garden of Allah* (1911), set in North Africa. The set designer also put an array of

Ill. 16. Backdrop from the libretto of *The Yellow Jacket*. Courtesy of the Library of Congress.

animals on the stage, including "storks, peacocks, horses and pigs," which amplified its exoticism.[23]

Throughout this period, white performers in yellowface dominated the stage and primarily controlled what it meant to be Chinese in the performing arts. They relied on technological advances in makeup that allowed them to look more "authentic." Furthermore, these actors expanded on the Chinese immigrant stereotype from the 1850s through the 1880s and began to reemphasize the exoticism and even allure of Chinese life through costuming and sets. These devices, in combination with other aspects of performance, created a more totalizing racialization on the stage; yet performance was available to ironies and paradoxes that could potentially threaten white hegemony over the stage.

China, Chinatowns, and Racialized Space

With the passage of the Chinese Exclusion Act and the rise of Tin Pan Alley, popular song began to locate the Chinese in new ways, expanding on the race-based vocabulary that had developed earlier in the nineteenth century. Although these songs were similar to those produced during the 1850s through the 1880s in response to Chinese immigration, and they maintained images of Chinese racial inferiority and effeminacy, there were some key differences.[24] An important shift occurred from treating the Chinese as subjects of a problem to objects of desire, and the resulting ambiguities provide an interesting lens through which to view American anxieties at the turn of the century. Some songwriters softened the more acerbic mid-nineteenth-century images and hinted that perhaps the Chinese lived in a simpler world that whites had lost and from which they might learn. Exoticism re-created Chinese life in the United States and abroad into a fantasy world that could be used as a criticism of modernization or could function as a form of escapism. By the late 1890s, Chinatowns finally became a musical subject and appeared as a site of both danger and pleasure. Simultaneously, China, which Americans had been describing in song for over seventy years (and Europeans for almost two hundred years), reemerged as a lush paradise untouched by the effects of colonialism. Together, these lyrical motifs altered stereotypes in ways that, at best, helped explore cultural differences and, at worst, perpetuated attitudes of racial inferiority through appeals to people's baser instincts.

What was new about the way in which Tin Pan Alley treated Chinese subjects was its use of locale, both the real and imagined. In particular, Chinese spaces, supposedly untouched by modern life, were seen as ways to contrast American life, the good and the bad. Lyricists often employed common devices to describe both Chinatowns and China as semi-mythical places. In the chorus of "Down in Chinatown" (1914), the narrator refers to "dreamy summer nights" (a subtle reference to the perception of widespread opium use) in the Chinese immigrant section of an unnamed American city.[25] Ben Bronfin and Joseph Nussbaum's "Chinese Moon" (1926) combined romantic signifiers, such as sunsets and moons, and exotic elements, including poppies (another reference to opium) and incense.[26] References to temples and joss houses, as in the earlier song "Josh, John" (1854), appeared in a small number of songs dealing with China. In the opening line of "Towsee Mongalay" (1915), Grahame Jones portrays China as "where the temple bells tinkled out the languid hours." The "heathen" spaces that had been seen as so frightening in earlier depictions of the Chinese had become almost quaint.[27]

There were important differences between descriptions of China and ones of Chinese communities in the United States. Chinatowns were often defined by their businesses, especially restaurants, opium dens, and laundries.[28] China, in contrast, was described as a paradise, even its urban centers. Residents lived either in huts, a term used by many writers to describe the homes of non-Western peoples generally, or in bungalows, a one-story house that had originated in India and was eventually transplanted to the United States. Exotic flowers and plants (such as bamboo, willow trees, lilies, and lotuses) and birds also appeared in lyrics as markers of more pastoral aspects of China. Lee Johnson, who had written music for *The First Born*, described Canton in "Mamma's China Twins" (1900):

Where the pretty flowers bloom 'neath shady bowers.
'Round their hut vines entwine, 'neath Oriental skies.
Rice boats on the river passing by their door,
Fragrant China lilies bloom along the shore.[29]

As with the European pastoral tradition from the seventeenth and eighteenth centuries that erased the economic and social difficulties rural laborers faced in Western Europe, these bucolic images of China created an illusion of beauty and abundance that appealed to American audiences frustrated with modernity.[30] This practice also relieved listeners in other ways—by obscuring the effects of Western colonialism on the Chinese landscape. Since the Opium War (1839–1842), skirmishes with American and European forces and unequal treaties contributed to dynastic instability and the hardships the Chinese faced on a daily basis. Although American writers did not blame the United States or Europe for this situation, many did describe China's squalidness and poverty in newspapers and travel writings. Songwriters such as Johnson, however, ignored this reality and imagined China as part of a simpler and more primitive world that would appeal to audiences.[31]

The erasure of American colonial exploits through the use of exoticism was a technique employed in songs and musical plays about Americans and Europeans visiting China. Unlike earlier accounts, these works did not address the lives of merchants, missionaries, diplomats, or military officers in China but rather the new phenomenon of honeymooning, an increasingly common practice among newlyweds that began in the 1880s.[32] Tourism in East Asia had increased in the twentieth century, with wealthy Europeans and Americans taking steamship cruises for several months at a time, sailing from port to port. Catering to this new romantic type of travel, composers promoted images of an idyllic and exotic China, which helped to sell it as a honeymoon destination.

The first such production was George Dance and Howard Talbot's *A Chinese Honeymoon,* which premiered in London in 1901 and traveled to New York City the following year. The timing and success of *A Chinese Honeymoon* is especially intriguing because it coincided with the Boxer Rebellion, in which Chinese insurgents attacked European and American missionaries and destroyed property. The psychological damage was enormous—for instance, no Chinese exhibitors (fifteen applied) were allowed to participate in the 1901 Pan-American Exposition in Buffalo, New York. There was not even a Chinese theater.[33] Yet *A Chinese Honeymoon* tells the story of a Mr. and Mrs. Pineapple who, along with their bridesmaids, travel to China for their honeymoon. Problems develop when Mr. Pineapple, who has not given up his bachelor ways, kisses Soo Soo, the daughter of Emperor Hang Chow and is forced to marry her. Soo Soo, however, is in love with Mr. Pineapple's nephew, Tom Hatherton, who has left the British army to be with her. To escape her unhappy marriage to Mr. Pineapple, Soo Soo takes a mysterious drug to feign death so that Mr. Pineapple will be forced to perform suttee, an Indian and not Chinese devotional practice of ritual suicide performed by women (not men) upon their husband's death. Hatherton stands in for Mr. Pineapple so that he can be with Soo Soo for eternity, but in the nick of time the British ambassador arrives and prevents the immolation. The production ends with everyone paired with a prospective mate, including Hatherton with Soo Soo and the emperor with Mrs. Brown, Mr. Pineapple's housekeeper from his bachelor days.[34] This happy ending is unusual when compared with that of other productions (most notably Puccini's *Madama Butterfly*) and seen in the context of American fears about the contamination of the white race as a result of interracial sex. Nevertheless, *A Chinese Honeymoon* was revived many times and led to several spin-offs, including the songs "A Chinese Honeymoon Waltz" (1901) and "A Chinese Honeymoon Lancers" (1902).[35] Later, there were several other honeymoon-themed songs: "That's the Sign of a Honeymoon" (1908), "A Chinese Honeymoon" (1914), "On a Chinese Honeymoon" (1923), and "A Shanghai Honeymoon" (1926).[36]

Chinatowns were also alluring places in American popular songs, but these songs had a darker edge in contrast to those set in China. For many, Chinatowns were vice-ridden slums that, despite the efforts of Chinese immigrants to make their community look more appealing, reinforced the belief that Chinese immigration was a threat to American life. The dangers, however, that supposedly abounded in this community were also intriguing, and Chinatown became both a physical and an imaginative space for many whites to try new things. Starting with Charles H. Hoyt's musical play *A Trip to Chinatown* (1892), Chinatowns became another venue to depict Chinese immigrants on the stage, this time focusing on a whole community as opposed to one comedic character on the frontier. By 1900, there was a spate of Chinatown plays such as *The Queen of Chinatown* (1899; which included conflicts between Chinese and Irish immigrants), *The King of the Opium Ring* (1899; which had no Chinese characters), *A Night in Chinatown* (1900), and *Chinatown Charlie* (1906).[37] In these productions and songs, laundries, opium dens, and restaurants were popular settings. Laundries had appeared in songs about Chinese immigrants from the 1850s and 1880s and were found in African American/Chinese immigrant skits in the early twentieth century. Opium use and Chinese food, however, were reformulated and played to both positive and negative stereotypes.

Opium was a subject of great concern among health experts and whites in general, who were worried that Chinese immigrant men would somehow addict white women to this drug, which, by extension, would lead to the downfall of American civilization. Yet contrary to these concerns, popular songwriters used the euphoric, dreamlike state induced by opium smoking to create a fantasy world so that audiences could vicariously experience the sensations and feelings it produced. "It Is the Flavor from a Two-Cent Chinese Butt" (1879), arguably one of the first songs to associate the Chinese with opium, is in the voice of an American male addict somewhere in the Far West, who explains how difficult his life is in contrast to his drug-induced dreams. Only the song's title associates the Chinese with opium.[38] Songs about the pleasures of opium were much more common at the turn of the century. "Chinatown, My Chinatown" describes a nighttime underworld in an unnamed city, where reality was put aside and dreams became real, especially with the consumption of opium. This song, compounded by exotic musical elements, painted a seductive picture of Chinese immigrant communities.[39] Other songs—"All Aboard for Chinatown" (1915), "China Dreams" (1917), "Pipe Dream Blues" (1918), "In Blinky, Winky, Chinky, Chinatown" (1915), and "When the Lights Go Down in Chinatown" (1922)—treat Chinese immigrants and opium in a similar manner.[40] These songs also contained Chinese musical tokens, which added to the exotic scene put forth by the lyrics. In popular song, if nowhere else, the pleasures of opium went well with the imagined otherworldliness of Chinatown.

The perception of Chinese food was transformed from being inferior to American food during the 1850s through the early 1880s to being one of the major tourist attractions of Chinatown. Chinese food was still seen as different from "American" cuisine, but tasty as well. The food items most often mentioned in American popular songs were chop suey (a term popularized after the visit in 1897 of Li Hongzhang, a Chinese statesman, to describe a mixed vegetable and meat stir fry), rice, and tea.[41] During the opening number of the musical *Broken Idol* (1908), the male and female choruses sing about a variety of Chinese foods as a form of double entendre.[42]

> (Men)Chop suey's fresh today,
> So is our yokomain,
> If you don't believe it's true
> That for you, That for you,
> Ching Lung he needs the price,
> You need a bowl of rice,
> Try it once, you'll try it twice,
> Come up and we'll prove it's true.
> (Girls) You're nice but your rice won't do.

This Chinese New Year's celebration, however, was only the backdrop for the first act.[43] The rest of the musical play focuses on an English nobleman trying to act American in order to woo an American heiress, until she loses all her money.

Americans by the end of the nineteenth century expanded on the lyrical devices used to describe the Chinese and focused on two imaginative spaces: China and Chinatowns. Even Chinese music making, which previously had been used as a marker of inferiority, was portrayed in new ways. Chinese cities and Chinatowns were now filled with the sounds of Chinese musicians playing ragtime rather than noisy Chinese music (of course, negative attitudes about Chinese music persisted).[44] Beginning in the 1880s, the repulsion that once filled American popular music led the way to songs that emphasized what Americans found so fascinating about Chinese life both in the United States and abroad.

The Arrival of China Doll and Ming Toy

The appearance of Chinese women as musical subjects at the end of the nineteenth century was tied to the reemergence of exoticism and the anxieties surrounding race and gender. Chinese women had been found in song and on the stage since the beginning of the century and even during the pre-Exclusion era, when caricatures of Chinese immigrant men dominated. By the late 1880s, portrayals of Chinese women began to raise questions about the relationship between modernity and womanhood, employing gender and race to criticize women's suffrage and feminism. Some songwriters produced romantic works that depicted Chinese characters in ways similar to portrayals of white ethnic groups and gave them more human-like emotions. In these instances, even Chinese immigrant men were treated more sympathetically, although sexualized/racialized images such as Fu Manchu also emerged at this time. Chinese women were also objectified in ways that played to gender extremes and put them on par with playthings. Such characterizations existed for the pleasure of white men, but they were also important to white women both on and off the stage. By enacting what was seen as the ultra-femininity of Chinese women, actresses expressed themselves in ways that were traditionally seen as outside white respectability. Ironically, by supporting the ultra-femininity of Chinese female characters, these New Women had a venue through which to convey their own desires and needs for pleasure, and began to breakdown the rigid Victorian gender norms that had been used to confine them.

Depictions of "Oriental" women in music, and in particular, opera, have a relatively long history in the West. The plots of late eighteenth-century Orientalist operas, known as "Turkish captivity" operas, told tales of Asian rulers abducting European women. Within the first few decades of the nineteenth century, this storyline as well as the gender and race of the protagonists in Orientalist operas changed. These musical productions worked closely with Europe's colonial project and validated its superiority and right to conquer. Beginning in this period, Orientalist operas focused on a European, and later an American, soldier who travels to the "Orient" and falls in love with a local woman. Because of the stigma of interracial marriage and its potential threat to the purity of the European race, the relationship between "The Soldier and the Exotic," a phrase from the title of John Parakilas's article on Orientalist operas, does not last and ends with the death (often by suicide) of the female protagonist. The ending of Puccini's *Madama Butterfly*, with Cio-Cio-San committing suicide out of her devotion and passion for Pinkerton, is representative of this popular plot.[45]

The portrayal of Chinese women in American songs, skits, and musicals was in many ways similar to the depiction of non-Western women in the Orientalist opera tradition. Often works described these female characters as little more than pieces of porcelain or playthings for their lovers—and by extension, audiences. Some literally told stories about porcelain dolls that were either made in China or looked Chinese. In 1904, a musical play appeared at the Majestic Theatre in New York City titled *A China Doll*. This production focused on Pee Chee San, the daughter of Wing Lee, whose doll is stolen; she refuses to marry until it is found.[46] Although *A China Doll* has an actor playing the life-size toy, the "doll" in this production is also Pee Chee San. In the song "One Umbrella Would Be Big Enough for Two," she is described as being "little" and having "tiny little feet."[47] Although obstinate for refusing the marriage match her father arranges for her, Pee Chee San still falls in love with her father's choice, the Americanized Hi See. Later, Hi See (who, as in productions of *Aladdin*, was played by a woman) sings about "My Little China Doll," which critics saw as the hit of the production.[48] Ironically, this song described a beautiful porcelain figurine sitting in a store window, but unlike Pee Chee San, this doll has "golden locks upon her head." Hi See realizes that there is no one who looks like the china doll in the window for him to love. Of course, there were blonde "dolls," but the taboo of interracial sex forbade such relationships. By the final scene, Hi See and Pee Chee San declare their plans for marriage, and the thieves who stole her doll are caught. Several Tin Pan Alley songs kept this image alive into the 1920s—"When Two Little Hearts Beat Together" (1908) from the light operetta *The Rose Maid,* and Irving Berlin's "Porcelain Maid" (1922) from the *Music Box Revue* of the 1922–1923 season.[49]

As in the "China Doll" motif, the names and nicknames given to Chinese women bolstered the image of their childlike and feminine attributes that many American men found appealing and nonthreatening. Furthermore, these terms became catch phrases for stereotypes of Chinese women, and Asian women more generally. In more pastoral instances, lyricists described Chinese women as "maidens," reemphasizing the myth that China was part of the pre-industrial world untouched by modern life. For example, Jack E. Slattery's "Chen, My China Girl" (1927) claims that "Oriental maidens there [Hong Kong] never yet have bobbed their hair, / Never will in our country."[50]

Chinese women were also "girls" or "babies," terms that implied that they were innocent and pure and in need of protection. In "My Dreamy China Lady" (1916), Ching Lo's lover is called "little China girl."[51] Others were much more objectifying and sexually charged. The lover of "Little Peeweet" (1897) describes her as a "pretty thing." Ching Ling calls his love interest, in the song "In China" (1919), a "Geisha girl," once again combining Chinese and Japanese signifiers and emphasizing the supposed sexual availability of Asian women.[52]

Although songs and musical plays about Chinese lovers appeared throughout this period, spin-offs of Orientalist operas, in which a European or American man falls in love with a non-Western woman, were also common. The most famous of these operas was Puccini's *Madama Butterfly,* which premiered in the United States in 1906 and was based on the play by a similar name (*Madame Butterfly*) produced by David Belasco in 1900. The popularity of *Madama Butterfly* led to many popular songs about not only Japanese but other Asian women. In the 1920s, American songwriters produced two Chinese "Butterfly" songs. As in other songs about separated lovers, "My Chinese Butterfly" (1922) is written in the voice of a Chinese immigrant who longs to return to his "Butterfly" in Shanghai. Much more in line with *Madama Butterfly,* "Chinky Butterfly" (1925) is written in the voice of an American sailor who, despite leaving his "Butterfly" behind, wants to prove to the world that such relationships are possible. The ending is unclear about whether they will be reunited.[53]

Several Tin Pan Alley songs that alluded to this stock Orientalist storyline did not conclude with the death of the Chinese female character but were much more open ended and allowed for the possibility that these relationships could survive. The ambivalence in the songs was perhaps tied to several factors: the increase in the number of listeners whom songwriters believed would like this ending, the decrease in anxiety about Chinese immigration, and the popularity of Asian-styled fashions and other products. Aaron S. Hoffman and Andy Lewis's "Pinky Panky Poo" (1902) tells the story of a man, presumably American, who falls in love with a woman named Pinky Panky Poo. She does not understand English, but he continues to woo her and eventually asks for her hand in marriage. Her father, Hop Luey, is angry but is won over after getting drunk. "Fan San" (1919) is about another Chinese woman, this time living in Singapore, a British colony largely populated by Chinese, who is waiting for "a sailor." He sends her a note promising to return to marry her, but it is unclear whether he does so.[54]

One of the most famous plays starring a Chinese female character in an American–Chinese love story was *East Is West* (1919). This play, by Samuel Shipman and John B. Hymer, was not a musical, but it did contain Robert Hood Bowers's hit "Chinese Lullaby," sung by the female heroine Ming Toy

CHINESE LULLABY

FEATURED BY

FAY BAINTER

IN WILLIAM HARRIS JR'S, PRODUCTION

• EAST IS WEST •

WORDS AND MUSIC BY

ROBERT HOOD BOWERS

U. S. A.

Price, 40 cents, net

T

G. SCHIRMER, INC., NEW YORK

Ill. 17. Portrait of Fay Bainter from *East Is West*, on the sheet music cover for Robert Hood Bowers's "Chinese Lullaby" (1919). Courtesy of the Lester S. Levy Collection of Sheet Music, Special Collections, Johns Hopkins University.

throughout the production, first in Chinese, then in pidgin English, and finally in "good English" (see ill. 17).[55] *East Is West* describes the life of Ming Toy, whose father sells her to the "Proprietor of Love-Boat," a slave trader. Watching this transaction take place is American Billy Benson and his friend Lo Sang Kee, a Chinese American merchant. Benson wants to save Ming Toy from sexual slavery but refuses to purchases her; instead, he persuades Lo to buy her and bring her to San Francisco. On his return to the United States, Lo receives threats from the local missionary board, which notices Ming Toy winking and shimmying in the window of his home. In order to save his business from boycotts, Lo sells Ming Toy to Charlie Yong, a wealthy Chinatown restaurateur. Immediately after the transaction, Benson arrives at Lo's and is shocked to find that he has sold Ming Toy. Quickly, he finds her a job as his sister's maid and, with the help of Lo and others, secrets her away to his parents' home. At the Benson residence, Billy and Ming Toy finally admit their love for each other and their desire to marry, much to the chagrin of Billy's mother and father. In the final scene, it comes out that Ming Toy is the daughter of an American scholar/missionary and his Spanish wife, so her marriage to Billy Benson neither ruins the reputation of the Benson family nor threatens the purity of the white race. The dangers of racial mixing are averted, and everyone is happy.[56]

The character Ming Toy from *East Is West* was so popular that she appears in several songs, musical revues, and even two films. Roy Turk, Bert Grant, and Cecil Bernard came out with a song titled "Ming Toy" (1919) a few months after the premiere of *East Is West* (see ill. 18).[57] In this version, Ming Toy comes to the United States and marries a "Yankee beau," but the lyric leaves out the discovery that she is not Chinese. To add to the confusion of Ming Toy's nation of origin, the sheet music cover depicts a Japanese woman wearing a kimono. The *Passing Show of 1919* included a spoof of *East Is West* and spotlighted "So Long, Sing Song" (1919) by Harold Atteridge and Sigmund Romberg.[58] Unlike "Ming Toy," "So Long, Sing Song" does not have a happy ending, although it does not end with Ming Toy's death. Set in China, the song has Ming Toy's "Yankee boy" receive a letter from a woman in the United States who is waiting for his return. He decides to go back to the United States without Ming Toy and tells her that he might "see-saw back to you" someday. *East Is West* was so successful that in 1928, nine years after it had first appeared on Broadway, Florenz Ziegfeld bought the rights to make it into a full-fledged musical and signed on George and Ira Gershwin as its songwriters. The production was supposed to go up in fall 1929, but, most likely because of the Great Depression, it never premiered. The Gershwins published one song originally intended for Ziegfeld's *Ming Toy,* "In the Mandarin's Orchid Garden," a year later.[59]

The success of *East Is West* was also tied to Fay Bainter, whose portrayal of Ming Toy made her a star. She contributed to perceptions of Asian women in much the same way that Maude Allen's characterization of Salome in vaudeville or Geraldine Farrar's Cio-Cio-San in *Madama Butterfly* had. In at least one instance, Bainter was described as the "successor to Maude Allen."[60] Both before and after *East Is West*, Bainter played a wide variety of female roles, including the dual role of the Image/Mary Temple in the Japanese-themed play *The Willow Tree* in 1917. Although *The Willow Tree* was not an opera, its plot was analogous to those of Orientalist operas, with the Image, a female embodiment of the Japanese Willow Tree Spirit, dying so that her lover, Edward Hamilton, will return both to Great Britain, to fight in World War I,

Ill. 18. Roy Turk, Bert Grant, and Cecil Arnold's "Ming Toy" (1919). Courtesy of the Sam DeVincent Collection of Illustrated American Sheet Music, Archives Center, National Museum of American History, Behring Center, Smithsonian Institution.

and to his ex-girlfriend Mary Temple (who is also played by Bainter).[61] Bainter's Ming Toy was also tied to the racialized archetype of the eternal feminine from *The Willow Tree*, a combination of innocence and purity and the ultimate expression of love. In response to her character in *East Is West*, a writer for the *Washington Post* gushed, "Everyone loves her; everyone leaves the theater with an impression of having had love creep into their heart. And Fay Bainter, with her great art, with her big human heart and her joy in her work, makes this Ming Toy a creature who will be treasured in memory for the years to come."[62] At the same time, in the play the city and jazz music (emblems of the vices of modern life) helped Ming Toy to get in touch with her sexuality and to use her feminine attributes to her advantage. Unaware of the implications for her reputation as well as Lo Sang Kee's, Ming Toy enjoys winking at men in the street and shimmying to jazz music. Her behavior, however, angers Lo, who calls her an "American vamp," an allusion to Ming Toy's increasing Americanization and her loss of the natural womanliness associated with being Chinese.[63] Critics agreed. John Corbin, theater critic for the *New York Times,* wrote that "she bats her eyelids at any chance male like a painted harridan." He continued: "The heroine is just another version of the pretty, coquettish, adorably slangy, and swearing little heathen in trousers."[64] While at times the ideal of white femininity, Bainter's Ming Toy is also an American vamp in the guise of a Chinese woman.

Many other white actresses yellowed up to portray the racialized eternal feminine during this period. In *The Daughter of Heaven* (1912), the empress commits suicide rather than marry the Manchurian emperor who has conquered her country and killed her young son, the last emperor of the Ming dynasty.[65] Viola Allen, who in the 1890s made her career starring in Shakespearean tragedies, played the empress, a role that she said in an interview "so appeals to my every instinct as an artist and as a woman." Allen saw the role as a combination of Chinese stereotypes—religious fanaticism, ancestor worship, moral purity, repression, and a "passive protest against modern intellectuality." *The Daughter of Heaven* also touched on the core of all humanity that Allen (and others) believed had been lost: "the mother love for her little son sweeps away the barriers of repression and shows in Caucasian or Mongolian alike that the old threnody of human hearts and human love beats similarly in all ages and among all people."[66] Although a "Chinese" production, *The Daughter of Heaven* was also a critique of modernity and its effect on Europeans and Americans.[67]

In spite of the greater diversity of images of the Chinese in the post-Exclusion era and the emphasis on the sexual availability of Chinese women, it was not until later in the twentieth century that the Dragon Lady character made it into American popular music and performance in the way that China Dolls and Ming Toys had done previously. There were, however, glimmers of this more dangerous image of Chinese femininity, particularly in the portrayal of the offspring of interracial sex.[68] Chinese female characters, who in the 1910s and 1920s were tied to the vamp, evolved into the sensual and maniacal Dragon Lady archetype by the early 1930s. For example, Lenore Ulric's Lien Wha from *The Son-Daughter* (1919) is the daughter of a New York Chinatown doctor who sells her to another man in order to help fund revolutionaries living in China. A loyal daughter, she complies with her father's wishes; however, once her father and childhood lover are murdered for their involvement in the insurgency, Lien Wha strangles her bridegroom, who coincidentally is an imperial spy, in the final scene. The filial daughter, good and pure, is also capable of revenge and murder; she can be a dangerous woman. Ulric made a career of playing the "Other" woman—Luana (Hawaiian) in *The Bird of Paradise* (1912), Wetona (Native American) in *The Heart of Wetona* (1916), and Carla Valett (Hungarian) in *The Harem* (1924). Both on and off the stage, she was seen as a vamp, capable of becoming either extreme of the feminine ideal, but she was almost always racialized. Brooks Atkinson, the well-known theater critic for the *New York Times,* extensively described Ulric's vamp: "she enters like a vexed tigress. From that heated moment onward she storms up and down the stage, shaking that bushy mop of hair, tearing the air with passionate gestures, arranging the Ulrician torso in sinuous curves, smoldering with evil intentions and kissing like an acetylene torch." Ulric "swear[s] and make[s] obscene allusions"; she knows "the desirability of sex."[69]

Images of Chinese women in popular music were another important development at the turn of the century. Although these characters had appeared throughout the nineteenth century, they became much more prominent and were important sources for exploring race, gender, and modern life. The stereotypes of Chinese (and more broadly Asian) femininity in part marginalized Chinese women as Other and perpetuated stereotypes of the racialized eternal feminine and vamp. Furthermore, these same characterizations could be seen as critiques of women's suffrage and feminism by giving examples of the normal and natural woman. Paradoxically, these same stereotypes worked differently for white women both on the stage and in the audience. For these performers and audience members, Chinese impersonation was another way to break down Victorian morals, which promoted domesticity and purity, and helped to create the New Woman.

AFRICAN AMERICANS AND NEW RACIALIZATIONS

In a crucial way, the mixing together of Chinese and African American musical signifiers as discussed in the previous chapter made a great deal of sense. By the turn of the century, Chinese immigrants and African Americans were frequently compared with each other not only on the stage but also in political and scientific debates. Before then, productions with Irish and Chinese immigrant characters predominated, especially those containing stories of conflict between Irish laundrywomen and Chinese laundrymen, but after the mid-1880s, these kinds of numbers only appeared periodically.[70] While still facing discrimination, the Irish had established over the century their claims to whiteness and political power. In response, a small number of songwriters and dramatists began to associate the Chinese with another group—African Americans. Although the conflation of African Americans and Chinese immigrants had occurred as early as the 1850s in political debates about what should be the racial makeup of states in the Far West, it emerged more consistently in popular music and theater by the end of the nineteenth century.[71]

White artists borrowed from yellowface and blackface, and established the inferiority of both groups through comic interaction and conflict. Once again, white songwriters and performers had control over the portrayal of the Other, although even here there were opportunities for inversion. While Chinese immigrants were quintessential foreigners, African Americans were often seen as Americans, in part because slavery had erased any connection to a specific homeland but also because, for some whites as well as African Americans, African American culture was an important way to delineate the United States from European nations. Despite being seen as racially inferior, African Americans could lay claim to American identity and use their own interpretation of Chinese immigrants to emphasize this connection.

"Coon" songs, which were popular from the late 1880s through the 1910s, helped to re-imagine the anxieties many whites felt about African Americans in the post-Reconstruction world. In comparison to what was popular on the stage at the time, this genre was relatively innovative through the influence of ragtime music. Coon songs, however, were still based on a set of African American stereotypes like those in earlier minstrel shows that had reinforced white racism and justified segregation. These songs presented blacks as capable of violence and sexual aggressiveness, and desiring to become white. Lyrics described laziness, alcohol consumption, gambling, eating certain foods (such as chicken, watermelon, and opossum), and carrying razors, all of which maintained the belief that African Americans, especially African American men, needed to be controlled. Some African American songwriters and performers, including politically militant ones, also produced coon songs.[72]

The stereotypes found in coon songs also appeared in the few songs that addressed interactions between African Americans and Chinese. Paul J. Knox, a white songwriter who had written several coon songs at the turn of the century, told the story of an African American man who frequents a local Chinese laundry to purchase "hop," or opium, in "I Don't Care if I Never Wake Up" (1899).[73] "I Don't Care if I Never Wake Up" fits the coon song tradition, including such musical references to ragtime as syncopation and chromatic movement; its opening also contains Chinese musical tokens—repeated parallel fourths. In this song, an unnamed African American character admits that he likes opium because it allows him to live out his fantasies. His drug-induced dreams represent his ideas about white society, which focus on a combination of power and money. The fact that this African American character is "yellow," as argued in an article by James H. Dormon, denoted that he was light skinned ("high yellow" or "yeller") and could possibly pass as white. Yet he is unable to do so.[74] In this particular song, "yellow" had multiple meanings; it could symbolize that this character was "going Chinese" through opium consumption and that he was cowardly in his refusal to face reality. As further signs of inferiority, he is described as lazy, not holding down a job, and spending as much time as possible on drugs. Although it is unlikely white audiences did so, he could be seen as sympathetic because of his desire to escape the realities of being an African American man in a racist society.

A handful of songs explored the problems surrounding miscegenation through Chinese/African American marriages. Edward Madden and Theodore Morse's "Ching-a-Ling" (1907) looked at the anxieties and fluidity of racial identity in a set of absurd scenes that ends with a wedding.[75] Like Knox, both Madden and Morse were white songwriters who had written numerous coon songs together and with others artists from the 1890s through the 1910s. Morse also arranged "The Wedding of the Chinee and the Coon" (1897) for piano by African American songwriters Billy Johnson and Bob Cole, which also seems to be the inspiration for "Ching-a-Ling."[76] "Ching-a-Ling," which contains no ragtime elements or Chinese musical devices, tells how an African American man named Ephraim Brown falls in love with a Chinese woman, Ching-a-Ling, while she was praying in "a joss house." To win Ching-a-Ling, Brown offers to become Chinese for her by changing his name to "Ding-a-Ling," moving into a "Chinese bungalow," and growing his hair into a queue. Brown eventually wins her father's approval, who calls him a "black face Chinee." Because the characters in "Ching-a-Ling" are not white, its commentary on interracial marriage was perhaps much safer and more palatable for white audiences, who most likely believed that miscegenation led to moral and racial decay. It also plays on the presumably absurd and humorous notion of one becoming the Other and losing one's racial identity through intimate and prolonged contact. Here, however, Brown is only a blackface version of a Chinese man.

Like songs about the brutalization of Chinese immigrants in the 1870s, Tin Pan Alley songwriters depicted African Americans as either threatening or attacking the Chinese. This was another way to imagine the potential danger that African Americans were to white society and to represent vicariously through African American characters the anger many whites felt toward the Chinese. "Li Hung Chang" (1898), whose title comes from the name of Chinese statesman Li Hongzhang, is the story of an unnamed African American impressed into the British army (after being arrested for stealing from the Prince of Wales) to fight the Japanese in China.[77] The problem for this African American soldier is that "Chinamen and Japs all looked alike," so he kills anyone who is Asian. In the final scene, Li Hung Chang (Li Hongzhang) sees what he has done and sends him back to the United States. "Wing Lee's Ragtime Clock" (1899) from the musical By the Sad Sea Waves is about Chinese immigrant Wing Lee who buys a clock that ticks a ragtime rhythm.[78] Local African Americans hear about his clock and break into his laundry so that they can dance to it. The chorus inverts part of "Li Hung Chang," with Wing Lee screaming "all lookee samee to me." The attack by African Americans on Chinese and Chinese immigrants fulfilled beliefs in each group's lack of normal masculine traits, one excessive and the other wanting. Further, both songs claim, as in Ernest Hogan's hit "All Coons Look Alike to Me" (1896), that African Americans and Chinese immigrants look similar to others within their racial group, thus deflating their subjectivity and resigning them to stereotypes.

Whites, however, were not the only ones putting Chinese immigrants and African American characters together at the turn of the century. Through their inheritance of anti-Chinese caricatures, African American songwriters and performers also portrayed the interactions between these two groups. Although conforming to white perceptions, these portrayals were in part tied to the antagonistic relationship between African Americans and Chinese immigrants during the nineteenth and early twentieth centuries. San Francisco's burgeoning African American community in particular feared the effects of Chinese immigration on political, occupational, and educational opportunities. By 1870, Chinese immigrants outnumbered African Americans and often dominated certain jobs, such as railroad work, that African Americans had hoped to have for themselves. Religion and education were also sites of conflict between African Americans and the Chinese. On June 21, 1867, there were two reports in the San Francisco African American newspaper the *Elevator* of African American parents refusing to allow their children to go to school with Chinese immigrants and Native Americans. One article argued that because African Americans were Christians, they should not be forced to go to school with "idolatrous heathens." In the next sentence, the anonymous writer somewhat contradicts this statement by remarking that the children of all good Christians should not attend school with "the scum of the community, let them be white, black, yellow or red." For this writer, religion should be the only dividing factor in gaining access to public education. Conflicts between African Americans and Chinese occurred in other parts of the United States as well.[79]

African Americans' parodies of Chinese immigrants were related to interracial conflict and awareness of the power of blackface caricatures, but their intention was somewhat different from that of their white or Chinese American counterparts. Through Chinese impersonations, African Americans were able to ally themselves with whites by marking the Chinese as different from the white norm, as they themselves had been marked. These characterizations, however, focused on both racial inferiority and the foreignness and inability of the Chinese to assimilate. This image contrasted with blackface caricatures that not only confirmed white perceptions of racial inferiority but also imagined African American culture as central to what it meant to be American.[80]

By the late 1870s and 1880s, theatrical columns mentioned the names of African Americans who performed Chinese caricatures. In 1879, the *New York*

Dramatic News and Society Journal reported that Billy Kersands, one of earliest black minstrels, gave a "very amusing" Chinese impersonation in Stockton, California.[81] Five years later, the African American performer popularly known as Japanese Tommy joined George W. Harding, the stage manager for the Boston Dime Museum and dialect comedian and vocalist, to present the skit "Fun in a Chinese Laundry."[82] Japanese Tommy, born Thomas Dilworth, was reportedly three feet six inches tall and had started performing in 1853 with Christy's Minstrels (also the year that Commodore Matthew Perry opened Japan to American trade, which was probably the source of Dilworth's name). Later he joined up with several African American minstrelsy troupes during the 1880s.[83]

From the 1890s through the 1920s, there were several African-American Chinese impersonators in vaudeville, many of whom made their careers by being Chinese on the stage. The duos Tom Brown and Siren Nevarro (also spelled Navarro), George Catlin and Bob Kelly (nicknamed Dad), and Sam Cook and Jim Stevens impersonated Chinese immigrants; the latter two also produced African American/Chinese laundry skits. Because the actors were African American, they faced numerous conflicts with white stage managers and agents, especially the United Booking Office, which controlled who was able to work on almost all the major vaudeville circuits. Although often relegated to the worst time slots, these performers were able to find work in vaudeville, except in the South.[84] Periodically, they also appeared in African American musicals, another phenomenon from the 1890s whereby African Americans wrote, produced, and starred in their own works. Many of these productions called for a Chinese laundryman or cook character; sometimes, as was the practice of the time, Chinese skits or songs were interpolated in the middle of an already loosely defined plot. Conflicts between Chinese immigrants and African Americans were common in many of these productions as well.

Among these performers, Tom Brown was one of the first to give Chinese impersonations. Born in Indianapolis, Indiana, in 1868, he initially appeared with McCabe and Young's Minstrels in the late 1880s, and then with Richard and Pringle's Minstrels, with whom he first started impersonating Italian and Jewish immigrants and "doing a Chinaman under cork."[85] In 1898, he portrayed the character Chinaman (as well as Detective Billy Binkerton and the characters Rube, Italian, and Hebrew) in *Trip to Coontown*, the first full-length African American musical.[86] In actuality, *Trip to Coontown* was more like a revue than a modern musical and was only loosely held together by a story about a con man, Jim Flimflammer (Billy Johnson), who is trying to steal Silas Green Jr.'s (Robert A. Kelley) pension. While on tour, the writers of *Trip to Coontown*, Bob Cole and Billy Johnson, added the song "The Wedding of the Chinee and the Coon" (1897), which was sung by Brown, Kelley, Johnson,

Cole (as Willie Wayside, a tramp), and J. A. Shipp (as Silas Green Jr., the son of Silas Green Jr.) to give Brown an opportunity to show off his Chinaman caricature.[87] "The Wedding of the Chinee and the Coon" tells the story of several intercultural conflicts between two lovers as they plan for their wedding. For instance, during one of the verses, the wedding party debates who should perform the service, an African American or Chinese clergyman. In the midst of this discussion, one African American attendee decides to cut off the queue of the "Chinese preacher." This is similar to incidents in songs written by whites from the 1850s through the early 1880s. Despite these problems, "The Wedding of the Chinee and the Coon" ends with the possibility that more mixed marriages will occur in the future.

> This strange amalgamation
> twixt these two funny nations
> gwine to cause an awful jamble soon—
> Twill cause a great sensation
> over the whole creation
> The wedding of the Chinee and the coon.

Although seeming to locate African Americans and Chinese immigrants in a similarly imagined place within American society, the lyrics do not discuss the effect of this "amalgamation." Here, Cole, Johnson, and Brown suggest an inevitable increase in miscegenation by using an African American/Chinese marriage, which, like the one in "Ching-a-Ling," would be seen as less threatening to white society.

By the turn of the century, Brown had joined up with dancer Siren Nevarro and continued to perform Chinese and other impersonations with her as a duo in vaudeville. From their advertising headshots, it appears they both wore a *shan ku*, with Brown wearing a hat that probably had a queue attached.[88] They did other numbers as well, such as one described by a reviewer as an "Indian Song," but the act was known for its Chinese impersonations.[89] In 1906 and 1909, respectively, they took a break from vaudeville and performed in Ernest Hogan's musical *Rufus Rastus*, which was interspersed with specialty acts such as theirs, and Bert Williams's *Mr. Lode of Koal*. Brown and Nevarro remained together in vaudeville until sometime in 1914, when they split up. Later that year, Brown briefly joined up with J. Rosamond Johnson, but he was unable to maintain his previous popularity and thereafter only appeared on stage periodically until his death in 1919. Nevarro continued to do Chinese dances as a solo act for about a year but disappeared from theater columns by 1916.[90]

Brown and Nevarro's number in Bert Williams's *Mr. Lode of Koal* (1909) participates in complex cultural work that deserves particular comment. During the second act, Bert Williams's character is sitting on the stage drinking beer while Brown and Nevarro are doing a Spanish dance. When Williams falls asleep, Brown and Nevarro come out on stage again as the Chinese immigrant characters Gimlet and Whirlina and sing "Chink Chink Chinaman" (see ill. 19).[91] This song, which contains a few Chinese musical tokens, describes a Chinese immigrant who owns a chop suey restaurant in a white neighborhood but moves to the African American part of town because he cannot stand white music. He eventually realizes that the musical and social habits of whites and African Americans are the same because both groups continually sing "chink chink chineeman" in his restaurant.[92] This song gives insight not only into the content of popular music, especially that produced by African Americans, but also into what was being sung as part of a more general oral culture. Several folklorists have collected children's ditties from the 1880s through the 1960s that are similar to "Chink Chink Chinaman" and were most likely used to tease and harass Chinese immigrant men.[93] These little rhymes also circulated in the African American community. African American educator and feminist Mary Church Terrell recalled that while she was living in Yellow Springs, Ohio, in the late nineteenth century, both black and white children sang out "Ching Ching Chinaman, do you eat rats?"[94] Williams's version of "Chink Chink Chinaman" brings African Americans and whites together because they enjoy singing the same racist ditties.

Like Brown and Nevarro, other African American duos that performed Chinese numbers appeared at the beginning of the twentieth century. In these acts, however, only one of the two performers portrayed a Chinese immigrant and the other was an African American dandy. Cook and Stevens, an African American duo on vaudeville from 1906 through 1919, produced a laundryman number, first known as "Chinese and the Coon" and later as "The Chinee and the Coon, No Checkee, No Washee" (see ill. 20).[95] Sam Cook, nicknamed Chink, impersonated Chinese immigrant men first with Billy Kersands's Minstrels in 1903; during the 1920s, he continued his caricatures with another partner listed only as Smith and in two touring shows, 7–11 (ca. 1922) and Hit and Run (1924).[96] Cook and Stevens's skit was described in Variety in 1906 as a "talking act" with coon songs interspersed. As the critic noted: "One does a Chinaman with an attention to accurate dialect and characterization that is unique and makes for good comedy effect in contrast with the Negro comedian."[97] The humor of "Chinese and the Coon" also centered on a lost laundry ticket and a series of misunderstandings between an immigrant laundryman and his customer.[98]

Not all African American impersonations tried to highlight Chinese foreignness. More than a decade later, Cook with his new partner Smith gave another rendition of a Chinese immigrant man who refused to give an African American customer his laundry without a ticket. The Variety reviewer at the American Roof Garden in New York City in 1919 wrote that "the dialogue"

CHINK CHINK CHINAMAN

Words by
ALEX ROGERS.

Music by
BERT A. WILLIAMS.
Arr. by J. Rosamond Johnson.

Ill. 19. Alex Rogers and Bert A. Williams's "Chink Chink Chinaman" (1909). Courtesy of the Library of Congress.

Ill. 19. (*continued*)

Ill. 19. (*continued*)

COOK AND STEVENS, *colored comedians, clever you must admit*
On any old bill they are a positive hit
Originality is a virtue with these two
Kings in their line is very true.

AND *you must be made of wood if you don't laugh right out*
Something's doing in laughland when they are about.
They sing coon songs and sing them right
Expect to laugh when they are in sight.
Very near everybody has heard of their original act
Every one praises it as a matter of fact.
Now, remember the name ana some afternoon
See COOK & STEVENS, the original Chinee and the Coon

EDWARD S. KELLER, Agent.

Ill. 20. Cook and Stevens advertisement from the *New York Age,* December 24, 1908. Courtesy of the Library of Congress.

was "witty throughout" and that both characters were "splendidly rendered." This skit also had a new twist on race. After refusing to hand over the laundry, the Chinese character played by Cook removed his queue and told his customer that this Chinese laundryman shtick was a "joke." It appears that the Chinese launderer is fully Americanized and is only pretending to be this caricature. The deception outrages Smith's character, who declares that all Chinese are "yellow." In another turn, the dialogue stops and Cook sings a song with a suggestive title: "Equality" (n.d.). In response to this section of Cook and Smith's act, the critic from *Variety* wrote: "This should be eliminated, however, as it is not in good taste with race conditions as they are in this country."[99]

Perhaps inspired by Cook and Stevens, Catlin and Kelly gave their own rendition of a Chinese/African American laundry skit. George Catlin reportedly had credentials for performing Chinese material. In his memoir, fellow performer Tom Fletcher recorded that Catlin had lived in China for some time and could even speak Chinese (though he did not name which dialect). He also wrote that although Catlin was "dark" and wore a "long moustache," he was apparently able to create a realistic Chinese caricature with greasepaint and spirit gum.[100] His qualifications, however, may in fact have come from his years of performing stock Chinese immigrant caricatures in African American musicals. In 1899, Catlin performed a short Chinese routine during the first act of Bert Williams and George Walker's musical *The Policy Players,* based on policy playing, an illegal turn-of-the-century form of the lottery. Catlin also portrayed a Chinese immigrant character in Williams and Walker's *The Sons of Ham* (1900), *In Dahomey* (1903), and *Abyssinia* (1905).[101] Kelly and Catlin's "The Coon and the Chink" brought together the stereotypes of African American and Chinese immigrant men, which both had been performing for almost a decade. Like Catlin, Kelly had starting performing in African American musicals during the late 1890s; he had also spent considerable time in vaudeville. For Kelley and Catlin, "The Coon and the Chink" was particularly successful, lasting from 1908 until they disbanded around 1917.[102]

Although no script exists of Cook and Stevens's and Kelly and Catlin's vaudeville routines, in 1912 the New York publishing firm Dick and Fitzgerald reproduced a one-act called "The Coon and the Chink."[103] Since the 1850s, Dick and Fitzgerald had sold books on popular entertainment for the home and probably wrote a version of "The Coon and the Chink" for their white clientele. Just as it was common practice in the music industry to co-opt African American works, Dick and Fitzgerald attributed the skit to "Walter Carter," perhaps a pseudonym for one of their staff writers. Nevertheless, Carter's version gives insight into what Cook and Stevens's and Kelly and Catlin's numbers might have looked like. "The Coon and the Chink" is a series of send-ups between an African American dandy, Pete Jackson or Coon, and a Chinese laundry owner called Chink. The first page gives a physical description of the two characters, playing on well-established stereotypes of the time. Coon was supposed to be "tall, lanky, ignorant and unpolished," whereas Chink was short, thin, middle-aged, and "very stupid and ignorant in disposition." Makeup and costumes added to these caricatures. Coon was to wear "comedy black-face," which many African Americans used well into the 1930s and 1940s, and an ill-fitting dandy costume. Chink wore a "typical close shaven wig with queue" and a traditional "coolie" costume.

The dialogue in "The Coon and the Chink" evoked well-circulated images of Chinese immigrant and African American men that no doubt appeared in Kelly and Catlin's and Cook and Stevens's vaudeville numbers. First, both spoke in their respective stage dialects, which had been created over the course of the nineteenth century. Coon was also dangerous, threatening to beat up Chink for refusing to return Coon's laundry without a ticket. Later, Coon does a little stage business about searching for a jackknife in a bowl of chop suey, which "smells jes like possum-soup."[104] Chink's foibles focus on his foreignness and inability to understand American ways. For example, Chink sews up the wrong end of Coon's socks, and when Coon shows him the mistake, Chink yells at Coon in gibberish. The skit ends with a song, before which Coon gets drunk and asks Chink to help him put together a vaudeville act.

The bringing together of Chinese immigrants and African Americans on the stage functioned in two distinct ways. A handful of white songwriters and performers used these characters to reaffirm the inferiority of both groups and to highlight the foreignness of Chinese immigrants. African American artists, however, focused on differentiating themselves from the Chinese and asserting their role in the creation of American identity and culture.[105] By the 1930s, this custom crossed over into film.[106] Although affirming constructions of Chinese inferiority and foreignness, songs by African Americans exemplified music's increasing complexity after 1880 and illustrated the rethinking of where men and women of Chinese descent belonged, both in America and in a hierarchy of races.

ALTHOUGH WIDELY HELD ATTITUDES about race, gender, modern life, and Chinese cultural practices remained restricting, much had changed in the portrayal of Chinese subjects by the late 1880s. American popular composers pondered in new ways where (and whether) the Chinese belonged in relation to other races and ethnicities. They also treated positively a couple of subjects that previously had been used to mark Chinese inferiority, presented China and Chinatowns as counter-images to the evils of modernization, added female and other new characters to the repertoire of stock figures, and took miscegenation as a fact rather than a fear. Racism still prevailed, but in more subtle and complex forms.

It was this atmosphere that presented a challenge and an opportunity for Chinese and Chinese American musicians and actors who wanted to perform in vaudeville.

CHAPTER 6

The Rise of Chinese and Chinese American Vaudevillians, 1900s–1920s

BY THE BEGINNING OF THE TWENTIETH CENTURY, Chinese and Chinese American performers began to appear in vaudeville throughout the United States, moving beyond community theater houses, world expositions, and human displays. Many of these vaudevillians avoided magic and acrobatics, which white audiences had highly praised, and produced acts that incorporated popular songs, dance routines, comedic skits, and impersonations. In fact, their routines were very similar to those performed during the same time period by Euro-Americans and African Americans. Chinese and Chinese American acts, however, also challenged racial beliefs. Using strategies similar to those employed by African Americans in minstrel shows and, later, in vaudeville and musical theater, Chinese and Chinese American vaudevillians were not simply the subject of songs and productions; they also performed and, in so doing, promoted their own ideas about American and Chinese identity on the stage.

Vaudeville, with its roots in blackface minstrelsy, circus, burlesque, and variety, first appeared by the 1880s in cities such as Boston and New York. In an effort to bring in more customers, owners tried to gentrify their theaters, which originally had catered to a male urban working-class audience, by bringing in less vulgar acts and halting the sale of liquor on the premises. Although vaudeville made no pretense of presenting acts similar to those found in concert halls, it did offer programming geared to white, middle-class families, most notably women and children. Over the next several decades, vaudeville became nationalized and streamlined, which allowed for the establishment of theatrical circuits and a central booking agency, the United Booking Office. An evening's entertainment also became regimented, with seven to ten acts appearing on the bill in a set order and dominated by a headliner. With its wide array of acts, vaudeville emerged as one of the most popular entertainment venues in the United States by the end of the nineteenth century.[1]

Success in vaudeville was very difficult to achieve, and that proved to be the case especially for most Chinese and Chinese American vaudevillians. Some performed for several years throughout the United States, Canada, and even Europe, while others lasted only part of a season. All of them, however, faced similar preconceptions about their nation of origin and their ability as performers. Nineteenth-century writers acknowledged the magical and acrobatic skills of the Chinese but questioned their ability to sing "more sophisticated" Western music. The racial hierarchy that whites had created over the previous century used the arts as markers of cultural development. Furthermore, because musical production was seen as a manifestation of civilization and Chinese music was often still seen as noise, questions arose about the musical aptitude of men and women of Chinese descent. By the end of the nineteenth century, these attitudes were so pervasive that American audiences could not believe that Chinese and Chinese Americans could sing a Tin Pan Alley song, a music that many elites condemned because of its commercialization, simplicity, and nonsensical lyrics.

Among the obstacles faced by Chinese and Chinese American performers were persistent doubts about their ability to speak and sing English in a coherent manner. Chinese dialect in yellowface performances and print media during the nineteenth century created the enduring idea that Chinese immigrants were incapable of speaking English without a heavy accent. Like Irish and German immigrant caricatures, Chinese characters in popular culture were frequently portrayed as unable to pronounce particular letters, such as r in the word American, or they were made to appear ignorant through statements such as "Me no shabee" (I don't understand). A key distinction between "white" immigrant and Chinese immigrant stereotypes was that, in the former case, language was employed to highlight the foibles committed along the road to assimilation. For the Chinese, however, dialect reinforced their racial inferiority and inability to become American.[2]

Exclusionary laws affected these performers as well. Beginning in the mid-1910s, acts from China that had white agents were allowed into the United States under bond for up to three years if they were performing in vaudeville, which was almost a decade earlier than Chinese American impresarios were permitted the same stipulations for Cantonese opera singers.[3] Chinese Americans also faced problems with the Immigration Bureau when they secured engagements in Europe and Canada. Like other men and women of Chinese descent, these vaudevillians needed permission to reenter the United States, meaning they had to prove that they were American born or had legally entered the country. This procedure, which took place at reentry, was lengthy, at times forcing people to wait several months. For vaudevillians, whose performances often were scheduled only twenty-four to forty-eight hours apart, this was a problem. Through the negotiations of theatrical agents, performers, and immigration inspectors, a system was created in which Chinese American vaudevillians proved their citizenship before leaving the United States. Interviews with friends and family members were conducted and official documents were collected before departure in order to receive a passport or certificate of identity. Vaudevillians also corresponded with regional immigration officers, from whom they procured their documentation, and the Immigration Bureau in Washington, D.C., which in turn wrote border agents about their departure and reentry. Despite the amount of paperwork and correspondence required, this process helped speed up border crossings and international travel for all Chinese American performers.[4]

Restrictions and anti-Chinese attitudes were only one part of the story, however. Chinese immigrant performers appropriated Christian doctrine and democratic ideals to ease their acceptance on the stage as well as in society more generally. During the nineteenth century, avenues for cross-cultural contact facilitated an interest by some Chinese in American popular music. Missionaries had built churches and schools in which immigrants and their children learned to sing, play musical instruments, and read and write English. Public schools, which in some areas were segregated, allowed these students to join bands and choirs and attend music classes. By the twentieth century, Chinese and Chinese Americans were being exposed to American popular culture in other ways. Some Chinese Americans catered to tourists and opened restaurants with floorshows by white entertainers. Many learned new material by watching actors and actresses on stage and in film, purchasing sheet music, and listening to the phonograph and radio. Like other would-be performers, they paid for dance and music lessons.[5]

As with African American vaudevillians, Chinese and Chinese Americans had to navigate carefully between well-developed preconceptions and their own artistic desires in order to succeed in vaudeville. To do this, they blended aspects of Chinese culture with American stereotypes to give white audiences what they wanted and expected, while simultaneously challenging those stereotypes. The most common devices they used were pidgin English, songs about Chinatowns, and Chinese-inspired costumes, props, and backdrops, which audiences had already seen and enjoyed. At the same time, they sang in several European languages, performed songs with no reference to race or ethnicity, gave Irish and Scottish impersonations, blackened up, and danced new and popular routines. These numbers, although often humorous, explicitly demonstrated the ability of performers of Chinese descent to reproduce non-Chinese images on the stage and to refute Chinese stereotypes tied to race, national identity, and musical ability.

Chinese and Chinese American vaudevillians opened up audiences to new ideas about Chinese immigrants and their acceptance into American society. While appropriating stereotypes, their performances directly questioned

notions of inferiority and foreignness. They met only limited success with critics and audiences, but their ability to negotiate constructions of Chinese and
American culture helped create new opportunities in music, theater, and, by
extension, film for all Asian and Asian American performers in the early twentieth century.

OPENINGS

In many ways, these Chinese and Chinese American vaudevillians are
representative of the diversity within the Chinese community and provide a
fascinating picture of race in the United States. San Francisco, home to one of
the largest Chinese immigrant communities by the end of the nineteenth
century, was also home to many Chinese American performers. Through missions, schools, and the city's significant performing arts scene, Chinese Americans were not only exposed to the tools required to enter vaudeville but also
found venues in which they could perform their material and groom their talent. A large number came from other cities as well—Honolulu, Portland,
Chicago, and New York City. An overwhelming majority of these performers
were second generation, but others had come from China as children or were
part of Chinese troupes that had traveled the world over. An even smaller
number born in the United States and Europe were the product of mixed
marriages. Although bound by their Chinese heritage and shared experiences
with anti-Chinese attitudes in the United States, what brought these individuals together was their love for music and the stage.

At the beginning of the twentieth century, the appearance of actors and
actresses of Chinese descent performing in an American popular idiom was
novel and intriguing for both theater managers and audiences alike. Lee Tung
Foo, also known as Frank Lee, was the first. Born in Watsonville, California,
in 1875, Lee moved with his family several times before settling in Ripon,
California, where his father forced him to give up school and go to work to
support the family. Eventually he arrived in Oakland, California, where he
worked as a servant for Zeno Mauvais, local music store and publishing firm
owner, and joined the choir of the local Presbyterian mission. With help from
missionaries, he became a student of a prominent vocal teacher in the Bay
Area, Margaret Blake Alverson, in 1897, and after several years of study, he
embarked on a career as "the first Chinese baritone" in vaudeville.[6]

By the 1910s, there were numerous Chinese American acts in vaudeville,
often with a few members from the Bay Area. Like Lee, they had trained in
music, theater, and dance with guidance from local band and chorus directors
and music teachers. Lee Tung Foo's brother Lee Tung Li (Henry Lee or Lee
Tung Lai) also trained with Margaret Blake Alverson and sang at the Presbyterian mission in Oakland. Later he joined the choir of the Chinese Congregational Church in San Francisco, where he was "discovered" by local

restaurateur Tony Lubelski, along with Hugh K. Liang (Leong Hui Kim). Liang had helped establish the choir at San Francisco's Chinese Congregational Church and was one of the original members of the Cathay Club Boys Band, the first Chinese American marching band, founded in 1911. At Lubelski's Odeon Café, Liang and Lee started singing with the duo Edgar Don Sang (Don Tin Yaw or Don Tin Yew) and Chan Shu Ying (Chan Suey Ting) from Chicago, who had already spent several years in small-time vaudeville touring Ohio and Pennsylvania. By 1912, they became known as the Chung Hwa Comedy Four (also known as the Chung Hwa Four or the Chinese Quartet).[7]

White actors on the stage, in film, and later in radio were also a source of new material during the early twentieth century. Rose Moy (Rose Yuen Ow) sang and danced in vaudeville with her husband and partner Joe Chong (Yow Joe or Chong Yow Haw) from 1915 through 1929. In an interview with Him Mark Lai and Philip P. Choy of the Chinese Historical Society of America in 1970, Moy recounted working at businesses that afforded her opportunities to watch performers before she broke into vaudeville. While still a teenager, she sold tickets at a local silent film house in San Francisco, whose shows, as was the practice at the time, probably included performances by vaudevillians. Later that year, she started working at Tait's Café, a San Francisco restaurant that included a dinnertime floorshow by white acts. Although Moy primarily handed out candies and biscuits to customers, the owner reportedly asked her if she wanted to learn some of the dances being performed at the Café and offered to pay for her lessons. Later Moy and Joe Chong, her boyfriend at the time, auditioned for the owner and were given jobs. By 1915, Raymond Hitchcock, a fellow performer and producer, offered to bring them to New York City and helped them break into vaudeville.[8]

Many first-generation Chinese found themselves in the performing arts as a result of diverse experiences. Some relied only on the training they had been exposed to in school and through commercial venues. According to his immigration case file, Tom (or Thomas) Guy Wing was born somewhere outside of Canton, where he lived with his mother. Because his father was an American citizen (born in Butte, Montana) and lived in the United States, his parents decided to send him to New York City in 1919, where he attended school and helped his father run a restaurant. In 1929 (and much to his father's chagrin), Wing became a chorus member in Honorable Wu's "Chinese Nights Revue," also known as the "Chinese Showboat Revue" or the "Chinese Whoopee Review," and traveled to France, where he performed for several months. Honorable Wu was the stage name for Harry Gee Haw, another vaudevillian from San Francisco who had started singing and dancing professionally in 1914. In an interesting twist of fate, Haw was a friend of Hugh Liang from the Chung Hwa Comedy Four, and when the quartet traveled to New York City in 1912, Haw asked to go along as an understudy. En route to New York, the group stopped in Chicago to visit the families of Edgar Don Sang and Chan Shu Ying, and it was there that Haw met Don Sang's sister, Minnie Don Fong. Haw and Don Fong decided that they would start a song and dance team of their own, which lasted for a few years. By the mid-1920s, Haw had created the first Chinese American revue in vaudeville and had toured the United States, Canada, and parts of Europe.[9] It appears that Wing had no professional theatrical training except for what he picked up along the way in school and later from knowledgeable old-timers such as Haw.[10]

World-renowned Chinese acts, which were mostly from the acrobatic and magic tradition, sometimes were the starting place for performers who wanted to sing American popular songs in vaudeville. Chee Toy, who was originally known as Chee Tai (a name change that suggests an awareness of attitudes toward Asian femininity), was the daughter of the internationally known magician Ching Ling Foo (Chee Ling Qua) and traveled throughout the world with his troupe of acrobats and jugglers (see ill. 21). During the late nineteenth century, Ching Ling Foo and his troupe had performed in European-owned theaters in northern China before coming to the United States in 1898 for the Trans-Mississippi Exhibition in Omaha, Nebraska. As a small child, Chee Toy had joined her father on the stage and sang little ditties in English for audiences. By the early 1910s, she sang and played the piano as a solo number in her father's act. Where she learned American popular music is not clear; her father, however, could have arranged for lessons while they were working in major cities such as New York or London. She likely also benefited from observation and impromptu backstage training by fellow performers.[11]

Those of mixed heritage found similar ways to break into vaudeville, but they faced censure from both whites and Chinese immigrants because of their parentage. The presence of Amerasians and Eurasians on the stage brought forth the anxieties many whites felt about the supposed threat that Chinese immigration posed to the United States, and the possibility that it would lead to the degeneracy of the American (meaning white) race. Laws passed in several states, beginning with California in 1880, codified these sentiments.[12] Immigration inspectors along the border were also alert to the possibility of persons of mixed heritage trying to enter the United States as "white" as opposed to "Chinese," the racial category used by the Immigration Bureau for all white–Chinese offspring. For example, George Wong, an acrobat with the Seven Romas, asked that the Immigration Bureau grant him permission to travel to Toronto, Canada, where the Seven Romas were to perform. The immigration inspector at Buffalo, New York, noted that because of Wong's excellent English, he "either was born in the United States or has lived here the greater part of his life." Wong's English skills aside, his appearance further confused his racial identity. The immigration inspector remarked that not only did Wong have "light brown hair" and "blue eyes," but "except for his oblique

Ill. 21. Portrait of Chee Toy from the sheet music cover for A. Seymour Brown's "I Don't Want To (Oh, Come On)" (1913). Courtesy of the Sam DeVincent Collection of Illustrated American Sheet Music, Archives Center, National Museum of American History, Behring Center, Smithsonian Institution.

eyes his Chinese blood would not be suspected." Born in Hoboken, New Jersey, he was the product of a Chinese–Irish union and, based on this description, probably could have passed as "white."[13] Chinese immigrants to a certain extent also promoted monoracialism and often denied the existence of mixed marriages or unions and their offspring.[14]

Mixed-race performers angered at least one Chinese American vaudevillian, who felt that these "pretenders" undermined the job opportunities for "real" vaudevillians of Chinese descent. Born in Salem, Massachusetts, James Archung (Ar Chung or Ah Chung) was of Irish and Chinese descent. His father, Joseph, was from Hong Kong, where he met two leather manufacturers who brought him to Salem. There he attended school, trained as a tanner, and finally married Bridget Griffin. They had thirteen children (James was their fifth).[15] Like his father and the rest of his family, James went to school in Salem, worked as a shoe cutter, married a local woman named Lillian Visall, and had two children. Something, however, inspired him to leave his hometown and family. By 1912, he was singing at local function halls in the New York City area, where he met up with members of the Chung Hwa Comedy Four, who, after the sudden death of Chan Shu Ying, were in desperate need of a fourth singer.[16] Although he had a long and successful career with the Chung Hwa Comedy Four, Archung faced sharp criticism from Henry Lee's brother, Lee Tung Foo. In letters to his music teacher, Lee emphasized his own authenticity and derided the Chung Hwa Comedy Four, calling Archung a "Mulatto." Lee also accused Leon Allah (Alarcon), who replaced his brother Henry in 1914, of being Mexican. He was in fact of Filipino descent.[17] Other vaudevillians, such as Bernice Ahi and Emma Hong in Honorable Wu's "Chinese Nights Review," were of mixed descent, but it is unclear what Chinese immigrants and Euro-Americans thought of these particular performers and if the latter even realized that they were not "one hundred percent Chinese."

What inspired these Chinese and Chinese Americans to embark on a career in vaudeville is not entirely known, but it seems to be a mixture of those same ambitions and passions felt by every performer, combined with a need to represent a self not found in yellowface and other Chinese acts. As with other groups of actors, they learned and honed their talents in several ways. Band and voice lessons, choir at school or at the local church, and even spur-of-the-moment coaching from fellow vaudevillians were important resources. Opportunities to watch different acts on the stage and in film, buy sheet music, and listen to phonograph records and the radio also gave would-be performers some ideas for acts of their own. Through hard work and training, Chinese and Chinese Americans were able to break into vaudeville without being relegated, as they had been earlier in the nineteenth century, to dime museums, Cantonese operas, and magic or acrobatic acts.

TYPES OF ACTS

A favorite routine of Lee Tung Foo's was his impersonation of a Scotsman. The act was so good, in fact, that it became one of his signature numbers, illustrating how Chinese and Chinese American vaudevillians used race as part of their acts. Moreover, it also shows how much race was an "act." The numbers that these vaudevillians put together were inextricably tied to the stereotypes found in yellowface and Chinese-themed Tin Pan Alley songs. On the one hand, these vaudevillians were limited by what audiences and theater managers expected of them, assumptions that were based on decades of anti-Chinese attitudes. On the other hand, while constrained by these stereotypes, Chinese and Chinese American performers pushed the limits of these images by using certain performance strategies that both supported and challenged what whites thought of them and their ability to perform. The ways in which their routines did this can be broken down into five distinct theatrical practices—costuming, music, language, dancing, and impersonations. Of course, just the mere appearance of Chinese and Chinese Americans on the stage challenged current beliefs about the fixed boundaries of race and nation by giving audiences "real" Chinese bodies to watch. At the beginning of the twentieth century, Chinese and Chinese Americans on the stage contested these notions while at the same time playing to them. The incongruity was all part of the act.

Costuming has always been important in helping performers project an image separate from themselves. Although Chinese and Chinese American vaudevillians could never really escape perceptions of their race, they used costumes to subvert constructions of racial and national identity. White actors who performed in yellowface relied on costumes and makeup to suggest race, but Chinese and Chinese American performers did not have this luxury and used costumes both to exaggerate their background and to expose the limitations of racial categories. With one exception, Chinese and Chinese Americans did not use the baggy blouses and short pants that were common among yellowface impersonators.[18] Instead, they chose either formal wear, like tuxedos or ball gowns, or elaborate Chinese costumes designed to be colorful and attractive rather than authentic. Lee Tung Foo, who bought his Chinese costume and embellishments in San Francisco, advertised that his "Oriental COSTUMING is Very ELABORATE and Effective" (see ill. 1). To add to its theatrical appeal, Lee had Alverson sew "brilliants" (either sequins or small mirrors) to his vest.[19] During certain numbers, Lee Tung Foo, the Chung Hwa Comedy Four, and Prince Lai Mon Kim wore tuxedos (see ill. 22). Although a tuxedo was common attire for professional singers and instrumentalists, Chinese American vaudevillians stood out for wearing the uniform of classical musicians—a costuming choice emphasizing that they should be taken seriously as performers, regardless of race.

Chinese and Chinese American women had to grapple with perceptions of Asian femininity and sexuality, which was apparent in their choice of costuming and hairstyle. Princess Jue Quon Tai (Rose Eleanor Jue) wore several elaborate costumes during her act, which included a special backdrop to add exoticism and novelty (see ill. 23).[20] Born in Los Angeles and raised in Portland, Oregon, Jue combined a royal title with her Chinese stage name, much in the tradition of nineteenth-century human curiosities. In 1915, she debuted as a "foreign princess" who had run away from her fourth-ranked mandarin father while attending the San Francisco World Exposition. In her headshots and advertisements, she wore a Western-style evening gown or a summer day dress with a picture hat. Her hair in these numbers, although

Ill. 22. Portrait of Chung Hwa Comedy Four in tuxedos. Courtesy of the National Archives, Washington, D.C.

sometimes hidden by a hat, was also modern, sometimes cut in a bob. For other numbers, she sustained the ideals of femininity and wore a large Chinese-style embroidered wrap or a jacket with pants and matching shoes. Her hair was parted down the middle, and above each ear was a little bun with flowers.[21] In another photograph for *Theatre Magazine*, Jue posed as a "singsong girl," on her knees holding a *sanxian*, a three-stringed lute, and looking up at the camera, a pose very similar to that of Fay Bainter's Ming Toy on the sheet

Ill. 23. Portrait of Jue Quon Tai. Courtesy of Harry Ransom Humanities Research Center, University of Texas at Austin.

music cover of "Chinese Lullaby" (see ill. 17).[22] Like the men, Chinese American women used both formal modern attire and hyper-Chinese costuming. Women, however, added another dimension to their clothes by playing to the innocence, modesty, and sexual allure of the "Oriental" female form, which was similar to yellowface characterizations of Chinese women in productions such as *The Yellow Jacket* or *East Is West*. Jue Quon Tai's act and photographs also represented some measure of control on her part in that she created a caricature of a caricature—a standard of femininity that was blatantly unrealistic. Ironically, the ideal of Asian femininity was in direct contrast to white womanhood of the early twentieth century, and it was promoted and marketed to question the New Woman.

Beyond the visual element, what really stood out for critics and audiences was the novelty of Chinese and Chinese Americans singing. Many reviews reflected the stereotypes, constructed during the nineteenth century, that encouraged the racialization of musical ability and excluded Chinese Americans from mainstream venues. For example, Lee Tung Foo often received extensive commentary on his singing ability because his act was considered so novel and groundbreaking. It seems almost silly, but it was such a widespread belief that men and women of Chinese descent could not understand European or American music that people were truly dumbfounded to hear him. In a review from *Keith's News,* the anonymous author admitted that at first he thought it was impossible for someone who was Chinese to sing well, but after hearing Lee perform, he realized he was wrong. "When there appeared upon the vaudeville market a chinaman who was said to be able to sing, and sing remarkably well in a rich, clear baritone voice, everyone scoffed at the idea, for it is a well known fact that the Chinese scale has only a few tones, and the music of China is a clash and discord that would be anything but acceptable to American theatergoers." Lee, however, "is all that was said of him and when it was found that he was a baritone vocalist of much ability and, what is more, that he sings in English, his services became very much in demand and he is now the talk of the vaudeville world."[23]

If one singer was a surprise, imagine the audience reaction to a Chinese American quartet! What distinguished the Chung Hwa Comedy Four from other Chinese American singers was that they sang in harmony much like other barbershop quartets of the period. Throughout the nineteenth century, music amateurs and experts had debated whether the Chinese could produce or even understand harmony, which was considered part of the foundation of Western music. In their reviews, vaudeville critics admired the Chung Hwa Comedy Four, making only inferences to the fact that the group countered previously held attitudes about the Chinese. The New York–based reviewer for the *Billboard* wrote that "the Chung Hwa Four, as the name implies, is a quartette of celestials who harmonize exceedingly well, and offer several well-rendered solo numbers." In Chicago, another critic wrote that "the Chung Hwa Four, billed as China's quartette of harmony, lived up to their title. The Orientals are gifted with remarkable voices, which blend nicely in an offering of ragtime and popular ballads."[24] Some of the Chung Hwa Comedy Four's success depended on their challenging of ideas about the Chinese and Western harmony, and this challenge was reflected in the tone of disbelief that frequently accompanied reviews.

Chinese and Chinese American vaudevillians also countered stereotypes simply by singing and speaking in English without an accent. The belief that all men and women of Chinese descent spoke with an accent was so strong that the lack of one was enough for critics to make note. In the *Billboard,* a correspondent from Cincinnati wrote that the Chung Hwa Comedy Four's "pronunciation is good, meaning English."[25] A different reporter wrote that in Princess Jue Quon Tai's speech, mannerisms, and dress, "the nearest Jue ever got to China was the west coast of America."[26] Prince Lai Mon Kim (William Kim Lai), "the Only Chinese Tenor Playing the American Stage," shocked one critic, who wrote, "Prince Lai Mon Kim a Chinese Tenor, made a splendid impression, singing ballads in English, with an enunciation so perfect one can hardly believe he is a foreigner."[27] Like Jue and members of the Chung Hwa Comedy Four, Lai Mon Kim was not from China but had been born in Portland, Oregon.[28]

Critics were also surprised at the English skills of Chinese and Chinese American women. Lady Tsen Mei (also known as Chung Moy, Lady Sen Mei, and later, Josephine Kramer), more so than any other Chinese or Chinese American vaudevillian, emphasized in her performances the relationship between race, exoticism, and femininity (see ill. 24). Born in Canton in 1888, she and her father, who was reportedly studying to be a doctor, moved to Philadelphia around 1900.[29] When she first appeared in vaudeville in 1915, reviewers commented on not only her poise and gracefulness but also her language ability. "Her perfect enunciation," noted one reviewer "constitutes the first favorable surprise and her general poise, carriage and graceful gesturing the next with her cultured voice insuring her success."[30] A Chicago reviewer deemed her a much better singer than many whites in vaudeville. "Her voice is clear and sweet toned, and the enunciation perfect. In this respect she could teach many of her Caucasian sisters a lesson."[31] Chee Toy received similar praise. During the Ching Ling Foo and Company's premiere at the Hammerstein Theater in New York City, a critic for the *New York Tribune* admitted to some surprise at her performance, especially in comparison to the more traditional Chinese numbers of others in the troupe: "little Chee Toy can easily give pointers to some of our American vaudeville singers in the fine art of singing ragtime [probably meaning coon songs]."[32] Later she played the piano and sang again in English.

Dancing was another novel aspect of several Chinese American acts during the first half of the twentieth century. Euro-Americans believed that Chinese immigrants avoided dancing because only low-class individuals, such as actors or prostitutes, danced in China. An 1896 article from the *Century,* titled "The Chinese of New York," argued that the Chinese "never" danced "neither in China nor in America." It qualified this statement by noting that a Chinese immigrant could become a dancer if he or she was "so far

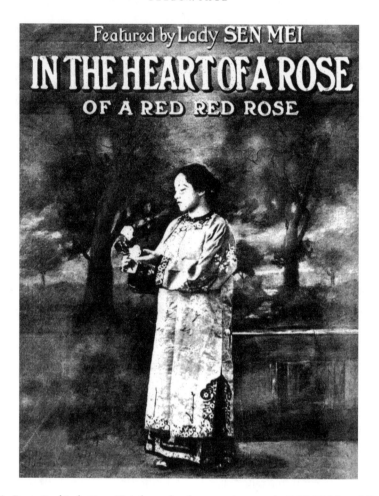

Ill. 24. Portrait of Lady Tsen Mei, from the sheet music cover for J. W. Walsh and George De Carme's "In the Heart of the Rose" (1912). Courtesy of the Sam DeVincent Collection of Illustrated American Sheet Music, Archives Center, National Museum of American History, Behring Center, Smithsonian Institution.

denationalized as to be considered a foreign graft on the Western Stalk." This, however, "occur[red] not once in a thousand cases."[33] Stylized movements and acrobatics were important to religious and state rituals, operas, and other performing arts traditions in China, but not social or ballroom dance. Since at least the fifteenth century, men and women of European descent danced in a manner that allowed everyone to participate and was seen as a form of relaxation, celebration, or physical culture. This practice, however, did not exist in China until the 1920s, when European and American dance instructors started teaching social dance in major metropolitan areas.[34] In vaudeville, elaborate versions of these same social dances were reproduced on the stage, many of which were influenced by African American and Latin music at the turn of the century. During the 1910s, Irene and Vernon Castle also popularized updated nineteenth-century dances and introduced "cleaned-up" versions of new dances such as the tango and one-step.[35]

By the mid-1910s, Chinese American dancing duos appeared in vaudeville, much to the surprise of audiences. Performing from 1914 through 1918, Harry Gee Haw (later known as Honorable Wu) and Dong Fong Gue (Minnie) sang and danced in a variety of styles—foxtrot, black bottom, waltz, and cakewalk, which they combined with what were described as Chinese stylized movements. Critics praised both their singing and dancing. In Chicago, a reviewer wrote: "this clever little Chinese couple not only sing well but are exceptionally good dancers, doing the cake-walk and fox-trot like regular old-timers."[36] Chong and Moy's act was similar to Haw and Gue's and consisted of popular songs and American dances with Chinese embellishments. In 1917, one critic wrote in the *Billboard* that their dances were "strange and modern" (a reference probably to their incorporation of "Chinese" movements), but "both excel[led] in grace and finish of execution."[37]

Most of the songs by Chinese and Chinese Americans in vaudeville were those that were popular with contemporary audiences and produced by Tin Pan Alley. Lee Tung Foo was one of the few who sang ballads from operettas, such as "Brown October Ale" and "Armourer's Song" from Reginald De Koven's *Robin Hood* (1890).[38] Overall, the content of the songs performed by Chinese and Chinese Americans ran the gamut from romantic love and patriotism to more racialized numbers. The act of singing about romantic love, which was often seen as a universal emotion, and patriotism supported other aspects of their acts, which questioned constructions of race and nation that precluded men and women of Chinese descent from being seen as American. For example, in the years before the United States became involved in World War I, Chee Toy sang "I Didn't Raise My Boy to Be a Soldier" (1915), a well-known plea for peacefully resolving the turmoil in Europe and keeping the United States out of the war.[39] Chinese and Chinese Americans also sang several love songs. Poldi Long (also known as Nee Sa Long), the daughter of acrobat and magician Long Tack Sam and his Austrian wife Leopoldini Rossler, performed Roy Turk, Jack Smith, and Maceo Pinkard's song about love and courtship, "'Gimme' a Little Kiss Will 'Ya' Huh?" (1926).[40] James Archung sang "Sipping Cider thru' a Straw" (1919) as a solo with the Chung Hwa Comedy Four. "Sipping Cider thru' a Straw" is not a ballad but a comedy lisping song in which the vocalist is required to imitate a lisp during the chorus, all the while singing about a romance that arose over two straws and a glass of cider.[41]

Chinese American performers also sang Tin Pan Alley songs in Cantonese. It is interesting that singers from China did not do this, probably because they were not from Guangdong Province (the region from which most Chinese immigrants came to the United States) and wanted to avoid being pigeonholed as "traditional" Chinese performers. For instance, Chee Toy did not do ethnic impersonations, nor did she sing Chinese songs or American popular songs translated into a Chinese dialect. She did, however, give renditions of songs such as "On the Shores of Italy" (1914), but without Italian costuming and dialect.[42] Chinese Americans did use Cantonese on the stage, another source of ambivalence, especially when contrasted to their English dialogue and singing. The most popular song was "Chinatown, My Chinatown," which Chinese Americans sang in both English and Cantonese.[43] Lee Tung Foo also created a "Chinese song" made up of a medley of Chinese-themed Tin Pan Alley songs.[44] Lai Mon Kim translated Irving Berlin's "Ragtime Violin" (1911) and sang Chinese folk songs. A critic in Cincinnati noted that Lai "fared much better with the Ragtime Violin sung in Chinese, than with the ballads." Although a tenor, Lai had "difficulty in sustaining the [high] notes."[45]

Of all the different aspects of their routines, impersonations were the most direct challenges to American assumptions that racial and national identities were fixed and natural categories. Imitations of ethnic and racial types were first made popular in the United States through blackface minstrelsy and continued throughout the twentieth century. Chinese and Chinese Americans, as with other groups such as African Americans, inherited these stereotypes, but used them to question these same images. Although some were reported to produce caricatures of famous vaudevillians, Chinese and Chinese American racial and ethnic impressions went even further by demonstrating that they themselves could generate such images once controlled by whites and seen as real. Irish, Scottish, and African American impersonations were all part of the repertoire of Chinese and Chinese American vaudevillians. Whether this was in response to connections already created among these groups—the perceived similarities between Scottish and Chinese music, the association of and competition between Irish and Chinese immigrants, and the lumping together of African Americans and the Chinese through popular and scientific racism—is not exactly clear. Irish Americans and African Americans were also producing Chinese caricatures and had been since the nineteenth century. Nevertheless, these particular choices turned American stereotypes on their head and added to the ambiguities of images already being generated on the stage.

Coon songs and blackface characterizations were found periodically in Chinese and Chinese American acts. Chee Toy was noted for singing coon songs in the United States and in Europe. One critic wrote, upon Chee Toy's debut with her father in 1912: "the orchestra struck up the music of Robert E. Lee [presumably the plantation song, "Waiting for the Robert E. Lee" (1912)] and the little Chinese Miss sang it with a purity of diction many American soubrettes might emulate."[46] Chinese Americans in blackface was, yet again, another novel device used to gain access to the stage, but, as Michael Rogin argues in his analysis of Jewish Americans in *Blackface, White Noise*, it also spoke to the relationship between blacking up and Americanization.[47] At least one act, Yen Wah and Chan Tock (Tak Wha Chan), did blackface impersonations in vaudeville from 1922 through 1927. In 1921, Yen Wah had first appeared as a solo act before he joined Chan Tock a year later.[48] Their act consisted of dance, comedic patter, singing, and imitations. In January 1922, a critic noted that Yen and Chan did "a Negro Specialty, singing 'blues' numbers" and "executing a cakewalk." He found them to be so realistic that he was unsure whether they were Chinese Americans who were "sufficiently authentic to make them as colored men" or African Americans in yellowface, adding once again to the complexity of conceptions of race on the stage.[49]

Although performers such as John "Chinee" Leach had produced Chinese-Irish send-ups in the 1870s, the appearance of Irish impersonations by Chinese Americans surprised and, through their humor, pleased audiences. When Lee Tung Foo first toured the East Coast of the United States starting in 1906, the *Boston Post* reported that he was "the Find of the Season." In part, this was because "his songs, especially 'My Irish Molly,' have delighted Howard [Theater] audiences all week."[50] Another anonymous critic in Pittsburgh agreed. "The Chinaman's Irish dialect impersonation is said to be a screamingly funny act."[51] The novelty of a Chinese American singing a song with an Irish accent was enough to amuse most critics, but Yip Lee from Honorable Wu's "Chinese Nights Review" went a little further, offering an ironic and funny twist on the connections between Chinese and Irish immigrants. After stepping out onto an empty stage, he "announc[ed] he would sing a native tune in his native language." Yip then broke out into the Irish number "Mother Machree" (1910), a song about a son's love for his mother.[52]

A number of Chinese American vaudevillians also impersonated a Scottish Highlander character or performed Scottish songs and dances. The Chung Hwa Comedy Four and Mina Long, Long Tack Sam and Leopoldini Rossler's eldest daughter, danced the Highland Fling, a reel (also called a Strathspey reel) known for its Scottish kick movement and heel touching on the calf and shin.[53] Jue Quon Tai sang Harry Williams's "Bonnie Annie Laurie" (1909), during which she wore what one reporter in Chicago described as "American idea of evening dress," not a kilt.[54]

Critics especially liked the Chung Hwa Comedy Four's Scottish impersonations in which members wore kilts and spoke and sang with a brogue. The success of this number was the result not only of the comedic elements they employed but also of the novelty and, to at least one reviewer, the silliness of Chinese Americans doing Scottish impersonations. "They sing a number of good vocal interpolations and wind up with a Scottish number which goes big probably due to the absurdity of Chinamen appearing in a Scottish song with costumes to match."[55] A few years later and perhaps after the novelty of Chinese Americans impersonating Scottish Highlanders had worn off, another reviewer remarked on the troupe's ability to speak in "perfect dialect even to the long trilled R."[56] The writer's comment about their ability to pronounce r is important because in pidgin English, the letter l replaced the letter r in, for example, "Amelican." As in their other numbers, the Chung Hwa Comedy Four's Scottish impersonations impressed critics, but this was still filtered through the fact that they were of Chinese descent.

Lee Tung Foo reached a significant turning point in his career with the introduction of a Scottish number based on the performer and songwriter Harry Lauder (see ill. 25). After Lee's return from Europe in 1909, his playbills began to read "Lee Tung Foo, The Chinaman with Harry Lauder on the Brain."[57] In a letter to Margaret Blake Alverson, he explained the premise of his Scottish number: "You know I don't imitate him [Harry Lauder] at all. I got the Scottish way and little dialect that's all and the quaint way I deliver the song."[58] Their correspondence also includes Lee's jokes, which alluded to Lauder. "There is one thing I can safely say and that is I go better in Scotland than he [Lauder] would in China. That's a cinch, u may not believe it, but there is some Scotch in me, honest, nearly half a pint."[59] Lee's Scottish and Chinese acts became the hallmark of his performances.

As with Lee Tung Foo's impersonations, the routines put together by Chinese and Chinese Americans in vaudeville were both funny and painful responses to the stereotypes found in the yellowface tradition. Unfortunately, many of these acts flew beneath the radar of writers on popular culture because they were not performed in big-time vaudeville or were only part of a larger act with a headliner.[60] To gain access to the vaudeville stage, Chinese and Chinese Americans exploited their "Chineseness" to draw interest to their acts through Chinese-themed songs, sets, and costumes. Simultaneously, they fashioned numbers in a manner that clearly allowed them to be different from what audiences expected and that countered race-based ideas on musical ability. In the end, Chinese and Chinese American vaudevillians spoke to the complexities of popular culture, which, in its moments of relative openness, tolerated these contradictions on the stage and the exposure of audiences to alternative points of view on racial and national identity.

CHINESE AND CHINESE AMERICAN VAUDEVILLIANS from the early twentieth century marked an important generational shift away from nineteenth-century Chinese performers in the United States, who worked in more traditional idioms or as human curiosities. In the period between 1900 through 1930, these vaudevillians clearly faced adversity and the daunting task of over-

Ill. 25. Portrait of Lee Tung Foo in a Scottish costume. Courtesy of the California History Room, California State Library, Sacramento.

coming or conforming to American popular conceptions. As documented in Arthur Dong's film *Forbidden City, U.S.A.*, whites still hung onto these attitudes well into the 1940s and were still shocked at the sight of Asian Americans singing and dancing.[61] To negotiate anti-Chinese attitudes, these vaudevillians created acts that contained elements of previous yellowface caricatures, but they avoided the earlier period's grosser "Heathen Chinee," laundryman, or servant stereotypes. At the same time, their acts undermined American ideas about the Chinese through sends-ups of other ethnicities and the use of popular songs and dances.

The surprisingly large number of Chinese and Chinese American performers—although primarily in small-time vaudeville—is a welcome addition to a mostly forgotten moment in America's past. At times, they proved that anyone could reproduce ethnic and racial impersonations and challenged white control over the stage. By demonstrating a command of Western musical and theatrical practices, Chinese and Chinese American vaudevillians were able to question race-based ideas of music. Although they still faced an enormous amount of discrimination and prejudice, the experiences of their generation were far removed from those of their forbearers, the Chinese and Chinese immigrants who had been the objects of so much misunderstanding and hatred in the nineteenth and early twentieth centuries.

Conclusion

In 1990, THE NEWS that Cameron Macintosh's London hit, *Miss Saigon*, was coming to the United States was received with both great enthusiasm and sharp criticism from Asian Americans and the theatrical community. *Miss Saigon*, an updated version of Puccini's *Madama Butterfly* (1904) by Alain Boubil and Claude-Michel Schönberg, tells the story of an American G.I. named Chris who falls in love with a Vietnamese prostitute, Kim, only days before the fall of Saigon and the withdrawal of American troops. Chris, through circumstances beyond his control, is forced to leave Kim behind during the evacuation of the U.S. embassy. Three years later, Chris has married an American woman, Ellen, while Kim along with Chris's son Tam and The Engineer, previously her pimp at the Vietnamese club Dreamland, are in Bangkok, where she works as a bargirl. On discovering that Kim is alive and that he has a son, Chris travels to Bangkok with Ellen but has no clear vision of how to balance his love for both women and his feeling of responsibility to Tam as his father. After realizing that Chris has married another woman, Kim sacrifices her life in the final scene so that Tam can go home with Chris and Ellen and become an "American" boy.[1]

On the basis of Macintosh's early success with Boubil and Schönberg's *Les Misérables* (1987), it was expected that the arrival of *Miss Saigon* on Broadway followed by a series of national tours would bring in huge revenues. For Asian American actors, it would also mean steady pay and jobs in an industry dominated by "white" roles or stereotypical, Asian/Asian American bit parts. Despite what was perceived to be its positive aspects, the plot and casting of *Miss Saigon* were intrinsically problematic for Asian American artists and activists. The storyline, characterizations, and music perpetuated stereotypes of the Vietnamese (and more broadly, Asians/Asian Americans) as degraded, violent, and sexually available to Americans. In particular, the casting of Jonathan Pryce to play The Engineer, a character of both French and Vietnamese descent, first in London and later in New York City, was also a point of contestation. Actor's Equity, the union for performers in the United States, had jurisdiction over whether foreign performers, excluding major stars, could appear in the United States and regulated the portrayal of nonwhite characters, ensuring, for instance, that African American roles were played by African Americans and not whites in blackface.[2] Pryce, however, was performing in yellowface, and with Macintosh threatening that he would not bring *Miss Saigon* to the United States if Pryce was not allowed to play The Engineer, Actor's Equity permitted *Miss Saigon* to be performed on Broadway in the same way it had been in London.

Debates surrounding Pryce as The Engineer focused on the producer's artistic freedom and the importance of having Asian Americans playing Asian or Asian American roles. Pryce, who for several performances in London even used prosthetics to slant his eyes and yellowish pancake, was participating in the tradition of yellowface—white bodies playing Asian/Asian American roles and controlling what it means to be nonwhite on the stage. Although blackface had disappeared by the 1960s, yellowface was still going strong—for example, Mickey Rooney's Mr. Yunioshi in *Breakfast at Tiffany's* (1961) and David Carradine's Kwai Chang Caine (the offspring of a Chinese woman and an American sailor) in the 1970s television series *Kung Fu*. Both Caine and The Engineer, however, represented the offspring of interracial sex, another group that was far too often ignored in discussions of race by both Asian Americans and Euro-Americans, who argued from monoracialist points of views. Regardless, several Asian American activists believed that because there were so few Asian and Asian American roles on Broadway, an actor of Asian descent should be cast as The Engineer.[3]

In response to the plot and casting of *Miss Saigon*, Asian Americans used the term *yellowface* to reveal the ways in which the entertainment industry caricatured *all* men and women of Asian descent and to question the perpetuation of Asian stereotypes through yellowing up, storylines, and music.[4] Tied to blackface and the portrayal of African Americans on the stage by whites in the nineteenth century, the term *yellowface* appears as early as the 1950s to describe the continuation in film of having white actors playing major Asian and Asian American roles and the grouping together of all makeup technologies used to make one look "Asian."[5] Thanks to the power of film executives in casting, Asian and Asian Americans who had decades of theatrical experience in vaudeville were unable to find work or were relegated to stereotypical roles—laundrymen, prostitutes, or servants. The stereotype that men and women of Asian descent were incapable of creating complex and subtle characters in film (not to mention their inability to speak English well) was once again recirculated. Many actors who went into film after the decline of vaudeville in the 1930s (such as Lee Tung Foo, Lady Tsen Mei, and Harry Gee Haw) participated in creating those same stereotypes that their work in vaudeville had confounded.

In conjunction with Asian American activism during the late 1960s and

1970s, Asian Americans used the idea of yellowface to reveal the perpetuation of Asian stereotypes and the fact that producers and directors still vied for white actors to play Asian and Asian American roles. Organizations such as the Oriental Actors of America (founded in 1968) emerged to protest this treatment and the lack of jobs for Asian American actors. Other Asian Americans created theatrical companies, the first of which was East-West Players in 1965, to give Asian American actors opportunities to perform and to support Asian American playwrights.[6] A wide array of Asian Americans even protested Fu Manchu and Charlie Chan movie marathons on local television stations.[7]

Almost two decades later, yellowface reemerged again as part of the rallying cry to condemn a racist tradition. Articles used the notion of yellowface to discuss *Miss Saigon* and later to make more generalized remarks about stereotypical images of Asians and Asian Americans in the media. In the 1994 article "The Heat Is on *Miss Saigon* Coalition: Organizing across Race and Sexuality," Yoko Yoshikawa discussed the protests against the Lambda Legal Defense Fund, a national organization dedicated to gay and lesbian rights, and its use of *Miss Saigon* for a fundraiser. Yoshikawa wrote: "Pryce had been acting in yellow-face, with prosthetically altered eyelids and tinted make-up."[8] Academics also incorporated the term into their analyses of Asian/Asian American stereotypes. In her discussion of Mary Pickford's portrayal of Cho-Cho-San in the film version of *Madame Butterfly* (1915), Gina Marchetti noted that Pickford had "adopt[ed] 'yellow face' for her role." Robert Lee, in the introduction (aptly titled "Yellowface") to *Orientals*, discussed this term as a form of discourse in popular culture for constructing an American Other.[9] Ironically, despite its appearance in the writings of academics and activists, *yellowface* still does not appear in the *Oxford English Dictionary* or any other major American dictionary.

THE HISTORY OF AMERICAN POPULAR CULTURE provides an important lens for viewing the social and cultural complexities of race and the ways that stereotypes from past musical performances live on today. Yet music and its performance also provide forums for expressing, debating, and providing alternatives to widely held racial attitudes, a method commonly used in the nineteenth and early twentieth centuries by Chinese and Chinese Americans. Unlike those who protested *Miss Saigon*, Chinese Americans at the turn of the nineteenth century did not appear in the streets with picket signs, but they did write articles condemning these stereotypes. For example, Julius Su Tow, secretary of the Chinese consulate general in New York City, was quoted in *Literary Digest* as saying that the majority of American playwrights "do not understand or know the real life and customs" of the Chinese people and produce plays that are "usually ridiculous and insulting in the eyes of the Chinese themselves."[10] During the 1920s and 1930s, the Chinese government condemned and boycotted the misrepresentations of its people in American films such as *The Thief of Bagdad* (1924) and *Welcome Danger* (1929).[11] For the most part, however, Chinese and Chinese Americans used the stage as an educational tool, gearing their performances to American theater habits and showing an alternative image of Chinese history and musical/theatrical abilities. Others exploited the ambivalence found in Chinese stereotypes and used the nature of performance to subvert them.

The diversity of writers, musicians, and performers who participated in the construction of the Chinese on the stage was integral to the formation and disintegration of yellowface. Today, discussions of yellowface are a form of empowerment that reveals stereotypes for what they are—white fantasies of the way Chinese bodies should look and sound based on a dichotomous relationship that differentiates "us" from "them." Let us consider three moments—the conception of Chinese music as noise (roughly during the eighteenth and nineteenth centuries), the various musical versions of Bret Harte's "Heathen Chinee," and Lee Tung Foo's twentieth-century vaudeville act. In the first instance, eighteenth- and early nineteenth-century European and American writers, with few exceptions, described Chinese music as lacking any of the traits maintained in Western music, and hence reinforcing beliefs in Chinese racial and cultural inferiority. This, in turn, influenced later, more "scientific" analyses in the nineteenth century; it limited the ways in which composers represented the Chinese musically; and it raised questions about the ability of the Chinese people to learn Western music, which they presumed to be more sophisticated and to represent a higher stage of civilization.

Written in 1870, Bret Harte's poem "Heathen Chinee" also broadly affected American music and theater. The poem, although originally a criticism of American and Chinese immigrant gamblers in the Far West, circulated anti-Chinese stereotypes that supported segregation, violence, and exclusion on the national level. Many performers and songwriters incorporated this song into their own productions, a few of which included token Chinese musical devices, a practice that was mostly absent from earlier anti-Chinese music that had grown out of the California Gold Rush. Inclusion of these sounds helped reinforce a sense of Chinese foreignness and inferiority, and created a more totalizing musical effect. Later in the century, such signifiers became more extensive and pervasive and helped create new modes of musical expression on the American stage.

The appearance of performers such as Lee Tung Foo in vaudeville at the beginning of the twentieth century, however, questioned previous anti-Chinese attitudes, among them ones expressed in music histories, travel narratives, and popular song. At times playing to notions of Chinese exoticism, Lee complicated notions of identity and musical inferiority through his ability to sing popular songs at a professional level, to speak English well, and to imitate Scottish and Irish characters. His success led the way for other Asians and Asian Americans who wished to participate in the making of American popular culture, and it undercut those stereotypes that had barred them from the stage.

These three examples do not exhaust the complexities of the story. Over the course of the nineteenth century, there were several important shifts in music about and by the Chinese—shifts that reflected changes in American social and cultural life. In the 1880s, with the Chinese Exclusion Act removing the possibility of any further significant immigration from China and the consolidation of the music industry into Tin Pan Alley, attitudes softened from the virulently anti-Chinese stance of earlier songs and led to a wider range of characters, especially female ones. More contradictory attitudes also crept onto the popular stage, with Chinese exoticism sometimes serving as an implicit criticism of the problems and disruptions of modern American life. Chinese characters also displayed presumably universal human emotions, such as love and a sense of loss, in contrast to the dehumanized portraits of them in Gold Rush era music. Some songs even explored miscegenation in a fairly accepting way.

Further complicating this account is the manner in which African American musicians and performers used images of the Chinese for their own ends. At a time when Irish-Chinese send-ups were being replaced by Chinese/African American ones, the appearance of African American Chinese impersonators allowed African Americans to use Chinese stereotypes as a way of underscoring the Americanness of black people and the inherent foreignness of Chinese immigrants. African American songwriters also combined Chinese musical signifiers with their own musical traditions, allowing for experimentation and innovation. Louis Armstrong's jazz version of "Chinatown, My Chinatown" is one such example.

In 1931, Louis Armstrong and his orchestra recorded "Chinatown, My Chinatown" and, like those before them, reworked the song to fit their musical style. A song originally written in 1910 to replace "Apache Chinese" in *Up and Down Broadway* and later sung by Chinese American vaudevillians in English and in Cantonese, "Chinatown, My Chinatown" had seen many alterations and modifications over the past twenty years, including those by several jazz musicians. Armstrong's "Chinatown, My Chinatown" used only the song's chorus, with scatted vocals by Armstrong himself and a riffed "argument" between George James on soprano saxophone and Louis Armstrong on trumpet. Representative of hot jazz from the 1920s and 1930s, this version not only maintained a driving beat but also included some of Armstrong's characteristic sustained high notes and a rapid-fire call and response between Armstrong's trumpet and the rest of the orchestra. Ironically, Armstrong and his orchestra cut out the Chinese musical tokens from the opening of

"Chinatown, My Chinatown" and relied solely on the lyrics to communicate that this was a song about a Chinese immigrant community. Since the late eighteenth century, however, slurs, syncopation, and dissonance could be found in European works that tried to embody the Other; they were not only found in jazz. In response to these complexities, where does Armstrong and his orchestra's "Chinatown, My Chinatown" fit into the spectrum of constructions of racial and national identity in the United States during the first half of the twentieth century? How do we as scholars address the contradictions surrounding a song such as "Chinatown, My Chinatown?"

The processes of generating stereotypes in music and on the stage coexisted with their subsequent subversion throughout the nineteenth and early twentieth centuries. American producers continually tried to create more totalizing Chinese and Chinese American images through a variety of devices—words, staging, makeup, costumes, and later, musical notation and instrumentation. A few also found China to be a source of innovation or a rhetorical device to address a range of social and cultural issues, including immigration and race, in the United States. Chinese and Chinese Americans used similar strategies to promote alternative notions of racial and national identity and of Chinese heritage. Today, however, scholars, activists, and performers use the term *yellowface* as a means of revelation, illuminating past and present stereotypes that have mystified Asian and Asian American realities.

Appendix A. American Popular Songs with Chinese Subjects or Themes

Songs in this list were written by American songwriters or published by an American music publishing company. No doubt there are other songs in these categories that I have not yet found.

Song Title	Date	Songwriters
1800–1849		
Twelve Variations to Ching Chit Quaw	ca. 1800	Rayner Taylor
Moo-Lee-Chwa	ca. 1802	Karl Kambra and Dr. Scott
Peyho Boatmen, or, Higho Highau	ca. 1802	Karl Kambra and Dr. Scott
Chinese Rondo, The	1828	Mathias von Holst
Chao Kanc, Galop Chinois	1841	Gustave Blessner
Chinese Bell Quadrilles, The	1844	Anonymous
Come Be My Love, a Chinese Song	1846	John Hill Hewitt
Glorious Victory, A	ca. 1846	J. W. R.
Aladdin Galop	1847	P. J. Bishop
Chinese Junk Galop, The	1847	J. J. William Bruhns
Aladdin Quadrilles	1840s	J. H. Tully
Chinee Bumboatman, The	1840s	Anonymous
1850–1859		
Kim-ka, Grand March Chinois	1852	A. Waldauer
Chinese Polka	ca. 1852	Frederick Southgate
Musical Chow Chow	1853	Francis H. Brown
California as It Is and Was	1854	John A. Stone
Honest Miner, An	1854	John A. Stone
Joaquin, the Horse-Thief	1854	John A. Stone
Josh, John	1854	John A. Stone
National Miner, The	1854	John A. Stone
Prospecting Dream	1854	John A. Stone
Seeing the Elephant	1854	John A. Stone
John Chinaman	1855	Anonymous
San Francisco	1855	John Swett
John Chinaman's Appeal	1856	Mart Taylor
California Bank Robbers	1858	John A. Stone
California Stage Company, The	1858	John A. Stone
Chinese Dance Polka	1858	B. Von Smit
Tom Pouce Quadrille	1850s	J. B. Duvernoy
1860–1869		
Fined Five Dollars	1860	J. W. Conner
John Chinaman in California	1861	Variant of "John Chinaman's Appeal"

APPENDIX A (*Continued*)

Song Title	Date	Songwriters
Bill-Poster's Dream, The	1863	E. T. Johnston
Fee-Faw-Fum and Ho-Hang-Ho	ca. 1863	Anonymous
Love in Canton	1867	Anonymous
Hong-Kong Gong, The	1868	H. P. Danks and George W. Elliott
John Chinaman, My Jo	1868	J. W. Conner
John Chinaman's Marriage	1868	Anonymous
Great Pacific Railway, The	1869	William E. Krause
What the Engines Said	1869	Anonymous
Hay Sing, Come from China	1860s	Anonymous
Long John, Chineeman	1860s	Anonymous
1870–1879		
John Chinaman	ca. 1870	P. P. Bliss
Hanki Panki	1870	Anonymous
Heathen Chinee, The	1870	F. Boote and Bret Harte
Heathen Chinee, The	1870	Charles Towner and Bret Harte
Nigger-vs.-Chinese	1870	Harry F. Lorraine
Chinese Galop	1871	W. L. Hayden
Chinese Giant, The	1871	J. A. Hardwick
Chinese Song, The	1871	Anonymous
Coolie Chinee, The	1871	Sep. Winner
Heathen Chinee, The	1871	Henry Tucker and Bret Harte
Heathen Chinee Waltz, The	1871	I. J. Bradford
John Chinaman	1871	Anonymous
John Chinaman, Esquire	1871	Anonymous
Since the Chinese Ruint the Thrade	1871	Anonymous
Twelve Hundred More	1871	Anonymous
Chinese Song, The	1872	Tony Pastor
Big Long John	1873	Luke Schoolcraft
Chinese Shoemaker, The	1873	Bobby Newcomb
Chinese Song	1873	John Thompson
Ching Foo	1873	Anonymous
Flum Fee Chow Foo	1873	Anonymous
Heathen Chinee	1873	Luke Schoolcraft
That Excellent Judge	1873	Tony Pastor
Trip to California, A	1873	Anonymous
Chinese Labor	1876	Barry Blackburn
Days of '49, The	1876	C. Rhoades (Bensell) and E. Zimmer
Heathen Chinee	1876	Sam Devere
Poor Chinee!	1876	T. W.
Ah Ling's True Love	1877	R. J. Pigot
Ah Sin, Chinee Song	1877	Harry R. Williams
Sang Lee	1878	George M. Vickers
Chinese Twins, The	1879	Anonymous

APPENDIX A (*Continued*)

Song Title	Date	Songwriters
Chop Sticks	1879	Arthur De Lulli (Euphemia Allen)
Chop Sticks Galop, The	1879	Arr. George F. Morris
Excelsior	1879	Ackland Von Boyle
Great Chinese Reception, The	1879	Jim J. Nelson
It Is the Flavor from a Two-Cent Chinese Butt	1879	Dave Roche
Pompey Little Pig-Tailed Chinaman	1879	Ackland Von Boyle
What! Never?	1879	Ackland Von Boyle
Artful Chinee, The	1870s	Frank Curtis
Bowery on Saturday Night, The	1870s	Charley Davies
Chin-Chin-Chow	1870s	Anonymous
Chinese Ball, The	1870s	Frank Golden
Chinese Wrestlers	1870s	Kennedy and Magee
1880–1889		
Chinese Patrol	1880	H. Fliege
Chinese Serenade	1880	H. Fliege
When McCormack Rules the State	1880	Anonymous
Aladdin	1881	Louis Dorn
Aladdin	1881	Matilda Scott-Paine and James Russell Lowell
Chinee Laundryman, The	1881	Frank Dumont
Chinese Song	1881	Charles Glidden
Crossing the China Sea	1881	Palmer Cox and Ellen P. Cross
Heathen Chinaman	1881	Anonymous
Heathen Chinese, The	1881	John McVeigh
Bully Chinaman	1882	John C. Leach
Chinese Song	1882	Arr. Frank Kellogg and Tom Shephard
Chun Wow Low	1882	John C. Leach
Hop Lee	1882	Frank Depro
Is That Mr. Rielly?	1882	Pat Rooney
Lee Poo Tay	1882	Anonymous
Me Be Like Mellican Man	1882	Thomas P. Westendorf
American Butterfly, The	1883	Louis Meyer
Ching Ching	1883	Charles Barton
Little Ah Sid	1883	J. P. Skelly
Aladdin Galop	1884	Aubrey De Vere
Chinese Wedding March	1884	S. Markstein
Mary Blaine	1884	Ben Warrren
Chinese War March	1885	Theodore Michaelis
Extra, Extra	1885	Dave Braham and Edward Harrigan
Get Out, Yellow-Skins, Get Out!	ca. 1885	Anonymous
Big Chinaman Quadrille	1886	C. A. White

APPENDIX A (*Continued*)

Song Title	Date	Songwriters
Blended Tea	1888	J. J. Cauchois
Lady Picking Mulberries, The	1888	Edgar S. Kelley
Wave High the Red Bandana	1888	Emma Washburn
1890–1899		
Wing Tee Wee: The Sweet Chinee	1890	Hubbard T. Smith
Chinese Picnic, The	1891	John St. George
Trip to Chinatown, A	1891	Percy Gaunt
Chinaman's Dream	1893	C. J. Wilson
Put Me Off at Buffalo	1895	John and Harry Dillon
Li Hung Chang March	1896	J. Bodewalt Lampe
Chinese Boys	1897	William Bross
Chinese Song and Dance	1897	William Bross
Li Hung Chang	1897	Otto Auerbach
Little Peeweet	1897	H. W. Petrie and Arthur J. Lamb
Wedding of the Chinee and the Coon, The	1897	Bob Cole and Billy Johnson
Chop Suey: Chinese March Patrol	1898	William Frederick Peters
Li Hung Chang	1898	Ben Harney
Chinese Lullaby, A	1899	Harvey Worthington Loomis and Edwin Star Belknap
I Don't Care If I Never Wake Up	1899	Paul J. Knox
Mesmerize Magee: A Dope Song	1899	M. M. Ellis
Wing Lee's Rag-Time Clock	1899	Al. Trahern
Queen of Chinatown	ca. 1899	Emil O. Wolff
Two Chinoiseries	1890s	H. Van Gael
1900–1909		
Chinatown Serenade	1900	W. A. Pratt
Every Race Has a Flag but the Coon	1900	Will. A. Heelan and J. Frederick Helf
In Chinatown	1900	M. Bernard
Mamma's China Twins	1900	Lee Johnson
Mandarin's Courtship	1900	William Loraine
Nations in Review, The	1900	Max Faetkenheuer and William G. Rose
Chinese Honeymoon Waltz, A	1901	Arr. Ernest Vousden
Ching a Ling a Loo	1901	Max Hoffman
Hop-Lee	1901	Ellis R. Ephraim
Ma Li Hung Chinese Queen	1901	Saint Suttle
Ragtime Laundry, The	1901	W. C. Powell
Cheerful Chinaman, The	1902	Theodore F. Morse
Chinese Honeymoon Lancers, A	1902	Arr. Karl L. Hoschna
Chinese Salmagundi, A	1902	Noel Lehsif
Chop Suey	1902	Chris Lane
Chop-Suey	1902	C. Backley
Chop Sticks	ca. 1902	De Zulli

APPENDIX A (*Continued*)

Song Title	Date	Songwriters
Fan-Tan	1902	Bert R. Anthony
Pinky Panky Poo	1902	Andy Lewis and
		Aaron S. Hoffman
Ah Sid	1903	H. and J. K. Taubman
Chinky-Chinks	1903	Spencer Morse
Hop-Lee	1903	H. L. Heartz
In the Land of Far Cathay	1903	Anonymous
Ragtime Chinaman	1903	Joseph E. Howard and
		R. W. Peck
Uncle Sam's Invitation	1903	W. L. Needham
Butterinski, The	1904	W. J. McGrath
China Tragedy, A	1904	Clayton Thomas and
		R. S. Hichens
Foong Foong Fee	1904	George M. Cohan
In a Pagoda	1904	John W. Bratton
March of the 'Frisco Chinks	1904	George M. Cohan
Moon Eyes	1904	Howard A. Winburn and
		George A. Norton
Soap Suds	1904	J. Mariager
Bric-a-Brac Rag	1906	Maurice Porcelain
Chinese Wedding Music	1906	Louis C. Jacoby
Mandarin, The	1906	William P. Brayton
Mandarin, The	1906	Charles A. Carvel
Plinky Plunk	1906	William Luton Wood
Ching-a-Ling	1907	Theodore Morse and
		Edward Madden
Moon Face	1907	Abe Olman
My Lotus Flower	1907	Seymour Furth and
		Edgar Selden
Chinese Cracker, A	1908	Herbert Robinson
Chinese Lantern	1908	B. P. Austin
Dance of Sing Ling Foo, The	1908	Charles Alphin
Little China Doll, A	1908	Egbert Van Alstyne and
		Harry Williams
When Two Little Hearts Beat	1908	Bruno Granichstaedten and
Together		Robert B. Smith
Chee Wee: A Chinese Novelty	1909	Thomas Allen
Chinese Love Song	1909	John L. Golden
Chink Chink Chinaman	1909	Bert A. Williams and
		Alex Rogers
Chung Lo: A Chinese	1909	Neil Morét
Monkeydoodle		
Say-Yoh	1909	Avery Werner and
		Vernon Eville
1910–1919		
Chinatown, My Chinatown	1910	Jean Schwartz and
		William Jerome

Appendix A (*Continued*)

Song Title	Date	Songwriters
Pekin Rag	1910	Harry W. Martin
That Chinatown Rag	1910	George W. Meyer and Jack Drislane
That Chinese Rag	1910	Al Stedman
Roll a Little Pill for Me	1911	Norma Gray
Dopy Rag, The	1912	W. C. Powell and Sam L. Rosen
Heathen Chinee, The	1912	W. J. McCoy and Bret Harte
Chinese Music	1913	J. S. Zamecnik
Chinese Suite	1913	Platon Brounoff
China Boy	1914	Lew Pollack and Ed Rose
Down in Chinatown	1914	J. Walter Leopold and J. Casper Nathan
Look Out for Mr. Wu	1914	George M. Cohan
My Rose of Old Pekin	1914	Bill Henly and Dave Whiteside
Ta-Tao	1914	William H. Penn
All Aboard for Chinatown	1915	Win Brookhouse and Frank Davis
Characteristic Folk Dances	1915	Platon Brounoff
Chin-Chin Open Your Heart and Let Me In	1915	A. Seymour Brown
Chinese Blues	1915	Oscar Gardner and Fred D. Moore
Chop Suey Rag	1915	Edward Hayne
Chop Suey Sue	1915	Will Marion Cook
In Blinky, Winky, Chinky Chinatown	1915	Jean Schwartz and William Jerome
Mandarin, The	1915	Norman Leigh
Meet Me in Frisco and We'll Go Out to the Fair	1915	William A. Fentress
On a Chinese Honeymoon	1915	George F. Olcott
Sing Sing Tango Tea	1915	Sigmund Romberg and Harry Atteridge
Towsee Mongalay	1915	Grahame Jones
Dragon's Eye, The	1916	Byron Gay
Fan Tan Man	1916	Herman Rose, Fred D. Moore, and Oscar Gardner
Hong Kong	1916	Hans Von Holstein, Alma M. Sanders, and Richard W. Pascoe
My Dreamy China Lady	1916	Egbert Van Alstyne and Gus Kahn
While the City Sleeps	1916	Jack Denny and William A. Downs

Appendix A (*Continued*)

Song Title	Date	Songwriters
Ah Sin: Eccentric Two-Step Novelty	1917	Walter Rolfe
Chin-Chin Chinaman	1917	James F. Hanley, Joe Goodwin, and Ballard MacDonald
China Dreams	1917	Egbert Van Alstyne, Gus Kahn, and Raymond Egan
China We Owe a Lot to You	1917	Milton Ager and Howard Johnson
Chinese Letter Song	1917	William White and E. Ray Goetz
Ching Chong	1917	Lee S. Roberts and J. Will Callahan
Chu-Chin-Chow	1917	Dave Stamper and Gene Buck
Danse Orientale à la Chinoise	1917	Harriette Cady
From Here to Shanghai	1917	Irving Berlin
My Little Sing Song Girl	1917	A. J. Stasny and Earl Burtnett
Pekin	1917	Fred Fischer and Howard Johnson
Yock-a-Hilo-Town	1917	Monty C. Brice and Walter Donaldson
Follow Me (Chinese Song)	1918	Nathaniel Osborne and Will H. Smith
In Dear Old China Town	1918	R. C. Young
Mandarin: Fox Trot	1918	Muriel Pollock
Pipe-Dream Blues	1918	Spencer Williams, Marguerite Kendall, and J. Russel Robinson
Under the China Moon	1918	Malvin Franklin and E. Ray Goetz
U.S. Spells Us!	1918	Hazel M. Bell
You're a Broken China Doll	1918	Robert and Dave Allan
Broken Blossoms	1919	A. Robert King and Ballard MacDonald
Buddha	1919	Lew Pollack and Ed Rose
China Dragon Blues	1919	Will Donaldson and Irving Caesar
China Lily—Think of Me	1919	Bob Chamberlin
Chinese Chop Sticks	1919	Stanly Crawford
Chinese Lullaby	1919	Robert Hood Bowers
Chong (He Come from Hong Kong)	1919	Harold Weeks
Chow Mein: A Chinese Episode	1919	Frank E. Hersom
Fan San	1919	Alex Sullivan and Lynn Cowan
Fast Asleep in Poppyland	1919	Byron Gay
Fu	1919	George P. Howard

APPENDIX A (*Continued*)

Song Title	Date	Songwriters
Goodbye Shanghai	1919	Jean Schwartz and Alfred Bryan
I'm Sneakin' to Peek in Pekin	1919	Monte Carlo, Alma M. Sanders, and Richard W. Pascoe
In China	1919	Otto Motzan and A. J. Stasny
In Chinatown	1919	Harvey Worthington Loomis
In the Bamboo Tree	1919	George Scarborough and David Belasco
Lo-Ki	1919	Irving Bibo, Ed Rose, and Henry Bergman
Mandarin Dance	1919	Leo Kempinski
Ming Toy	1919	Bert Grant, Cecil Arnold, and Roy Turk
Peek-in Pekin	1919	Lorenz Hart and Richard Rodgers
Red Lantern, The	1919	Fred Fisher
Shanghai	1919	Dave Stamper and Gene Buck
Shantung	1919	L. Wolfe Gilbert and Dan Caslar
So Long, Sing Song	1919	Sigmund Romberg and Harold Atteridge
Who Comes in My Garden	1919	George Scarborough and David Belasco
You Cannot Make Your Shimmy Shake on Tea	1919	Irving Berlin
1920–1929		
China Moon	1920	Frank Thornton and Don Everett
Chinaman's Song, The	1920	Percy Fletcher and Oscar Ashe
Chinese Firecrackers	1920	Irving Berlin
Chinese Wedding Bells	1920	Henry Murtagh and Wootson Davis
Ching a Ling's Jazz Bazaar	1920	Ethel Bridges and Howard Johnson
Ching-a-Ling	1920	Will Morrissey and Edward Madden
Cup of Tea, A	1920	Efrem Zimbalist and Joseph Herbert
Down in Chinatown	1920	Joe Meyer and George P. Hulten
Hi-Lo	1920	George Fairman
Idle Dreams	1920	George Gershwin and Arthur Jackson

APPENDIX A (*Continued*)

Song Title	Date	Songwriters
In the Land of Rice and Tea	1920	Charley Straight and Paul Biese
Jazzy Jazzy Sound in All Chinatown	1920	Louis Borromeo, Al. Hether, and Herman Bush
My China Man	1920	Hal Ehrig, Lou Breau, and Charles Byron
Mystery of Night, The	1920	Lucien and Gwynne Denni
Pekin	1920	Norman Wilbur and J. Brandon Walsh
Pretty Ming Toy	1920	Sigmund Romberg and Alex Gerber
Rickshaw	1920	James Monaco
Rose of China	1920	Paul Biese, Clark Tyler, and Rex Lardner
So Long Oolong	1920	Bert Kalmar and Harry Ruby
Yan-Kee	1920	George Gershwin and Irving Caesar
Yo San	1920	Jean Hazard and Moy Tully
Chi-Nee	1921	Spot Cravello and Irene Delaney
Ching-Ching-Chan: The San Pan Man	1921	Raphael Cliford
Down in Midnight Town	1921	Andrew B. Sterling, Edward P. Moran, and Harry Von Tilzer
Good-bye Shanghai	1921	Joseph Meyer and Howard Johnson
Sing Song Girl	1921	Armand Vescey, Jerome Kern, and P. G. Wodehouse
Sing-a-Loo	1921	Lew Brown and Sidney D. Mitchell
Tea Cup Girl	1921	Weston Wilson
Tea Leaves	1921	Richard A. Whiting and Raymond B. Egan
Wang-Wang Blues	1921	Gustave Mueller, "Buster" Johnson, and Henry Busse
Blinky Winky	1922	Jack Caddigan and Chick Story
Chin Choo of China Land	1922	J. Allegro, M. Isaksen, and Edward La Voie
China Eyes	1922	Charles A. and William G. Arthur
Chinese Billikens, The	1922	Alexei Archangelsky and Dailey Paskman
Chinese Flower	1922	Robert Hood Bowers and Francis DeWitt
Chingtu	1922	Fred Sarchet and Ed Rooks

APPENDIX A (*Continued*)

Song Title	Date	Songwriters
Dreamy Chinee	1922	Harold C. Berg, Howard Simon, and Richard W. Pascoe
Limehouse Blues	1922	Philip Braham and Douglas Furber
Mah-Jongg Blues	1922	Stuart B. Dunbar and Lester Stevens
My Chinese Butterfly	1922	Vincent Dattilo, Gene Cullinan, and Thomas R. Murray
Oh Sing-a-Loo Whad' Ya Do with Your Que?	1922	Lew Pollack, Lew Brown, and Sidney D. Mitchell
Poppy Jade Song	1922	Netta Naomi Andrews and Arthur W. Fisk
Porcelain Maid	1922	Irving Berlin
When the Lights Go Down in Chinatown	1922	Malvin M. Franklin and Alex Gerber
Charlie Chin	1923	Lewis Frederick Stafford
Chinaman Blues	1923	Gene Burdette
Chinese Dance	1923	Harry Crismore
Ching, Ching, Chinaman	1923	Louis F. Gottschalk and Eve Unsell
Choo Fong	1923	Fred C. Stoutenburg
Dear Old Chinatown	1923	Earl Comyns and Vincent C. Plunkett
Half Past Ten (Sop-Tim-Bom)	1923	Paul Ash and Neil Morét
Hi-Lee Hi-Lo	1923	Ira Schuster and Eugene West
Hoptown Chinatown Hop	1923	Billy Baskette, James Dealy, and Doc Hunsbedt
In a Chinese Temple-Garden	1923	Albert W. Ketèlbey
On a Chinese Honeymoon	1923	C. J. Hausman and W. L. Shockley
Pekin	1923	Zeph Fitz-Gerald
Shanghai Lullaby	1923	Isham Jones and Gus Kahn
Sing-Loo	1923	Theo. V. Norman and Herman Ruby
Songs from the Chinese	1923	Granville Bantock
Within the Walls of China	1923	Katherine Allan Lively
China Girl	1924	Henry Halstead, Don Warner, and Louis Singer
Chinese Lotus	1924	Floryane Thompson and Virginia Haugh
Chinese Quarrel, A	1924	Walter Neimann
Hong Kong Dream Girl	1924	Harry Barris and George E. Springer

APPENDIX A (*Continued*)

Song Title	Date	Songwriters
Shanghai Shuffle	1924	Gene Rodemich and Larry Conley
Since Ma Is Playing Mah Jong	1924	Billy Rose and Con Conrad
Chinky Butterfly	1925	Lee David and Billy Rose
Who'll Chop Your Suey When I'm Gone	1925	Sidney Bechet and Rousseau Simmons
Beautiful Fan, A	1926	Alberta Nichols, J. Fred Coots, and Maurie Rubens
Chinese Moon	1926	Joseph Nussbaum and Ben Bronfin
Melican Man, Fox Trot	1926	Leland A. White, Mary Black, and Lucile Burton
Shanghai Honeymoon	1926	William L. Shockley, Charles J. Hausman, and Lester Melrose
So Does Your Old Mandarin	1926	Ray Henderson, Sam M. Lewis, and Joe Young
Song of Shanghai	1926	Vincent Rose, Richard A. Whiting, and Raymond B. Egan
Up and Down in China	1926	Willard Robison
Chen, My China Girl	1927	Jack E. Slattery
China Lady o' Mine	1927	Lew Farris and Leon Close
Come Back to Little Yo San	1927	Ora Carew, Nacio Herb Brown, and Grant Clarke
Draggin' the Dragon Drag	1927	Arthur Johnston and Roy Turk
In a Chinese Laundry	1927	George Mulfinger
In an Oriental Garden	1927	John E. Hayes
Shanghai Dream Man	1927	Benny Davis and Harry Akst
We Americans	1927	Ed. G. Nelson, Harry Pease, and Al. Dubin
Chan: Song of China	1928	Richard A. Whiting and Helen Lewis
Chinatown Rose	1929	Florence Good and Bernie Grossman
Chinese Coolie Hurries with a Rickshaw	1929	Frieda Peycke
Chinky Chinee Bogie Man	1929	Richard A. Whiting, Neil Morét, and Haven Gillespie
In the Mandarin's Orchid Garden	1929	George and Ira Gershwin

Abyssinia	1906	Hello 1919	1919
Africana	1927	Hello America	1918
Aladdin	1813	Hello Broadway!	1914
Aladdin	1826	Hip-Hip-Hooray	1915
Aladdin	1847	Hitchy-Koo of 1917	1917
Aladdin	1873	Honeydew	1920
Aladdin, Jr.	1894	In Dahomey	1903
All Aboard	1918	Innocent	1915
Amber Express, The	1916	Kid Boots	1924
Andre Charlot's Revue of 1924	1924	Kim-ka	1847
Ba-Ta-Clan (Ching-Chow-Hi)	1855	Lady in Red	1919
Balieff's Chauve-Souris	1922	Lady of the Lamp, The	1920
Broadway Rastus	1915	Little Johnny Jones	1904
Broken Idol, A	1908	Man from China, The	1904
Buzzin' Around	1920	Mandarin, The	1896
By the Sad Sea Waves	1899	Mandarin Zune, The	1886
Candy Shop, The	1909	Mecca	1920
Chee Chee	1928	Mr. Lode of Koal	1909
Chin-Chin	1914	Mulligan Guard Chowder	1879
Chin Toy	1920	Mulligan's Silver Wedding	1881
China Doll, A	1904	Music Box Revue, 1922–23	1922
China Rose	1924	My China Doll	1923
Chinese Honeymoon, A	1901	Old Lavender	1885
Chow Chow	1872	Passing Show of 1919, The	1919
Chris and the Wonderful Magic Lamp	1899	Pearl of Pekin	1888
Chu Chin Chow	1917	Policy Players	1899
Crystal Slipper	1897	Poor Little Ritz Girl	1920
Darktown Follies	1916	Pousse Café	1897
Darkydom	1915	Reign of Error, A	1899
Defender, The	1902	Rose Maid, The	1908
Devil, The	1922	Rose of China, The	1919
East Is West	1919	Rufus Rastus	1906
East of Suez	1922	San Toy	1899
First Born, The	1897	Shing Ching	1893
Fly with Me	1919	Ski-Hi	1908
Gay Paree	1926	Son-Daughter, The	1919
Geezer, The	1896	Sons of Ham, The	1900
Geisha, The	1896	Struttin' Sam from Alabam'	1927
George White's Scandals of 1920	1920	Tenderfoot, The	1903
Good Morning Dearie	1921	Travellers, The	1806
Hands Up	1915	Trip around the World	1921

APPENDIX B (*Continued*)

Trip to Chinatown, A	1892	*Yankee Mandarin, A*	1909
Trip to Coontown	1898	*Yellow Jacket, The*	1912
Up and Down	1922	*Ziegfeld Follies of 1917*	1917
Up and Down Broadway	1910	*Ziegfeld Follies of 1919*	1919
Voyage en Chine, Le	1879	*Ziegfeld Follies of 1920*	1920
Wift Waft Warblers	1921	*Ziegfeld Midnight Frolic*	1919
Yama	1907		

NOTES

INTRODUCTION

1. Lee Tung Foo, letter to Margaret Blake Alverson, London, 4 June 1908; "Vaude-ville," *Providence Journal*, 1 Jan. 1907, 16; "Proctor's Theatre," *Newark Evening News,* 18 Dec. 1906, clippings, Margaret Blake Alverson Papers, California State Library, Sacramento, Calif. All personal papers from Lee Tung Foo and Margaret Blake Alverson are from the California State Library in Sacramento, California, unless otherwise noted.

2. *News Democrat* (Providence, R.I.), 1 Jan. 1907, clippings, Margaret Blake Alverson Papers.

3. John Fiske, *Understanding Popular Culture* (New York: Routledge, 1990), 23–26.

4. Gilbert Chase, *America's Music: From the Pilgrims to the Present* (Urbana: University of Illinois Press, 1987), 323–561; Richard Crawford, *America's Musical Life: A History* (New York: W. W. Norton, 2001), 139–688; Richard Butsch, *The Making of American Audiences, from Stage to Television, 1750–1990* (New York: Cambridge University Press, 2000), 66–234.

5. Judith Butler, "Performative Acts and Gender Constitution: An Essay in Phenome-nology and Feminist Theory," in *Performing Feminisms: Feminist Critical Theory and Theatre,* ed. Sue-Ellen Case (Baltimore: Johns Hopkins University Press, 1990), 278.

6. Edward Said, *Orientalism* (New York: Vintage, 1979), 3, 118.

7. Colin Mackerras, *The Chinese Theatre in Modern Times* (Amherst: University of Massachusetts Press, 1975); Alan R. Thrasher, Joseph S. C. Lam, Jonathan P. J. Stock, Colin Mackerras, Francesca Rebolto-Sborgi, F. Kouwenhoven, A. Schim-melpenninck, Stephen Jones, Han Mei, Wu Ben, Helen Rees, Sabine Trebinjac, and Joanna C. Lee, "China," in *The New Grove Dictionary of Music and Musicians,* ed. Stanley Sadie (New York: Macmillan Press, 2001), 5:631–695; Bell Yung, *Cantonese Opera: Performance as Creative Process* (New York: Cambridge University Press, 1989); Tanaka Issei, "The Social and Historical Context of Ming-Ch'ing Local Drama," in *Popular Culture in Late Imperial China,* ed. David Johnson, Andrew J. Nathan, and Evelyn S. Rawski (Berkeley: University of California Press, 1985), 143–160.

8. Homi K. Bhabha, *The Location of Culture* (New York: Routledge, 1994), 66.

9. Antoinette Burton, *Burdens of History: British Feminists, Indian Women, and Imperial Culture, 1865–1915* (Chapel Hill: University of North Carolina Press, 1994).

10. Robert G. Lee, *Orientals: Asian Americans in Popular Culture* (Philadelphia: Temple University Press, 1999); John Kuo Wei Tchen, *New York before Chinatown: Oriental-ism and the Shaping of American Culture, 1776–1882* (Baltimore: Johns Hopkins Uni-versity Press, 1999); James S. Moy, *Marginal Sights: Staging the Chinese in America* (Iowa City: University of Iowa Press, 1993). See also Creighton Miller, *The Unwel-come Immigrant: The American Image of the Chinese, 1785–1882* (Berkeley: University

of California Press, 1969); Mari Yoshihara, *Embracing the East: White Women and American Orientalism* (New York: Oxford University Press, 2003); Christina Klein, *Cold War Orientalism: Asia in the Middlebrow Imagination, 1945–1961* (Berkeley: University of California Press, 2003); Judy Tsou, "Gendering Race: Stereotypes of Chinese Americans in Popular Sheet Music," *Repercussions* 6 (Fall 2001): 25–62.

11. Peter Stallybrass and Allon White, *The Politics and Poetics of Transgression* (Ithaca, N.Y.: Cornell University Press, 1986), 5 (emphasis in the original), 191.

12. John M. MacKenzie, *Orientalism: History, Theory, and the Arts* (New York: University of Manchester Press, 1995), 138–175; James Parakilas, "The Soldier and the Exotic: Operatic Variations on a Theme of Racial Encounter: Part I," *Opera Quarterly*, 10 (Winter 1993–94): 33–56; Derek B. Scott, "Orientalism and Musical Style," *Musical Quarterly* 82 (Summer 1998): 309–335; Ralph P. Locke, "Reflections on Orientalism in Opera and Musical Theater," *Opera Quarterly* 10 (Autumn 1993): 50–64.

13. Dale Cockrell, *Demons of Disorder: Early Blackface Minstrels and Their World* (New York: Cambridge University Press, 1997); Robert C. Toll, *Blacking Up: The Minstrel Show in Nineteenth-Century America* (New York: Oxford University Press, 1974); Eric Lott, *Love and Theft: Blackface Minstrelsy and the American Working Class* (New York: Oxford University Press, 1993).

14. Eileen Southern, *The Music of Black Americans: A History* (New York: W. W. Norton, 1971); Thomas L. Riis, *Just before Jazz: Black Musical Theater in New York, 1890–1915* (Washington, D.C.: Smithsonian Institution Press, 1989); Lawrence Levine, *Black Culture, Black Consciousness: Afro-American Folk Thought from Slavery to Freedom* (New York: Oxford University Press, 1977).

15. Josephine Lee, *Performing Asian America: Race and Ethnicity on the Contemporary Stage* (Philadelphia: Temple University Press, 1997), 30. See Dorinne Kondo, *About Face: Performing Race in Fashion and Theater* (New York: Routledge, 1997), 10; Karen Shimakawa, *National Abjection: The Asian American Body Onstage* (Durham, N.C.: Duke University Press, 2002), 19–22.

CHAPTER 1   IMAGINING CHINA

1. Jacques Attali, *Noise: The Political Economy of Music*, trans. Brian Massumi (Minneapolis: University of Minnesota Press, 1985). See Alain Corbin, *Village Bells: Sound and Meaning in the Nineteenth-Century Countryside*, trans. Martin Thom (New York: Columbia University Press, 1998); Mark M. Smith, *Listening to Nineteenth-Century America* (Chapel Hill: University of North Carolina Press, 2001).

2. Thomas Walker, Peter Branscombe, James R. Anthony, Curtis Price, Jack Sage, Manfred Boetzkes, Roger Savage, and Stanley Sadie, "Part One: Baroque Opera," 13–68; Daniel Heartz, Charles Troy, Michael Robinson, Peter Branscombe, Stanley Sadie, James R. Anthony, Martin Cooper, David Charlton, Curtis Price, Lionel Salter, Manfred Boetzkes, and Roger Savage, "Part Two: Pre-Classical and Classical Opera," 71–164, both in *History of Opera*, ed. Stanley Sadie (New York: W. W. Norton, 1989); Rudolf Rasch, "Tuning and Temperament," 193–222; Penelope Gouk, "The Role of Harmonics in the Scientific Revolution," 223–245; Joel Lester, "Rameau and Eighteenth-Century Harmonic Theory," 753–777, all in *Cambridge History of Western Music Theory*, ed. Thomas Christensen (New York: Cambridge University Press, 2002).

3. Hugh Honour, *Chinoiserie: Visions of Cathay* (New York: E. P. Dutton, 1962); Dawn Jacobson, *Chinoiserie* (London: Phaidon Press, 1993).

4. Krystyn Moon, "Yellowface: Creating the Chinese in American Popular Music, 1850s–1920s," Ph.D. dissertation, Johns Hopkins University, 2002, 8–17.

5. Johannes Nieuhoff, *Embassy from the East India Company of the United Provinces, to the*

Grand Tartar Cham Emperour of China, trans. John Ogilby (London: John Macock, 1669), 40. I have tried to use pinyin throughout this text; however, there are a few exceptions. People's names, song titles, and terms in quotation marks are spelled the way they were during the nineteenth and early twentieth centuries. Also, I have used "Canton" instead of "Guangzhou" because Canton was such a pervasive place-name in Western literature during this period.

6. Immanuel C. Y. Hsu, *The Rise of Modern China* (New York: Oxford University Press, 2000); John D. Spence, *The Search for Modern China* (New York: W. W. Norton, 1990).

7. "Music in China," *Musical Visitor,* 15 Apr. 1841, 33; "The Canton River, or River Tigris," *Living Age,* 4 Jan. 1845, 46; Benjamin L. Ball, *Rambles in Eastern Asia* (Boston: James French and Co., 1855), 130; "Chinese Theatricals," *Cornhill Magazine* 9 (Mar. 1864): 301; Peter Dobell, *Travels in Kamtchatka and Siberia* (1830; reprint, New York: Arno Press, 1970), 233; Julius Berncastle, *A Voyage to China,* vol. 2 (London: William Shoberl, 1850), 162.

8. Henry Ellis, *Journal of the Proceedings of the Late Embassy to China* (London: John Murray, 1817), 418. A. Small in Philadelphia also published this travel narrative in 1818.

9. Martha Noyes Williams, *A Year in China* (New York: Hurd and Houghton, 1864), 254–255.

10. William Tyrone Power, *Recollections of a Three Years' Residence in China* (London: Richard Bentley, 1853), 191–192.

11. John L. Nevius, *China and the Chinese* (New York: Harper and Brothers, 1869), 270–271.

12. Evariste Regis Huc, *A Journey through the Chinese Empire* (New York: Harper and Brothers, 1856), 2:277.

13. "Chinese and Japanese Music," *Dwight's Journal of Music,* 21 July 1860, 131.

14. Power, *Recollections,* 193; "Negro Songs," *Brainard's Musical World* 10 (Oct. 1873): 151.

15. Jon W. Finson, *The Voices That Are Gone: Themes in Nineteenth-Century Popular Song* (New York: Oxford University Press, 1994), 278–283.

16. John E. Duer, "Chinese Sketches," *Knickerbocker* 60 (Mar. 1860): 398. Duer, however, disagreed with those who believed that Scottish and Chinese melodies were similar.

17. "Chinese and Scotch Music," *Family Minstrel,* 1 June 1835, 67. Charles Burney made similar claims in *A General History of Music from the Earliest Ages to the Present,* in which he argued that Chinese and Scottish music are similar because both use whole tone scales and have no semitones. Charles Burney, *A General History of Music from the Earliest Ages to the Present* (1789; reprint, New York: Dover Publications, 1957), 2:45–47.

18. Peter Holland and Michael Patterson, "Eighteenth-Century Theatre," 255–298; Michael R. Booth, "Nineteenth-Century Theatre," 299–340, both in *The Oxford Illustrated History of Theatre,* ed. John Russell Brown (New York: Oxford University Press, 1995); Walker et al., "Part One"; Heartz et al., "Part Two"; Oscar G. Brockett, *History of the Theatre* (Boston: Allyn and Bacon, 1995), 125–127, 208–220, 237–259.

19. G. Tradescant Lay, *The Chinese as They Are* (Albany, N.Y.: E. G. Squier, 1843), 43–44, 74–77.

20. Seyfried, "Chinese Music," *Family Minstrel,* 1 May 1835, 49–50; "Chinese Amusements," *All the Year Round,* 28 Jan. 1865, 14–16.

21. For a discussion of the deification of Shakespeare in nineteenth-century America, see Lawrence Levine, *Highbrow/Lowbrow: The Emergence of a Cultural Hierarchy in America* (Cambridge: Harvard University Press, 1990), 13–81.

22. Osmond Tiffany, *The Canton Chinese, or the American's Sojourn in the Celestial Empire* (Boston: M. Monroe, 1849), 209.

23. Caroline H. Butler, "Recollections of China—No. IV," *Columbian Lady's and Gentleman's Magazine* 2 (Aug. 1844): 89 (emphases in the original).

24. "Chinese Theatricals," *San Francisco Chronicle,* 25 Sept. 1869, 3; "Home and Foreign Gossip," *Harper's Weekly,* 6 Nov. 1869, 715; Frederick J. Masters, "The Chinese Drama," *Chautauquan* 21 (July 1895): 441; Mrs. Frank Leslie [Miriam Squier], *California: A Pleasure Trip from Gotham to the Golden Gate, April, May, June, 1877* (1877; reprint, Nieuwkoop, Netherlands: B. DeGraaf, 1972), 156–158.

25. Wesley Woo, "Chinese Protestants in the San Francisco Bay Area," in *Entry Denied: Exclusion and the Chinese Community in America, 1882–1943,* ed. Sucheng Chan (Philadelphia: Temple University Press, 1991), 213–240.

26. Power, *Recollections,* 282–283.

27. I have been unable to locate this city in order to put it into pinyin. Ellis, *Journal of the Proceedings,* 130.

28. "Miscellaneous," *American Repertory of Arts,* 4 (Oct. 1841): 298.

29. Edward W. Syle, "Music among the Chinese," *Dwight's Journal of Music,* 11 May 1867, 28–29; Mary Richard, "Music and Missions: Shansi, China," *Musical Herald* 7 (June 1886): 180.

30. Erastus Wentworth, "Chinese Music," *Ladies' Repository* 20 (Mar. 1860): 154–155; "The Musical Capabilities of the Chinese," *Dwight's Journal of Music,* 27 Apr. 1867, 20; Syle, "Music among the Chinese," 28; Richard, "Music and Missions."

31. Syle, "Music among the Chinese," 28. See Edward W. Syle's correspondence with Sophie M. Du Pont, Samuel F. Du Pont Family Papers, Hagley Museum and Library, Wilmington, Del.

32. Robert S. Maclay, *Life among the Chinese* (New York: Carlton and Porter, 1861), 235–236.

33. Chase, *America's Music,* 103–104.

34. Raynor Taylor, "Twelve Variations to Ching Chit Quaw," *Musical Journal* 1 (ca. 1800): 37–40; Raynor Taylor, "La Mandarine, Ning Chew Nang, Chit Ching Quaw," in *La Mandarine* (London: Samuel, Ann, and Peter Thompson, ca. 1789); Ann Dhu McLucas, "Raynor Taylor," in *New Grove Dictionary of Music and Musicians,* 4:358; Stephen Siek, "Musical Taste in Post-Revolutionary America as Seen through Carr's *Musical Journal for the Pianoforte,*" Ph.D. dissertation, University of Cincinnati, 1991.

35. Karl Kambra and Dr. Scott, "Two Original Chinese Songs: Moo-Lee-Chwa and Higho Highau" (London: n.p., 1796).

36. John Barrow, *Travels in China* (Philadelphia: W. F. McLaughlin, 1805), 210–212.

37. Karl Kambra and Dr. Scott, "Two Original Chinese Songs Moo-Lee-Chwa and the Peyho Boatmen or Higho Highau," *Musical Journal* 4 (ca. 1802): 39–42.

38. Carl Engel, *An Introduction to the Study of National Music* (London: Longmans, Green, Reader, and Dyer, 1864), 50, 114, 220; "Our Musical Correspondence," *Western Musical World* 5 (Oct. 1868): 157; "Ein Chinesishes Lied, Genaunt Mik la Hwa," *Sonntag-Schul,* 12 June 1881, 1; Mosco Carner, *Puccini: A Critical Biography* (New York: Holmes and Meier Publishers, 1992), 521–523.

39. Mathias von Holst, "The Chinese Rondo" (New York: A. Fleetwood, 1828).

40. For Chinese festivals in Europe and the United States, see Moon, "Yellowface," 42–44, 80–82.

41. Andrew Cherry, *The Travellers; or, Music's Fascination; an Operatic Drama, in Five Acts* (Philadelphia: Mathew Carey, 1807), v.

42. Joseph-Marie Amiot, *Mémoires concernant l'histoire, les science, les arts, les mœurs, les usages, etc. des chinois: Par les missionaries de Pekin* (Paris: Nyon, 1780), 6:184–185; Domenico Corri and Andrew Cherry, *The Travellers, or Music's Fascination: A Dramatic*

Opera in Five Acts (London: 15 Little Newport, St. Leicester Square, ca. 1806), 22; Cherry, *Travellers*, 25.

43. Alan Nadel, "A Whole New (Disney) World Order: *Aladdin*, Atomic Power, and the Muslim Middle East," in *Visions of the East: Orientalism in Film*, ed. Matthew Bernstein and Gaylyn Studlar (New Brunswick, N.J.: Rutgers University Press, 1997), 184–203.

44. "The Story of Ala-ed-din and the Wonderful Lamp," in *Stories from the Thousand and One Nights*, trans. Edward William Lane and Stanley Lane-Poole (New York: P. F. Collier and Sons, 1937), 341–424.

45. Charles Farley, *Aladdin; or, The Wonderful Lamp: A Grand Romantic Spectacle, in Two Acts*, in *Cumberland's British Theatre*, vol. 36 (London: Davidson, Peter's Hill, n.d.); playbill for *Aladdin; or, The Wonderful Lamp*, New York Theater, New York, N.Y., 11 Jan. 1817, Playbill Collection, American Antiquarian Society, Worcester, Mass.; *Songs, Chorusses, &c. in the Grand Melo-Dramatic Romance called Aladdin, or, the Wonderful Lamp* (Boston: Boston Theater, 1818); "Charles Farley," in *A Biographical Dictionary of Actors, Actresses, Musicians, Dancers, Managers, and Other Stage Personnel in London, 1660–1800*, ed. Philip H. Highfill Jr., Kalman Burnim, and Eduard A. Langhans (Carbondale: Southern Illinois University Press, 1973), 5:152–157.

46. Playbill for *Aladdin! Or, The Wonderful Lamp!* Bowery Theatre, New York, N.Y., 23 Aug. 1843, Playbill Collection, American Antiquarian Society; "Aladdin; or the Wonderful Lamp," in *Modern Drama*, vol. 10 (New York: O. A. Roorbach Jr., 1856).

47. William Clapp, *A Record of the Boston Stage* (Cambridge, Mass.: Allen and Farnham, 1853), 471.

48. In the wake of the successful run of *Aladdin*, Steele and Comer wrote the unsuccessful *Dragon's Flight* (1847), which was loosely based on the popular Chinese belief that the emperor was the incarnation of a dragon and a descendant from the sun. The work was supposed to be informative, illustrating Chinese "mythology, music, customs, character, sentiment, humor, and proverb," a claim few productions made before the California Gold Rush, especially in regard to music. Unfortunately, no score or sheet music exists to confirm whether Chinese music was actually used. Claire McFlinchee, *The First Decade of the Boston Museum* (Boston: Bruce Humphries, Inc., 1940), 147–148; playbill for *Dragon's Flight or The Pearl Diver*, Boston Museum, Boston, 5 July 1847, Playbill Collection, American Antiquarian Society.

49. T. Comer and Silas S. Steele, "Come, Come Away" (Boston: Oliver Ditson, 1847); "In Darkness I Wander" (Boston: Prentiss and Clark, 1847); "Oh! Return My Mother" (Boston: Prentiss and Clark, 1847); "When the Golden Morn" (Boston: Prentiss and Clark, 1847); "Alone, Alone" (Boston: Prentiss and Clark, 1847); "Aladdin Quickstep" (Boston: Prentiss and Clark, 1847).

50. P. J. Bishop, "Aladdin Galop" (Boston: Stephen W. Marsh, 1847); J. H. Tully, "Aladdin Quadrilles" (Boston: Oliver Ditson, 1840s).

51. "Spirit of the Theatre," *Porter's Spirit of the Times*, 30 May 1857, 208; 6 June 1857, 224; George C. D. Odell, *Annals of the New York Stage* (1927–49; reprint, New York: AMS Press, 1970), 6:474–475; "Aladdin," in *Modern Drama*.

52. Playbill for *Female Guard, or A LAD in a Wonderful Lamp*, in Joseph N. Ireland, *Records of the New York Stage* (New York: T. H. Morrell, 1867), vol. 2, pt. 7; playbill for *Aladdin! Or, the Wonderful Lamp, Produced with New Scenery, Costumes, Machinery, Appointments, &c.*, New Arch Theater, Philadelphia, 25 Dec. 1863–1 Jan. 1864, Theater Collection, Huntington Library, San Marino, Calif.; Carl Hose, "Aladdin Schottische" (San Francisco: M. Gray, 1873); Odell, *Annals*, 5:89; John S. Kendall, *The Golden Age of the New Orleans Theater* (Baton Rouge: Louisiana State University Press, 1952), 521; playbill for *Aladdin; or, The Wonderful Scamp!*, Trimble Opera House, Albany, N.Y., 24 June 1871, Trimble Opera House Playbill Collection,

American Antiquarian Society; "Dramatic Feuilleton," *Sporting Times*, 27 Mar. 1869, 12; "The Stage," *Sporting Times and Theatrical News*, 8 May 1869, 7; 12 June 1869, 7; 28 Aug. 1869, 7; "Things Theatrical," *Spirit of the Times*, 14 Mar. 1874, 112; 18 Apr. 1874, 232.

53. Odell, *Annals*, 4:234, 365–367, 545; 5:22, 118, 194, 358.

54. Daniel-François-Esprit Auber and Eugène Scribe, *Songs, Duets, Trios, Chorusses, Etc., Etc., Etc., in the New Grand Fairy Opera of "The Bronze Horse"* (London: Wright Theatre Royal, 1836); A. Bunn, *The Bronze Horse*, in *Plays Submitted to Lord Chamberlain* (London: n.p., 1835), vol. 69; Daniel-François-Esprit Auber, "Overture to *The Bronze Horse*" (Boston: Oliver Ditson, n.d.).

55. Eugene Tompkins, *History of the Boston Theatre, 1854–1901* (1908; reprint, New York: Benjamin Blom, 1969), 80–81; playbill for *Bronze Horse or the Spell of the Cloud King*, in Ireland, *Records of the New York Stage*, vol. 2, pt. 10. The Seguin Operatic Troupe and the Boston Museum also presented adaptations of *The Bronze Horse* during the 1840s. See Katherine K. Preston, *Opera on the Road: Traveling Opera Troupes in the United States, 1825–60* (Urbana: University of Illinois Press, 1993), 227; McFlinchee, *First Decade of the Boston Museum*, 139.

56. "Gallery of Illustration," *Musical World*, 19 Aug. 1865, 511–512; 14 Oct. 1865, 641; *Musical Standard*, 7 Oct. 1865, 110.

57. Richard Traubner, *Operetta: A Theatrical History* (New York: Doubleday, 1978), 30–31; Jacques Offenbach and Ledevic Halevy, *Ba-Ta-Clan: A Masquerade in One Act*, trans. Ian Strasfogel (New York: G. Schirmer Inc., 1971).

58. "Musical and Dramatic," *Watson's Art Journal*, 21 Nov. 1868, 60; "Theatrical Record," *New York Clipper*, 28 Nov. 1868, 270.

59. "The Stage," *Sporting Times and Theatrical News*, 25 Sept. 1869, 7.

60. "Theatrical Record," *New York Clipper*, 28 May 1870, 63; 18 Nov. 1878, 270; "Dramatic Doings," *New York Dramatic News and Society Journal*, 4 Nov. 1876, 2.

61. "Theatrical Record," *New York Clipper*, 14 Nov. 1874, 263.

62. Playbill for *Kimka; or, The Adventures of an Aeronaut*, Howard Athenaeum, Boston, 19 and 30 June 1854, Playbill Collection, American Antiquarian Society.

63. *Kim-ka*, in *The Chinese Other, 1850–1925*, ed. Dave Williams (New York: University Press of America, 1997), 7.

64. The Ravels continued to produce *Kim-ka* up until at least 1857. "Spirit of the Theatre," *Porter's Spirit of the Times*, 23 May 1857, 192. The Montplaisirs Ballet Troupe put up *Kim-ka* in 1854 at an unnamed theater in San Francisco. "Editor's Table," *Pioneer; or, California Monthly Magazine* 1 (July 1854): 51.

65. "Theatrical Record," *New York Clipper*, 6 Dec. 1873, 286.

66. "Spirit of the Theatre," *Porter's Spirit of the Times*, 30 Mar. 1861, 64; "Theatrical Record," *New York Clipper*, 3 Sept. 1870, 174; 19 July 1873, 126; 15 Apr. 1876, 23.

67. Playbill for *Kimka; or, The Adventures of an Aeronaut*, 19 and 30 June 1854.

68. Tchen, *New York before Chinatown*, 106–113, 134–145.

69. "Diary of the Julian Serenaders, 1853–1855," John Hay Library, Brown University, Providence, R.I.

70. Odell, *Annals*, 5:370–371.

71. "Things Theatrical," *Spirit of the Times*, 12 Feb. 1853, 613.

72. "Theatrical Record," *New York Clipper*, 29 Jan. 1870, 343; 5 Mar. 1870, 383; Odell, *Annals*, 8:441, 586 (emphasis added).

CHAPTER 2   TOWARD EXCLUSION

1. Cockrell, *Demons of Disorder*, 62–139; Lott, *Love and Theft*, 22–26.

2. Toll, *Blacking Up*, 169–170; Lee, *Orientals*, 15–50.

3. Alexander Saxton, *The Indispensable Enemy: Labor and the Anti-Chinese Movement in*

California (Berkeley: University of California Press, 1971); Andrew Gyory, *Closing the Gate: Race, Politics, and the Chinese Exclusion Act* (Chapel Hill: University of North Carolina Press, 1998); Najia Aarim-Heriot, *Chinese Immigrants, African Americans, and Racial Anxiety* (Urbana: University of Illinois Press, 2003).

4. The U.S. Congress was required to review the Chinese Exclusion Act every ten years, leaving open the opportunity to overturn it. They passed the Geary Act in 1892, barring Chinese immigrants again and requiring certificates of identity, which they then renewed in 1902. In 1904, Congress eliminated the renewal clause and made Chinese exclusion permanent. The flow of men and women from China, however, was not completely shut off, because many came to the United States as relatives of residents and citizens, certain kinds of nonlaborers (missionaries, diplomats, and merchants), students, and "paper sons." Congress did not overturn this act until World War II, but then it set an immigration quota of 105 persons a year.

5. John A. Stone, "California Bank Robbers," in *Put's Golden Songster* (San Francisco: D. E. Appleton and Co., 1858), 39–42. For musical notation to this song, see "California Bank Robbers," in *The Songs of the Gold Rush*, ed. Richard A. Dwyer, Richard E. Lingenfelter, and David Cohen (Berkeley: University of California Press, 1964), 144–146.

6. Stone committed suicide during the winter of 1863–1864 in Greenwood, California. Dwyer, Lingenfelter, and Cohen, *Songs of the Gold Rush*, 7–8.

7. "Theatrical," *Daily Herald* (San Francisco), 10 Nov. 1854, 2; 20 Nov. 1854, 2; Dan Emmett, "Jordan Is a Hard Road to Travel" (Boston: Oliver Ditson, 1853).

8. Mart Taylor, "John Chinaman's Appeal," in *The Gold Digger's Song Book* (Marysville, Calif.: Marysville Daily Herald, 1856), 29–31; *San Francisco Call*, 26 Sept. 1886, 1; Venra M. DeWitt (granddaughter of Taylor), letter to the California State Library, 26 Jan. 1950, California State clippings, California State Library, Sacramento, Calif.

9. "Yankee Volunteer" (New York: Charles Magnus, n.d.); for the melody, see E. Hoffman, "Trinity Chimes" (New York: William A. Pond, 1864).

10. William Cowper, "A Negro's Complaint," in *The Poetical Works of Cowper*, ed. H. S. Milford (London: Oxford University Press, 1950), 371–372; William Cowper, "The Negro's Appeal," in *The Free Soil Minstrel,* comp. George W. Clark (New York: Martyn and Ely, 1848), 46–47. This was sung to the tune of "Isle of Beauty."

11. Another version of "John Chinaman's Appeal" (1856) appeared in other songsters. See "John Chinaman in California," in *The Pacific Song Book: Containing All the Songs of the Pacific Coast and California* (San Francisco: D. E. Appleton, 1861); "John Chinaman in California," in *Johnson's New Comic Songs,* no. 2 (San Francisco: D. E. Appleton Co., 1863).

12. Anonymous, "John Chinaman," in *California Songster,* ed. D. E. Appleton (San Francisco, Calif.: Noisy Carriers Books and Stationery, 1855), 44–45.

13. John A. Stone, "Josh, John," in *Put's Original California Songster,* 62.

14. "Josh," *Random House Historical Dictionary of Slang,* 2:314.

15. "John Chinaman's Marriage," in *Conner's Irish Songster!* (San Francisco: D. E. Appleton, 1868), 60–61.

16. *Directory of the City of Placerville and Towns of Upper Placerville, El Dorado, Georgetown, and Coloma* (Placerville, Calif.: Thomas Fitch and Co., 1862), 10–12.

17. Bret Harte, "Plain Language from Truthful James," *Overland Monthly,* 5 (Sept. 1870): 287–288. For more information on the popularity of "Heathen Chinee," see Robert McClellan, *The Heathen Chinee: A Study of American Attitudes toward China, 1890–1905* (Bowling Green: Ohio State University Press, 1971), 47–52.

18. Ronald Takaki, *Iron Cages: Race and Culture in Nineteenth-Century America* (New York: Oxford University Press, 1990), 215–249; Tchen, *New York before Chinatown,* 196–197.

19. See John McVeigh, "The Heathen Chinese," in *John McVeigh and Kate Montrose's Songster* (New York: A. J. Fisher, 1881), 4; anonymous, "Heathen Chinaman," in *The Hayles' on the Farm Songster* (New York: A. J. Fisher, 1881), 14; I. J. Bradford, "Heathen Chinee Waltz" (New York: J. L. Peters, 1871); anonymous, "The Chinese Song," in *Tony Pastor's "Down in a Coal Mine" Songster* (New York: George Munro Publishers, 1871), 59; J. P. Skelly, "Little Ah Sid" (Sacramento, Calif.: Weinstock and Lubin, 1883).

20. Henry Tucker and Bret Harte, "The Heathen Chinee," in *The "Heathen Chinee" Musical Album* (New York: Robert M. DeWitt, 1871), 1–2; F. Boote and Bret Harte, "The Heathen Chinee" (Boston: Oliver Ditson, 1870); Charles Towner and Bret Harte, "The Heathen Chinee" (Cleveland: S. Brainard's Sons, 1870).

21. Lee, *Orientals*, 32–43; Tchen, *New York before Chinatown*, 218–224.

22. Williams, *Year in China*, 161.

23. Frank Curtis, "The Artful Chinee" (Cleveland: S. Brainard's Sons, ca. 1870); anonymous, "Chinger Ring" (n.p., ca. 1833). See Lott, *Love and Theft*, 119.

24. George McKinley Murrell, letter to Eliza F. Murrell, El Dorado, Calif., spring 1851, Manuscript Collection, Huntington Library.

25. Ackland Von Boyle, "What! Never?" (Brooklyn, N.Y.: George Molineux, 1879), 2.

26. John C. Leach, "Chun Wow Low," in *Billy Mendel's and Bertha Trent's Ireland-vs.-Germany Songster* (New York: William J. A. Lieder, 1882), 49.

27. Lee, *Orientals*, 36–38; "Chow," *Random House Historical Dictionary of Slang*, 1:415–416; "Chow," *The Oxford English Dictionary*, ed. J. A. Simpson and E. S. C. Weiner (New York: Clarendon Press, 1989), 3:175.

28. Lester Levy, *Flashes of Merriment: A Century of Humorous Songs in America, 1805–1905* (Norman: University of Oklahoma Press, 1975), 157–159; "Editor's Table," *Pioneer*, 372; "Things Theatrical," *Wilkes' Spirit of the Times,* 19 Aug. 1865, 400.

29. As cited in Stuart W. Hyde, "The Chinese Stereotype in American Melodrama," *California Historical Society Quarterly* 34 (Dec. 1955): 359.

30. Ibid., 357–367; William Purviance Fenn, *Ah Sin and His Brethren in American Literature* (Beijing: College of Chinese Studies, 1933), 101–111; Dave Williams, *Misreading the Chinese Character: Images of the Chinese in Euroamerican Drama to 1925* (New York: Peter Lang, 2000), 115–139.

31. "Lydia Thompson and Her New Company," *Ray* (Boston), 25–30 Sept. 1871; 6–7 Oct. 1871; "City Summary," *New York Clipper,* 6 Apr. 1872, 7; 16 Aug. 1873, 158; "Things Theatrical," *Spirit of the Times,* 7 Mar. 1874, 88; "Dramatic Doings," *New York Dramatic News and Society Journal,* 19 July 1879, 4.

32. "Reviews," *New York Mirror,* 24 May 1879, 7; "Dramatic Doings," *New York Dramatic News and Society Journal,* 18 Oct. 1879, 5; Odell, *Annals,* 11:48–49, 65, 167, 403, 423; 12:203, 392, 398, 402, 546; 13:191.

33. Leach died in 1918. John "Chinee" Leach, John Leach clippings, 1870s–1909, Bancroft Library, University of California, Berkeley, Calif.; "Dramatic Doings," *New York Dramatic News and Society Journal,* 23 June 1877, 6; 13 Sept. 1879, 5; 6 Dec. 1879, 4; "Reviews," *New York Mirror,* 17 Jan. 1880, 3; playbill for *The Pearl of Pekin,* Los Angeles Theater, Los Angeles, Calif., 28 Jan. 1890, Behymer Collection, Huntington Library; John Ragan, "John Leach," *Who's Who in Hollywood* (New York: Factson File, 1992), 2:946; Odell, *Annals,* 12:96, 113–114, 307, 316, 319, 378; 13:457.

34. *Brooklyn Times,* 9 Sept. 1879, and *Albany Press,* 19 Sept. 1879, as cited in advertisements, *New York Dramatic News and Society Journal,* 18 Oct. 1879, 16.

35. "Leach as Chinaman," no journal or date, John Leach clippings.

36. "At the High Street," *Columbus Citizen,* 11 Oct. 1887, John Leach clippings.

37. "Round the Clock," *San Francisco Call,* 13 Dec. 1877, John Leach clippings.

38. "Piper's Opera House," *Territorial Enterprise,* 17 Apr. 1878, John Leach clippings.
39. "Out of Town Correspondence," *New York Dramatic News and Society Journal,* 11 Oct. 1879, 5.
40. There are many songs that use food and eating as a function of difference. Here are just a few: Stephen Foster, "My Old Kentucky Home" (Baltimore: Thomas G. Doyle, 1853); Henry C. Work, "Corporal Schnapps" (Chicago: Root and Cady, 1864); "Finnegan's Wake" (New York: William A. Pond, 1864).
41. Lee, *Orientals,* 38–39.
42. Harry F. Lorraine, "Nigger-vs.-Chinese" (St. Louis: Balmer and Weber, 1870).
43. Bobby Newcomb, "The Chinese Shoemaker," in *Billy West's "Banjo Solo" Songster* (New York: Robert M. DeWitt, 1873), 26. This songster also contains another song about Chinese immigrants in North Adams, Massachusetts, titled "Ching Foo" (1873).
44. Walter Muir Whitehall, *The East India Marine Society and the Peabody Museum of Salem: A Sesquicentennial History* (Salem, Mass.: Peabody Museum, 1949), 21; Syle, "Music among the Chinese," 28; *Lee and Walker's Musical Almanac* (Philadelphia: Lee and Walker, 1872), 75; *Descriptive and Illustrated Catalogue* (Philadelphia: C. F. Zimmermann and Son, ca. 1880), 11, 28.
45. Playbill for *Buckley Serenaders,* no theater, New York, N.Y., 16 Dec. 1853, in *Behind the Burnt Cork* by William J. Mahar (Urbana: University of Illinois Press, 1999), 52.
46. "Theatrical Record," *New York Clipper,* 2 Aug. 1873, 143; 29 Aug. 1874, 174; "B.P.O. Elks," *Footlights,* n.d., John Leach clippings.
47. Judy Yung, *Unbound Feet: A Social History of Chinese Women in San Francisco* (Berkeley: University of California Press, 1999), 15–51; Tchen, *New York before Chinatown,* 75–79.
48. Ronald Takaki, *Strangers from a Different Shore: A History of Asian Americans* (Boston: Little, Brown, 1998), 92–93.
49. I have only given the first three of eight verses and the chorus. "Since the Chinese Ruint the Thrade," in *The Poor Little Man and the Man in the Moon Is Looking, Love Songster* (San Francisco: G. W. Greene, 1871), 11.
50. Christine Stansell, *City of Women: Sex and Class in New York, 1789–1860* (Urbana: University of Illinois Press, 1987).
51. Lee, *Orientals,* 83–105.
52. Luke Schoolcraft, "Big Long John," in *Luke Schoolcraft's Shine on Songster* (New York: A. J. Fisher, 1873), 13.
53. Noel Ignatiev, *How the Irish Became White* (New York: Routledge, 1995); David R. Roediger, *Wages in Whiteness: Race and the Making of the American Working Class* (New York: Verso, 1991); John Kuo Wei Tchen, "Quimbo Appo's Fear of Fenians: Chinese-Irish-Anglo Relations in New York City," in *The New York Irish,* ed. Ronald H. Bayor and Timothy J. Meagher (Baltimore: Johns Hopkins University Press, 1996), 125–152.
54. Harry R. Williams, "Ah Sin" (Detroit: Roe Stephens, 1877).
55. For other instances, see Frank Depro, "Hop Lee," in *Frank Depro's Too-Too Wilde Songster* (New York: Champion Publishing, 1882), 24; John C. Leach, "Bully Chinaman," in *Ireland-vs.-Germany Songster,* 30; Newcomb, "Chinese Shoemaker," 26.
56. R. J. Pigot, "Ah Ling's True Love," in *Charles Konollman's New York Variety Songster* (New York: A. J. Fisher, 1877), 8.
57. "Piper's Opera House," *Territorial Enterprise,* 17 Apr. 1878, John Leach clippings.
58. George M. Vickers, "Sang Lee" (Philadelphia: I. L. Cragin and Co., 1878). Judy Tsou notes that the cover of "Sang Lee" included images of the title character smoking opium, which has nothing to do with the song itself ("Gendering Race," 58–59).
59. James H. Dormon, "Ethnic Cultures of the Mind: The Harrigan-Hart Mosaic," *American Studies* 33 (Summer 1992): 21–40; Katherine K. Preston, "Irish American

Theater," in *Irish American Theater*, ed. Katherine K. Preston, vol. 10 of *Nineteenth Century American Musical Theater* (New York: Garland Publishing, 1994), xiii–xxviii; Jon W. Finson, "Realism in Late Nineteenth Century American Musical Theater: The Songs of Edward Harrigan and David Braham," in *Collected Songs: Edward Harrigan and David Braham*, ed. Jon W. Finson, vols. 27–28 of *Music of the United States of America* (Madison, Wis.: American Musicological Society, 1997), xv–xxxvii.

60. David Braham and Ed Harrigan, *Mulligan's Silver Wedding* (1881), 171–173, as cited in Dormon, "Ethnic Cultures of the Mind," 35.
61. Anonymous, "John Chinaman," in *Tony Pastor's "Down in a Coal Mine" Songster*, 26.
62. As cited in Dormon, "Ethnic Cultures of the Mind," 34.
63. "When McCormack Rules the State," *Flora Moore's Irish Songster* (New York: New York Popular Publishing, 1880), 52; Pat Rooney, "Is That Mr. Rielly?" in *Pat Rooney's Madam Duvan Songster* (New York: New York Popular Publishing, 1882), 4.
64. Some Chinese immigrants were politically active at this time. See Qingsong Zhang, "The Origins of the Chinese Americanization Movement: Wong Chin Foo and the Chinese Equal Rights League," in *Claiming America: Constructing Chinese American Identities during the Exclusion Era,* ed. K Scott Wong and Sucheng Chan (Philadelphia: Temple University Press, 1998), 41–63.

CHAPTER 3   CHINESE AND CHINESE IMMIGRANT PERFORMERS

1. Fiske, *Understanding Popular Culture,* 25.
2. For other examples, see Ben Shephard, "Showbiz Imperialism: The Case of Peter Lobengula," in *Imperialism and Popular Culture*, ed. John M. Mackenzie (New York: Manchester University Press, 1986), 94–112; Paul Kramer, "Making Concessions: Race and Empire Revisited at the Philippine Exposition, St. Louis, 1901–1905," *Radical History Review* 73 (1999): 74–114.
3. Robert Bogdan, *Freak Show: Presenting Human Oddities for Amusement and Profit* (Chicago: University of Chicago Press, 1988); Andrea Stulman Dennett, *Weird and Wonderful: The Dime Museum in America* (New York: New York University Press, 1997); David R. Brigham, *Public Culture in the Early Republic* (Washington, D.C.: Smithsonian Institution Press, 1995).
4. Bogdan, *Freak Show*, 105–111.
5. Other noted Chinese human curiosities were Yan Zoo, the Chinese Juggler (perhaps also known as Chang-Fong); Chang Yu-Shing, the Chinese Giant; and Che-Mah, the Chinese Dwarf.
6. Passenger lists of vessels arriving at New York, New York, 1820–1897, microfilm, National Archives, Washington, D.C. Afong Moy could be the Anglicization of a typical Cantonese name. Tchen, *New York before Chinatown*, 103.
7. Walter Barrett [Joseph Alfred Scoville], *The Old Merchants of New York City* (1870; reprint, New York: Greenwood Press, 1968), 40–45; Registers of vessels arriving at the Port of New York from foreign ports, 2 Jan. 1830–31 July 1835, microfilm, National Archives, Washington, D.C.
8. "The Chinese Lady," *Providence Journal,* 31 Aug. 1835, 2; "Miss Afong Moy," *Daily Evening Transcript* (Boston), 16 July 1835, 2. See Tchen, *New York before Chinatown,* 104; Arthur Bonner, *Alas! What Brought Thee Hither? The Chinese in New York, 1800–1950* (Cranbury, N.J.: Associated University Presses, 1997), 1–3.
9. Playbill for *The Chinese Lady, Afong Moy*, North American Hotel, New Orleans, 28 Mar. 1836, Playbill Collection, American Antiquarian Society; "The Chinese Lady," *Sun* (Philadelphia), 13 Nov. 1834, 3. See Tchen, *New York before Chinatown,* 102.
10. Advertisements—Amusements section, *New York Commercial Advertiser,* 28 June 1836, 4; "Delays Are Dangerous," *Pennsylvanian,* 11 June 1836, 2.

11. Advertisements, *Daily Herald* (New Haven, Conn.), 5 Oct. 1835, 3.
12. "The Chinese Lady," *Pensacola Gazette,* 19 Mar. 1836, 2.
13. "City News," *New York Commercial Advertiser,* 7 Aug. 1847, 2.
14. The *New York Tribune* stated that she had been living in Monmouth County, N.J. "The Chinese Lady," *New York Tribune,* 10 Aug. 1847, 2; "Chinese Lady at Niblo's Saloon," *New York Herald,* 30 July 1847, 2; advertisements, *New York Commercial Advertiser,* 4 Aug. 1847, 3; advertisements, *Boston Post,* 4 Sept. 1847, 3.
15. "The Chinese Junk," *New York Herald,* 21 July 1847, 2. See "City News," *New York Commercial Advertiser,* 10 July 1847, 2; "City Items," *New York Tribune,* 11 Aug. 1847, 2; "City Intelligence," *Morning Courier and New York Enquirer,* 21 Aug. 1847, 2.
16. "The Chinese Junk," *New York Herald,* 28 July 1847, 2; 29 July 1847, 2; 31 July 1847, 2; "City Intelligence," *New York Weekly Herald,* 16 July 1847, 228.
17. *Morning Courier and New York Enquirer,* 7 Oct. 1847, 2.
18. "The Chinese Junk," *Albany Evening Journal,* 11 Aug. 1847, 2; "City News," *New York Commercial Advertiser,* 31 Aug. 1847, 2; "City Items," *New York Tribune,* 28 Sept. 1847, 2; 4 Oct. 1847, 2; "Law Courts," *New York Tribune,* 8 Sept. 1847, 2.
19. John R. Peters Jr., *Miscellaneous Remarks* (New York: John F. Trow, 1849); John R. Peters Jr. *Guide to, or Descriptive Catalogue of the Chinese Museum* (Boston: Eastburn's Press, 1845). See Charlotte Elizabeth Smith, "West Meets East: Exhibitions of Chinese Material Culture in Nineteenth Century America," master's thesis, University of Delaware, 1987, 40–45.
20. Advertisements, *New York Herald,* 22 Apr. 1850, 2; "Chinese Museum," *Morning Courier and New York Enquirer,* 24 May 1850, 2. When the Chinese Family returned to New York City from London on 29 Dec. 1851, Amoon's name appeared as "Amoy" and Mun Chung's as "Non Chung" in the passenger lists. Passenger lists of vessels arriving at New York, New York, 1820–1897. See Tchen, *New York before Chinatown,* 113–123.
21. Advertisements, *New York Herald,* 22 Apr. 1850, 2; 29 Apr. 1850, 3; Peters, *Guide,* 7.
22. Public Amusements, etc., column, *Boston Post,* 13 July 1850, 2.
23. "We'll Go Again," *Morning Courier and New York Enquirer,* 27 Apr. 1850, 2.
24. "All Sorts of Paragraphs," *Boston Post,* 17 Dec. 1847, 2; "The Chinese Exhibition," *Boston Evening Transcript,* 2 July 1850, 2; Public Amusements, etc., column,, *Boston Post,* 17 July 1850, 2; P. T. Barnum, *Struggles and Triumphs, or Forty Years' Recollections of P.T. Barnum* (New York: Penguin Books, 1981), 222; "The First Naturalized Chinaman," *Alameda Argus,* 2 Jan. 1879.
25. "The Chinese Exhibition," *London Times,* 2 May 1851, 3; "Fearful Accident," *London Times,* 20 Jan. 1851, 5; "Public Buildings, Places of Amusement, &c.," *Critic,* 3 May 1851, 218; "Amusements Incidental to the Great Exhibition," *Critic,* 10 May 1851, 245.
26. "Letters of M. Hector Berlioz," in *The Great Exhibition, and London in 1851* (London: Longman, Brown, Green, and Longmans, 1852), 602–606; Hector Berlioz, letter to Joseph D'Ortigue, London, England, 25 June 1851, in *Correspondance générale,* ed. Pierre Citron, Yves Gérard, and Hugh J. MacDonald (Paris: Flammarion, 1983), 4:72–73.
27. "Letters of M. Hector Berlioz," 603, 604–605.
28. In December 1851, the Chinese Family returned to Barnum's American Museum in New York City and then toured throughout the eastern half of the United States and Canada. What happened to the Chinese Family after this tour is uncertain. Advertisements, *New York Times,* 1 Jan. 1852, 5; advertisements, *New Orleans Commercial Bulletin,* 26 Jan. 1853, 2; John J. Weisert, *Mozart Hall: 1851 to 1866* (Louisville, Ky.: n.p., 1962), 4.
29. "The Chinese Jugglers," *Daily Herald* (San Francisco), 6 Oct. 1852, 2; "Theatrical," *Daily Herald* (San Francisco), 8–9 Oct. 1852, 2; advertisements, *Daily Herald* (San Francisco), 8–9 Oct. 1852, 3.

30. See Odell, *Annals,* 2:305, 4:668; P. T. Barnum, "Letter to Moses Kimball," in *Selected Letters of P. T. Barnum,* ed. A. H. Saxon (New York: Columbia University Press, 1983), 13.

31. The Chinese Artistes consisted of the following performers: Chin Gan (a Chinese dwarf), Wang Sing (Wang Ching), Ting Hee, Yan Gyn, Yan Yow, Tuck Quy, Chang Moon, Thong Mong (Tong Ming), Di Hon, Lo Pu, Loi Pha, Aur Oy, Ar Sam, Ar Hee (a nine-year-old boy), Amoy (a six- or seven-year-old girl), and Wan Nuy (the only woman).

32. Playbill for Chinese Artistes, City Hall, Worcester, Mass., 25–26 Apr. 1853, Playbill Collection, American Antiquarian Society; playbill for *À la Chinois,* in Ireland, *Records of the New York Stage,* vol. 2, pt. 8. See Lois Rodescape, "Celestial Drama in the Golden Hills: The Chinese Theatre in California, 1849–1869," *California Historical Society Quarterly* 23 (June 1945): 100–101.

33. *Memphis Daily Appeal,* 17–18 Jan. 1854, 3.

34. Amusements section, *New York Times,* 1 Feb. 1853, 1.

35. "The Chinamen," *New Orleans Commercial Bulletin,* 7 Dec. 1852, 2.

36. "Things Theatrical," *Spirit of the Times,* 5 Feb. 1853, 612.

37. Preston, *Opera on the Road,* 306.

38. Ronald Riddle, *Flying Dragons, Flowing Streams: Music in the Life of San Francisco's Chinatown* (Westport, Conn.: Greenwood, 1983), 104–105.

39. Marlon K. Hom, *Songs of Gold Mountain: Cantonese Rhymes from San Francisco Chinatown* (Berkeley: University of California Press, 1987).

40. Charles Warren Stoddard, *In the Footprints of the Padres* (San Francisco: A. M. Robertson, 1902), 188.

41. Benjamin F. Taylor, *Between the Gates* (Chicago: S. C. Griggs and Co., 1878), 108–109.

42. Leslie, *California,* 170.

43. L. Vernon Briggs, *California and the West, 1881, and Later* (Boston: Wright and Potter Printing, 1931), 91–92.

44. "A Chinese Reception," clippings, Toner Collection, Rare Book Division, Library of Congress, Washington, D.C.

45. Pardee Lowe, *Father and Glorious Descendent* (Boston: Little, Brown, 1943), 43–48.

46. Frank Soulé, John H. Gihon, and James Nisbet, *Annals of San Francisco* (New York: Appleton, 1855), 382–383.

47. "Raid on a Chinese Gambling House," *Alta California,* 29 Dec. 1869, 1. See Riddle, *Flying Dragons,* 107–108.

48. Albert S. Evans, *À la California: Sketch of the Golden Gate State* (San Francisco: A. L. Bancroft and Company, 1873), 135–136. See Riddle, *Flying Dragons,* 120–123.

49. "General Lee Yu Doo Buried," *New York Times,* 30 Oct. 1888, 3.

50. "Chinese Masonic Funeral," *New York Times,* 27 Jan. 1900, 14.

51. "Chu Fong Is Now Sing Foy," *New York Times,* 30 Sept. 1893, 1; "Chu Fong and His Bride," *New York Times,* 15 Oct. 1893, 1.

52. Woo, "Chinese Protestants"; Riddle, *Flying Dragons,* 125–127.

53. Otis Gibson, *The Chinese in America* (1877; reprint, New York: Arno Press, 1978), 82–83.

54. Charles Augustus Stoddard, *Beyond the Rockies: A Spring Journey in California* (New York: C. Scribner's Sons, 1894), 116.

55. Gibson, *Chinese in America,* 186–193; "The Chinese School Festival," *Alta California,* 8 June 1878, 1. See Riddle, *Flying Dragons,* 125–126.

56. Mary H. Wills, *A Winter in California* (Norristown, Pa.: n.p., 1889), 108. See Thomas W. Chinn, *Bridging the Pacific: San Francisco Chinatown and Its People* (San Francisco: Chinese Historical Society of America, 1989), 10; Riddle, *Flying Dragon,* 116–119.

57. "The Belleville Chinamen's New Year's," *Newark Daily Advertiser*, 17 Feb. 1871, 2; "Tin Pans and Gunpowder," *New York Times*, 19 Feb. 1882, 10; "Chinese New Year Festivity," *New York Times*, 8 Feb. 1883, 10; Stewart Culin, *The Religious Ceremonies of the Chinese in the Eastern Cities of the United States* (Philadelphia: Franklin Publishing House, 1887), 9.

58. Riddle, *Flying Dragons*, 123–125.

59. *Letters of Miska Hauser, 1853* (New York: AMS Press, 1972), 64–65; "The Procession," *Daily Herald* (San Francisco), 6 July 1854, 2.

60. Yung, *Cantonese Opera*; Mackerras, *Chinese Theatre in Modern Times*, 147–150; Isabelle Duchesne, ed., *Red Boat on the Canal: Cantonese Opera in New York China-town* (New York: Museum of Chinese in the Americas, 2000); Daniel Lee Ferguson, "A Study of Cantonese Opera: Musical Source Materials, Historical Development, Contemporary Social Organization, and Adaptive Strategies," Ph.D. dissertation, University of Washington, 1988; Sau Yan Chan, "Improvisation in Cantonese Operatic Music," Ph.D. dissertation, University of Pittsburgh, 1986; Lim Chew Pah, "The Two Main Singing Styles in Cantonese Opera: Bandzi and Jiwan," master's thesis, University of Washington, 1973.

61. Advertisements, *Daily Herald* (San Francisco), 16–24 Oct. 1852, 3. See Nancy Yun-hwa Rao, "Songs of the Exclusion Era: New York Chinatown's Opera Theaters in the 1920s," *American Music* 20 (Winter 2002): 409–412.

62. "Theatrical," *Daily Herald* (San Francisco), 17–24 Oct. 1852, 2; "American Theatre," *Alta California*, 18 Oct. 1852, 2. See Peter Chu, Lois M. Foster, Nadia Lavrova, and Steven C. Moy, *Chinese Theatres in America* (San Francisco: Bureau of Research Federal Theatre Project, 1936), 22–23.

63. "Theatrical," *Daily Herald* (San Francisco), 20 Oct. 1852, 2.

64. "The Chinese Opera, at Niblo's," *Spirit of the Times*, 28 May 1853, 169.

65. "City Intelligence," *New York Evening Post,* 16 and 21 July 1853, 2. See Tchen, *New York before Chinatown*, 86–90; Riddle, *Flying Dragons*, 18–21; Bonner, *Alas!* 5–9.

66. "The Chinese Tong-Hook-Tong Dramatic Company," *New York Herald,* 27 July 1853, 1; "City Intelligence," *New York Evening Post,* 3 Sept. 1853, 2; "The Chinese Theatrical Company," *Oriental, or Tung-Ngai San-Luk* 1 (Aug. 1855).

67. "Chinese Theatrical Company"; "Report of the Rev. E. W. Syle," *Spirit of Missions* 18 (Aug. 1854): 323–328. American agents for circuses, vaudeville, and world expositions later traveled to northern China to find acrobatic troupes and magicians.

68. "The Chinese Theatre," *Alta California,* 14 Dec. 1856, 2. See Rodescape, "Celestial Drama," 104–107; Riddle, *Flying Dragons*, 21–23.

69. Playbill for the *Chinese Dramatic Company*, Sacramento Theater, Sacramento, Calif., 23 May ca. 1855, Playbill Collection, Huntington Library.

70. Riddle, *Flying Dragons*, 22–24; Rodescape, "Celestial Drama," 104–106.

71. Riddle, *Flying Dragons*, 25–26; Rodescape, "Celestial Drama," 108–109; Chu et al., *Chinese Theatres*, 39–40.

72. "New Chinese Theatre," *New York Clipper,* 28 Dec. 1867, 298.

73. Philip P. Choy, "The Architecture of San Francisco Chinatown," *Chinese America: History and Perspectives* 4 (1990): 38–39; Chu et al., *Chinese Theatres*, 28–38; Riddle, *Flying Dragons*, 30–32, 36–38.

74. Chu et al., *Chinese Theatres*, 38–46; Riddle, *Flying Dragons*, 36–88.

75. "Things Theatrical," *Wilkes' Spirit of the Times,* 7 Mar. 1868, 48; Riddle, *Flying Dragons*, 63–66.

76. "Dedication of the New Chinese Theatre," *Alta California,* 24 Jan. 1868, 1; "Inauguration of the New Chinese Theatre 'Hing Chuen Yuen,'" *Alta California,* 28 Jan. 1868, 1; Riddle, *Flying Dragons*, 63–64.

77. Rao, "Songs of the Exclusion Era," 409–410; Rodescape, "Celestial Drama," 110–111; Chu et al., *Chinese Theatres*, 49–59.

78. Alice Henson Ernst, *Trouping in the Oregon Country: A History of Frontier Theatre* (Portland: Oregon Historical Society, 1961), 96–102; Howard F. Grant, *The Story of Seattle's Early Theatres* (Seattle: University of Washington Book Store, 1934), 17; Eugene Clinton Elliott, *A History of Variety-Vaudeville in Seattle, from the Beginning to 1914* (Seattle: University of Washington Press, 1944), 66; "Variety, Minstrel, and Circus," *New York Clipper*, 17 Mar. 1888, 2; "Queer Oriental Plays," *New York Tribune*, 20 Aug. 1893, 15; Harris Newmark, *Sixty Years in Southern California, 1853–1913* (New York: Knickerbocker Press, 1916), 585; "They Saw a Chinese Play," *New York Times*, 13 Feb. 1891, 1; "Local Meetings and Other Notices," *Journal of American Folk-Lore* 4 (Apr.–Mar. 1891): 183; "The Chinese Opera: Under the Auspices of the Folk-Lore Society," no paper or date, clippings, Harvard Theatre Collection.

79. "Chinese Actors at the Windsor," *New York Tribune*, 25 June 1889, 6; "The Chinese Play," *New York Times*, 25 June 1889, 4; William E. S. Fales, "The Chinese Mimes," *Harper's Weekly*, 29 June 1889, 528. See Bonner, *Alas!* 87–88.

80. "Got a Good Start Last Night," *New York Times*, 26 Mar. 1893, 4; Duvon Clough Corbitt, *A Study of the Chinese in Cuba, 1847–1947* (Wilmore, Ky.: Asbury College Press, 1971), 92.

81. "Theatre Case for the Courts," *New York Times*, 30 July 1895, 6; "Five Chinese Actors Arraigned," *New York Times*, 21 Jan. 1896, 14; "No License for Chu Fong," *New York Times*, 21 Mar. 1896, 9. In 1897, Li Toy, the manager of the Chinese theater in Boston, and his actors were able to convince a judge that Sunday performances were religious and therefore were allowable under the law. Chu Fong had also argued that his plays were of a religious nature, but he was unable to convince the judge. "Chinese Drama," *Boston Journal*, 9 Jan. 1897, 2.

82. "Chinese Concert Company Licensed," *New York Tribune*, 27 Mar. 1893, 9; "Doyers Street Theatre," *New York Times*, 8 May 1897, 2; "Ruined by a Right System," *New York Tribune*, 8 May 1897, 7. See Bonner, *Alas!* 88–93.

83. M. Alison Kibler, *Rank Ladies: Gender and Cultural Hierarchy in American Vaudeville* (Chapel Hill: University of North Carolina Press, 1999); Robert C. Allen, *Horrible Prettiness: Burlesque and American Culture* (Chapel Hill: University of North Carolina Press, 1991).

84. Riddle, *Flying Dragons*, 56, 68, 96; Alfred Trumble, *The "Heathen Chinee" at Home and Abroad* (New York: Richard K. Fox, 1882), 62–63; Henry Burden McDowell, "The Chinese Theater," *Century* 29 (Nov. 1884): 38.

85. Helen F. Clark, "The Chinese of New York," *Century* 53 (Nov. 1896): 106.

86. "Little Yut Gum, of Chinatown," *New York World*, 21 June 1896, 29; "Doyers Street Theatre," *New York Times*, 8 May 1897, 2; "The Bernhardt of the Celestial Realm," *Dramatic Mirror*, 4 July 1896, clippings, Harvard Theatre Collection.

87. Yung, *Unbound Feet*, 45, 111. See Riddle, *Flying Dragons*, 32; Rodescape, "Celestial Drama," 112.

88. Riddle, *Flying Dragons*, 95–96.

89. In re Ho King, *Federal Reporter*, District Court of Oregon, 15 Jan. 1883, 14:724–728.

90. "To Exclude Alleged Chinese Actors," *New York Tribune*, 2 Sept. 1898, 9; Chapman W. Maupin, *A Digest of Chinese Exclusion Laws and Decisions* (Washington, D.C.: Government Printing Office, 1899), 31–33; Frederick D. Cloud, *A Digest of the Treaty, Laws, and Regulations Governing the Admission of Chinese* (Washington, D.C.: Government Printing Office, 1908), 11. See Lucy E. Salyer, *Laws Harsh as Tigers: Chinese Immigration and the Shaping of Modern Immigration Law* (Chapel Hill: University of North Carolina, 1995), 154–155.

91. Chu et al., *Chinese Theatres*, 15; Riddle, *Flying Dragons*, 137–140.

92. "Two Chinamen Killed," *New York Tribune*, 7 Aug. 1905, 1; "Chinese Theatre Closed,"

New York Times, 31 Dec. 1909, 4; "Chinese Theatre again Open," *New York Times,* 6 Mar. 1910, 4; "End of Chinese Theatre," no paper, 4 Sept. 1910, clippings, Harvard Theatre Collection. See Bonner, *Alas!* 88–93.

93. Riddle, *Flying Dragons,* 138; "This Week's Vaudeville Reviews This Week," *Billboard,* 7 Oct. 1916, 9; playbill for *Vaudeville,* Boston Opera House, 7 May 1932, Warshaw Collection, Archives Center, Smithsonian Institution, Washington, D.C.

94. U.S. Department of State, *Admission of Chinese into the United States* (Washington, D.C.: Government Printing Office, 1936), 14; R. D. McKenzie, *Oriental Exclusion* (Chicago: University of Chicago Press, 1928), 121; Chu et al., *Chinese Theatres,* 74–75, 85–88. See bonds housed in the National Archives, Washington, D.C., for individual performers.

95. Ananda Coomaraswamy and Stella Bloch, "The Chinese Theatre in Boston," *Theatre Arts Monthly* 9 (Feb. 1925): 113–122; Chu et al., *Chinese Theatres,* 12–15, 72–88; Bonner, *Alas!* 93–95; Riddle, *Flying Dragons,* 140–156; Robe Carl White, Assistant Secretary of Labor, Washington, D.C., to Attorneys McGee and Mather, San Francisco, telegram, 2 Apr. 1927, in file 55374, box 257; Secretary of Labor, Washington, D.C., to M. Walton Hendry, Esq., Washington, D.C., 19 June 1925, box 356, file 50374, Subject Correspondence, 1906–32, Records of the Immigration and Naturalization Service, Department of Labor, National Archives, Washington, D.C. All National Archives records are Chinese Exclusion Acts case files from RG85 unless otherwise stated.

96. Curtis M. Hinsley, "The World as Marketplace: Commodification of the Exotic at the World's Columbian Exposition, Chicago, 1893," in *Exhibiting Cultures: The Poetics and Politics of Museum Display,* ed. Ivan Karp and Steven D. Lavine (Washington, D.C.: Smithsonian Institution Press, 1990), 344–365; Robert W. Rydell, *All the World's a Fair: Visions of Empire at American International Expositions, 1876–1916* (Chicago: University of Chicago Press, 1987); Burton Benedict, "Rituals of Representation: Ethnic Stereotypes and Colonized Peoples at World's Fairs," in *Fair Representations: World's Fairs and the Modern World,* ed. Robert W. Rydell and Nancy Gwinn (Amsterdam: VU University Press, 1994), 28–61.

97. Whitehall, *East India Marine Society,* 21.

98. E. C. Wines, *A Peep at China, in Mr. Dunn's Chinese Collection* (Philadelphia: Ashmead and Co., 1839), 44–45, 66–67; Peters, *Guide.*

99. Gertrude M. Scott, "Village Performance: Villages at the Chicago World's Columbian Exposition, 1893," Ph.D. dissertation, New York University, 1991, 96–110.

100. "Guide Book to the Joss House, Temple of China, Chinese Theater, Tea Garden, Café and Chinese Bazaar," Wah Mee Exposition Company, Chicago, 1893, in the Exposition Records of the Smithsonian Institution and the United States National Museum, Smithsonian Archives, Smithsonian Institution.

101. Odell, *Annals,* 15:405–407, 663–664; Scott, "Village Performance," 50–51, 114–115, 122–124.

102. "Chinese Actors on the Saratoga," *New York Tribune,* 11 Apr. 1893, 5; "Will Admit Chinamen," *Daily Inter-Ocean* (Chicago), 16 Apr. 1893, 7; "Chinese World's Fair Actors Must Go Back," *New York Tribune,* 18 Apr. 1893, 1; "Chinese Actors Shut Out," *New York Tribune,* 4 May 1893, 2.

103. Charles Stevens McClellan, *The Adventures of Uncle Jeremiah and Family at the Great Fair* (Chicago: Laird and Lee, 1893), 164.

104. Scott, "Village Performance," 96–110; Smith, "West Meets East," 73–75.

105. *California Midwinter Exposition Official Guide* (San Francisco: California Midwinter Exposition Committee, 1894), 100–102; "Leong Nam," *New York Times,* 1 June 1896, 4; "National Export Exposition, Philadelphia," *Harper's Weekly,* 9 Sept. 1899, 909; scrapbook, Helen May Butler Collection, Archives Center, Smithsonian Insti-

tution, Washington, D.C.; *Alaska-Yukon-Pacific Exposition Official Guide* (Seattle: Alaska-Yukon-Pacific Exposition Publishing Co., 1909), 65; *The Official Guide Book of the Panama California Exposition* (San Diego: Panama California Exposition, 1915), 39; E. L. Austin and Odell Hauser, *The Sesqui-Centennial International Exposition* (Philadelphia: Current Publications, 1929), 374. Despite applications from fifteen individuals and businesses, fair owners did not allow for any Chinese concession at the Pan-American Exposition in Buffalo, N.Y. This was, perhaps, tied to American anger toward the Chinese after the massacring of missionaries and the destroying of property during the Boxer Rebellion (1898–1901). "Applications for the Pan-American Concessions," *Pan-American Herald* (Buffalo, N.Y.), Aug. 1899–Nov. 1900.

106. *Official Guide Book to the Trans-Mississippi and International Exposition* (Omaha: Megeath Stationery Co., 1898); "A Wonderful Conjuror," *New York Dramatic Mirror*, 3 June 1899, 16; "The Sorrows of a Magician," *New York Daily Tribune*, 22 Feb. 1901, 4; Sidney W. Clarke, "Oriental Conjuring," *Magic Wand* 19 (Dec. 1928): 212–217. See Robert W. Rydell, "The Trans-Mississippi and International Exposition: 'To Work Out the Problem of Universal Civilization,'" *American Quarterly* 33 (Winter 1981): 587–607.

107. "China's Exhibits at the World's Fair," *World's Fair Bulletin* (St. Louis) 5 (Feb. 1904): 42; "December Record," *World's Fair Bulletin* (St. Louis) 3 (Jan. 1902): 27; "China and the World's Fair," *World's Fair Bulletin* (St. Louis) 3 (Aug. 1902): 34; "Dedication of China's Building Site," *World's Fair Bulletin* (St. Louis) 4 (Oct. 1903): 2–4; David R. Francis, *The Universal Exposition of 1904* (St. Louis: Louisiana Purchase Exposition Company, 1913), 1:215–216, 317, 598; 2:416; *China: Catalogue of the Collection of Chinese Exhibits* (St. Louis: Shallcross Print, 1904), in the Zim Collection, Archives Center, Smithsonian Institution. See Irene E. Cortinovis, "China at the St. Louis World's Fair," *Missouri Historical Review* 72 (Oct. 1977): 59–66.

108. "Chinese Village," *World's Fair Bulletin* (St. Louis) 5 (July 1904): 88; "The True and Complete Story of the Pike and Its Attractions," *World's Fair Bulletin* (St. Louis) 5 (Apr. 1904): 21; "November Record," *World's Fair Bulletin* (St. Louis) 3 (Dec. 1901): 12; "Chinese at World's Fair," *World's Fair Bulletin* (St. Louis) 3 (June 1902): 15; Rydell, *All the World's a Fair*, 180.

109. "Chinese Exhibits Will Arrive in San Francisco," *Exhibitors' Weekly Bulletin* (San Francisco), 28 Nov. 1914, 3; "China's Exposition Board Arrives in San Francisco," *Exhibitors' Weekly Bulletin* (San Francisco), 2 Jan. 1915, 1; "China Installs a Wonderful Exhibit," *Exhibitors' Weekly Bulletin* (San Francisco), 23 Jan. 1915, 2; *Official Souvenir View Book of the Panama-Pacific International Exposition at San Francisco, 1915* (San Francisco: Robert A. Reid, 1915).

110. Rydell, *All the World's a Fair*, 228–229; Smith, "West Meets East," 80–81.

CHAPTER 4   THE SOUNDS OF CHINESE OTHERNESS

1. Locke, "Reflections on Orientalism"; MacKenzie, *Orientalism*; Parakilas, "Soldier and the Exotic"; Scott, "Orientalism and Musical Style".

2. T. J. Jackson Lears, *No Place of Grace: Antimodernism and the Transformation of American Culture, 1880–1920* (New York: Pantheon Books, 1981).

3. Timothy Rice, "Comparative Musicology," in *New Grove Dictionary of Music and Musicians*, 6:178–179; Carole Pegg, Helen Myers, Philip V. Bohlman, and Martin Stokes, "Ethnomusicology," in *New Grove Dictionary of Music and Musicians*, 8:367–408; Philip V. Bohlman, "Representation and Cultural Critique in the History of Ethnomusicology," in *Comparative Musicology and Anthropology of Music: Essays on the History of Ethnomusicology*, ed. Bruno Nettl and Philip V. Bohlman (Chicago: University of Chicago Press, 1991), 131–151.

4. An example of such a work is Andrew Cherry's *The Travellers; or Music's Fascination*, as noted in chapter 1. Jacques Gernet, *China and the Christian Impact: A Conflict of Cultures*, trans. Janet Lloyd (New York: Cambridge University Press, 1985); Ysia Tchen, *La musique chinoise en France au XVIIIe siècle* (Paris: National Institute of Oriental Languages and Civilizations, 1974); Kii-Ming Lo, "New Documents on the Encounter between European and Chinese Music," *Revista de Musicologia* 16 (1993): 16–31; Jim Levy, "Joseph Amiot and Enlightenment Speculation on the Origin of Pythagorean Tuning in China," *Theoria: Historical Aspects of Music Theory* 4 (1989): 63–88.

5. Jean-Baptiste Du Halde, *A General History of China, Containing a Geographical, Historical, Chronological, Political and Physical Description of the Empire of China* (London: John Watts, 1736), 3:65–70, 193–237; Amiot, *Mémoires concernant l'histoire*, vol. 6.

6. Clifton Jackson Phillips, *Protestant America and the Pagan World: The First Half-Century of the American Board of Commissioners for Foreign Missions, 1810–1860* (Cambridge: East Asian Research Center, Harvard University, 1969), 172–205.

7. Lay, *Chinese as They Are*, 43–44, 74–77.

8. G. Tradescant Lay, "Remarks on the Musical Instruments of the Chinese with an Outline of Their Harmonic System," *Chinese Repository* 2 (May 1839): 38–53.

9. Edward W. Syle, "On the Musical Notation of the Chinese," *Journal of the North-China Branch of the Royal Asiatic Society*, no. 2 (1859): 176–179.

10. Engel, *Introduction to the Study of National Music*, 50; Carl Engel, *Music of the Most Ancient Nations, Particularly of Assyrians, Egyptians, and Hebrews* (London: J. Murray, 1870), 131.

11. *Catalogue for the International Health Exhibition* contained several more melodies than did J. A. Van Aalst, *Chinese Music* (Shanghai: Statistical Department of the Inspectorate General of Customs, 1884). It is not clear whether these songs were recorded in China or London, where a small group of musicians from Beijing were performing as part of the Exposition. *Illustrated Catalogue of the Chinese Collection of Exhibits for the International Health Exhibition, London, 1884* (London: William Clowes and Sons, 1884), 150–180; "Chinese Music," *New York Times*, 22 Jan. 1886, 6.

12. Van Aalst, *Chinese Music*, iii.

13. Ibid., 6, 37–38.

14. Ibid., 84.

15. A supporter of Antonín Dvořák's ideas on national music, Krehbiel collected African American folk songs that he felt should be the basis for an American school of composition. Herbert E. Krehbiel, *Afro-American Folksongs: A Study in Racial and National Music* (1914; reprint, Portland, Me.: Longwood Press, 1974).

16. "The 'Ahs' in a Girls' School," *New York Tribune*, 19 June 1887, 13.

17. "Lecturing on Chinese Music," *New York Tribune*, 28 Nov. 1891, 7; Herbert E. Krehbiel, "Chinese Music," *Century* 41 (Jan. 1891): 449–457.

18. Alexander J. Ellis, "On the Musical Scales of Various Nations," *Journal of the Society of Arts*, 27 Mar. 1885, 485–527; Jaap Kunst, "Introduction," in *Ethnomusicology*, ed. Jaap Kunst (1950; reprint, The Hague: Martinus Nijhoff, 1974), 2–24.

19. J. Walter Fewkes and Benjamin Ives Gilman, *A Few Summer Ceremonials at Zuni Pueblo*, vol. 1 (Boston: Houghton, Mifflin, 1891).

20. Benjamin Ives Gilman, "On Some Psychological Aspects of the Chinese Musical System," *Philosophical Review* 1 (Jan. 1892): 54–78; 1 (Feb. 1892): 154–178.

21. Not all music with Chinese subjects during this time was innovative or used sound to denote race. See John St. George, "The Chinese Picnic" (Boston: Oliver Ditson, 1891); B. P. Austin, "Chinese Lantern" (Erie, Pa.: Sprague Green, 1908).

22. Lay, "Remarks on Musical Instruments," 42–44; "About Gongs," *Orpheus*, 1 June 1870, 148; *Lee and Walker's Musical Almanac*, 74–75.

23. "Musical Comment," *New York Tribune* (Ill. supplement), 17 Oct. 1897, 16.

24. Francis Powers, *The First Born* (San Francisco: n.p., 1897); Williams, *Misreading the Chinese Character*, 124–125.

25. "Musical Comment," *New York Tribune*, 17 Oct. 1897, 16; Lee Johnson, "Chinese Highbinder Patrol" (San Francisco: Model Music Store, 1897). Later in 1897, Charles Ulrich's *Celestial Maiden* incorporated these songs as well. Playbill for *Celestial Maiden*, Burbank Theatre, Los Angeles, Calif., 20 Dec. 1897, album 37, Behymer Collection.

26. An untitled review, with no journal and date, press clippings, vol. 2, Behymer Collection.

27. Ibid.

28. "Musical Comment," *New York Tribune*, 17 Oct. 1897, 16; Van Aalst, *Chinese Music*, 44.

29. George C. Hazelton and Henry Benrimo, *The Yellow Jacket* (1912; reprint, New York: Samuel French, 1939); William Furst, *Piano Score of "The Yellow Jacket,"* arr. Paul Taubman (New York: Samuel French, 1941).

30. Sheldon Cheney, *The New Movement in the Theatre* (1914; reprint, New York: Benjamin Blom, 1971), 91–92, 173.

31. "Something New and Strange in Drama," *New York Times*, 3 Nov. 1912, X6.

32. Van Aalst, *Chinese Music*, 37, 42–43; George Carter Stent, "Chinese Lyrics," *Journal of the North-China Branch of the Royal Asiatic Society* 7 (1873): 120–123.

33. Van Aalst, *Chinese Music*, 38–39. Stent had also transcribed "Wang Ta Niang" with a completely different melody ("Chinese Lyrics," 95–105).

34. "Mood" music was often used during several types of scenes in silent films. Those characterized as "Chinese" were also used for "Japanese" scenes; at least one publisher recommended "Chinese Serenade" (1880) to be played during dancing, comedic sketches, or juggling. Otto Langey, "Chinese-Japanese," in *Motion Picture Moods for Pianists and Organists*, arr. and comp. Erno Rapée (New York: G. Schirmer, 1924), 331; H. Fliege, "Chinese Serenade," in *Album of Photo-Play Music*, arr. and comp. G. Martaine (New York: Academic Music, 1914), 1:5.

35. J. S. Zamecnik, "Chinese Music," in *Sam Fox Moving Pictures Music* (Cleveland, Ohio: Sam Fox Publishing, 1913), 5; Russell Sanjek, *Pennies from Heaven: The American Popular Music Business in the Twentieth Century* (New York: Da Capo Press, 1988), 11, 48–50.

36. Barrow, *Travels in China*, 212.

37. William P. Brayton, "The Mandarin" (Newburgh, N.Y.: Teachers Publication Society, 1906); Frank Davis and Win Brookhouse, "All Aboard for Chinatown" (New York: Shapiro, Bernstein and Co., 1915).

38. "New Show at Casino Is Big and Lively," *New York Times*, 19 July 1910, 7.

39. "The Billboard Song Hits," *Billboard*, 27 Feb. 1915, 12.

40. Jean Schwartz and William Jerome, "Chinatown, My Chinatown," in *Up and Down Broadway* (New York: Jerome H. Remick and Co., 1910); *Billboard* song chart, *Billboard*, 13 Mar. 1915, 14; 20 Mar. 1915, 14; 29 Mar. 1915, 14; 10 Apr. 1915, 14; "Vaudeville Reviews by Special Wire," *Billboard*, 25 Dec. 1915, 7.

41. Richard Crawford and Jeff Magee, *Jazz Standards on Record, 1900–1942* (Chicago: Center for Black Music Research, 1992), 14.

42. James J. Fuld, *The Book of World-Famous Music* (New York: Dover Publications, 2000), 170–171; Alfred V. Frankenstein, "'Chopsticks': A Musicological Mystery," *American Mercury* 25 (Mar. 1932): 372–378.

43. Arthur De Lulli (Euphemia Allen), "Chop Sticks" (New York: R. A. Saalfield, 1879); George F. Morris, "Chop Sticks Galop" (New York: C. H. Ditson and Co., 1879); Archie Gottler and Abe Frankl, "Ragging the Chopsticks" (New York: Leo Feist, Inc., 1919); De Zulli, "Chop Sticks" (Philadelphia: Eclipse Publishing, ca. 1902).

44. "Reviews," *Musical Herald* 1 (Dec. 1880): 288; H. Fliege, "Chinese Serenade" (New York: C. H. Ditson and Co., 1880); F. Alexander, "Turkish Patrol" (no city: M.M.C. Walker, 1880).

45. H. Fliege, "Chinese Serenade" (New York: C. H. Ditson and Co., 1880); A. Pferd-ner and H. Fliege, "General J. A. Garfield's March and Chinese Serenade" (Cincin-nati: John Church, 1884); H. Fliege, "Chinese Serenade," in *Les Trois Pianistes* (Baltimore: George Willig and Co., 1885); H. Fliege, "Chinese Serenade," in *Reper-toire of Celebrated Compositions* (Boston: White, Smith, and Co., 1885); H. Fliege, "Chinese Serenade," *Musical Herald* 3 (June 1882).

46. Playbill for *Boston Ideal Club*, Park Hall, Boston, 14 June ca. 1893, scrapbook of programs and clippings, 1871–1895, Harris Collection, John Hay Library, Brown University, Providence, R.I.

47. Fliege, "Chinese Serenade," in *Album of Photo-Play Music*, 5.

48. W. C. Powell, "The Ragtime Laundry" (Chicago: Victor Kremer, 1901); George W. Meyer, "The Chinatown Rag" (New York: F. B. Haviland, 1910). See William J. Schafer and Johannes Riedel, *The Art of Ragtime: Form and Meaning of an Original Black American Art* (Baton Rouge: Louisiana State University, 1973); Southern, *Music of Black Americans*, 308–329.

49. Edward Hayne, "Chop Suey Rag" (Chicago: Edward Hayne Music Publisher, 1915).

50. I. Caesar and Will Donaldson, "China Dragon Blues" (New York: T. B. Harms, 1919); Philip Braham and Douglas Furber, "Limehouse Blues" (New York: T. B. Harms, 1922).

51. Fred D. Moore and Oscar Gardner, "Chinese Blues," in *A Treasury of the Blues*, ed. W. C. Handy (1915; reprint, New York: Simon and Schuster, 1949), 184–185; Southern, *Music of Black Americans*, 330–338.

52. Willard Robison, "Up and Down in China," in *Six Studies in Modern Syncopation for Piano* (New York: Robbins Music Corp., 1926), 12–14.

Chapter 5   From Aversion to Fascination

1. Chase, *America's Music*, 323–428; Crawford, *America's Musical Life*, 429–494; Charles Hamm, *Yesterdays: Popular Song in America* (New York: W. W. Norton, 1979), 284–390; Butsch, *Making of American Audiences*, 57–172.

2. Carrie Tirado Bramen, "The Urban Picturesque and the Spectacle of Americaniza-tion," *American Quarterly* 52 (Sept. 2000): 444–477; Spence, *Search for Modern China*, 137–268; Takaki, *Strangers from a Different Shore*, 230–269.

3. Kay J. Anderson, "The Idea of Chinatown: The Power of Place and Institutional Practice in the Making of a Racial Category," *Annals of the Association of American Geographers* 77 (Dec. 1987): 580–598; Choy, "Architecture of San Francisco China-town"; David Chuenyan Lai, *Chinatowns: Towns within Cities in Canada* (Vancouver: University of British Columbia Press, 1988), 34–36.

4. Catherine Clément, *Opera, or the Undoing of Women* (Minneapolis: University of Minnesota Press, 1988), 43–59; Judith R. Walkowitz, "The 'Vision of Salome': Cosmopolitanism and Erotic Dancing in Central London, 1908–1918," *American Historical Review* 108 (Apr. 2003): 337–376; Gaylyn Studlar, "'Out-Salomeing Salome': Dance, the New Woman, and Fan Magazines," in Bernstein and Studlar, *Visions of the East*, 99–129; Yoshihara, *Embracing the East*, 77–100; Kibler, *Rank Ladies*, 1–54.

5. Aarim-Heriot, *Chinese Immigrants*, 1–14; Luther W. Spoehr, "Sambo and the Hea-then Chinee: Californians' Racial Stereotypes in the Late 1870s," *Pacific Historical Review* 42 (May 1973): 185–204; Dan Caldwell, "The Negroization of the Chinese Stereotype in California," *Southern California Quarterly* 53 (June 1971): 123–132.

6. Lee, *Performing Asian America*, 11–15.

7. For discussions of African Americans challenging the presence of white bodies in blackface on the stage, see Toll, *Blacking Up*, 195–229; Riis, *Just before Jazz*, 185–190.

8. *Pocket Catalogue* (Brooklyn, N.Y.: Arthur B. Albertis Company, n.d.), 31; Edith Dabney and C. M. Wise, *A Book of Dramatic Costume* (New York: F. S. Crofts and Co., 1930), 146–147; J. G. Hamley, *Chapeaugraphy; or, Twenty-Five Heads under One Hat* (London: W. F. Hamley, ca. 1885), 21; R. D. Chater (Hercat), *Chapeaugraphy, Shadowgraphy, and Paper-Folding* (London: Dean, 1909), 24.

9. Haejeon Kim, "Far Eastern Influence on Western Women's Dress in *Harper's Bazaar*, 1890–1927 (Sino-Japanese)," Ph.D. dissertation, University of Minnesota, 1989.

10. *Catalogue of Theatrical and Society Hair Goods* (Jersey City, N.J.: Philip Ostermayer, n.d.).

11. Lee, *Orientals*, 51–82.

12. *Pocket Catalogue*, 31; *Arthur W. Tams Costumes . . . Catalogue No. 7* (New York: Arthur W. Tams, n.d.), 10–11, 36, 42; Helena Chalmers, *The Art of Make-up* (New York: D. Appleton and Co., 1925), 111–115; Ivard Strauss, *Paint, Powder, and Makeup* (New Haven, Conn.: Sweet and Son, 1936), 169–170.

13. Hazelton and Benrimo, *Yellow Jacket*, 100–102, plate X; "The New Plays," *Theatre* 15 (Dec. 1912): 162–163.

14. Haresfoot and Rouge [pseudonym], *How to "Make-Up": A Practical Guide for Amateurs &c.* (New York: Samuel French, 1877), 38. "Haresfoot" and "Rouge" were makeup terms—rouge was (and still is) a kind of red paint placed on the lips and cheeks, and a haresfoot (or a hare's foot) was used as a tool for applying greasepaint by professional actors during the nineteenth and early twentieth centuries.

15. *A. M. Buch & Co., Dealers in and Manufacturers of All Kinds of Hair Goods, Theatrical and Street, Wig and Toupee Makers, and All Necessary Articles for the Stage* (Philadelphia: A. M. Buch, ca. 1880), 4; Nikola Helmer, *Helmer's Actor's Make-up Book* (New York: Harold Roorbach, 1888), 64; Richard B. Whorf, *Time to Make Up: A Practical Handbook in the Art of Grease Paint* (Boston: Walter H. Baker Company, 1930), 60; John F. Baird, *Make-up, a Manual for the Use of Actors, Amateur and Professional* (New York: Samuel French, 1930), 109–111; Walter L. Rodgers, *Rodgers' Make-up Book* (Chicago: Dramatic Publishing, 1930), 64; Rudolph G. Liszt, *The Last Word in Make-up* (New York: Contemporary Play Publications, 1938), 58–59; Arthur H. Schwerin, *Make-up Magic: A Modern Handbook for Beginners or Advanced Students* (Minneapolis: Northwestern Press, 1939), 63–64.

16. Ellen M. Gall and Leslie H. Carter, *Modern Make-up: A Practical Text Book and Guide for the Student, Director and Professional* (San Francisco: Banner Play Bureau, 1928), 72.

17. Cecil Holland, *The Art of Make-up for Stage and Screen* (Hollywood: Cinematex Publishing, 1927), 71–72.

18. Strauss, *Paint, Powder, and Makeup*, 172.

19. Chalmers, *Art of Make-up*, 111–115; Strauss, *Paint, Powder, and Makeup*, 96, 169–172.

20. Lee, *Orientals*, 113–117.

21. Hazelton and Benrimo, *Yellow Jacket*, 103, plate I.

22. "New Acts This Week," *Variety*, 3 Nov. 1926, 23.

23. "*Daughter of Heaven*, Leibler and Co.'s Second Annual Spectacle Pronounced the Most Magnificent Production Ever Seen on an American Stage," *Billboard*, 19 Oct. 1912, 6.

24. Hyde, "Chinese Stereotype," 357–367; Fenn, *Ah Sin*, 112–113; Williams, *Misreading the Chinese Character*, 115–139.

25. J. Casper Nathan and J. Walter Leopold, "Down in Chinatown" (Chicago: F.J.A. Forster Music Publisher, 1914).

26. Joseph Nussbaum and Ben Bronfin, "Chinese Moon" (New York: Frazer-Kent Inc., 1926).

27. Grahame Jones, "Towsee Mongalay" (New York: Jerome H. Remick and Co., 1915).

28. Hyde, "Chinese Stereotype," 357–367; Fenn, *Ah Sin*, 112–113; Williams, *Misreading the Chinese Character*, 133–139.

29. Lee Johnson, "Mamma's China Twins" (San Francisco: Lee Johnson and Co., 1900).

30. Raymond William, *The Country and the City* (New York: Oxford University Press, 1973), 17–33.

31. Spence, *Search for Modern China*, 137–268.

32. Ellen Rothman, *Hands and Hearts: A History of Courtship in America* (New York: Basic Books, 1980), 81–83, 175–176, 280–82.

33. "Applications for the Pan-American Concessions," *Pan-American Herald* (Buffalo, N.Y.), Aug. 1899–Nov. 1900.

34. "A Chinese Honeymoon," *New York Times*, 3 June 1902, 9; Kurt Gänzl, *The British Musical Theatre* (New York: Oxford University Press, 1986), 1:767–772.

35. George Dance and Howard Talbot, "A Chinese Honeymoon Waltz," arr. Ernest Vousden (Boston: White-Smith Music Publishing, 1901); Karl L. Hoschna, "A Chinese Honeymoon Lancers" (New York: M. Witmark and Sons, 1902).

36. Egbert Van Alstyne and Harry Williams, "That's the Sign of a Honeymoon" (New York: Jerome H. Remick and Co., 1908); Ivan Caryll and Bryan Williams, "A Chinese Honeymoon," in *Chin-Chin* (New York: Chappell and Co., 1914); C. J. Hausman and W. L. Shockley, "On a Chinese Honeymoon" (Chicago: Melrose and Montgomery Publishers, 1923); William L. Shockley, Charles J. Hausman, and Lester Melrose, "Shanghai Honeymoon" (Chicago: Melrose and Montgomery, 1926).

37. Fenn, *Ah Sin*, 113.

38. Dave Roche, "It Is the Flavor from a Two-Cent Chinese Butt," in *Campbell and Burke's Our Honest Workingmen Songster* (New York: New York Popular Publishing, 1879), 49. There was also "The Dopy Rag" (1912), which contained an image of Chinese immigrants and opium on the sheet music cover. W. C. Powell and Samuel L. Rosen, "The Dopy Rag" (Milwaukee: Joseph Flanner, 1912).

39. Schwartz and Jerome, "Chinatown, My Chinatown."

40. Frank Davis and Win Brookhouse, "All Aboard for Chinatown" (New York: Shapiro, Bernstein and Co., 1915); Raymond Egan, Gus Kahn, and Egbert Van Alstyne, "China Dreams" (New York: Jerome H. Remick and Co., 1917); Spencer Williams, Marguerite Kendall, and J. Russel Robinson, "Pipe Dream Blues" (Chicago: Lee S. Roberts, 1918); Jean Schwartz and William Jerome, "In Blinky, Winky, Chinky Chinatown" (New York: Waterson, Berlin, and Snyder Co., 1915); Malvin M. Franklin and Alex Gerber, "When the Lights Go Down in Chinatown" (New York: M. Witmark and Sons, 1922).

41. Requi Yu, "Chop Suey: From Chinese Food to Chinese American Food," *Chinese America: History and Perspectives* 1 (1987): 87–99.

42. Egbert Van Alstyne and Harry Williams, "Opening Act I," in *Broken Idol* (New York: Jerome H. Remick and Co., 1908).

43. "*A Broken Idol* at the Herald Square," *New York Times*, 17 Aug. 1909, 7; "Plays of the Month," *Theatre* 10 (Oct. 1909): xiii–xiv; Gerald Bordman, *American Theatre: A Chronicle of Comedy and Drama, 1869–1914* (New York: Oxford University Press, 1994), 293.

44. Howard Johnson and Milton Ager, "China, We Owe a Lot to You" (New York: Leo Feist, Inc., 1917); Raymond W. Peck and Joseph E. Howard, "Rag-Time Chinaman" (Chicago: Joseph E. Howard and Co., 1903); Harold Weeks, "Chong (He Come from Hong Kong)" (New York: Leo Feist, Inc., 1919).

45. Parakilas, "Soldier and the Exotic"; Locke, "Reflections on Orientalism."
46. Bordman, *American Theatre*, 238.
47. Robert B. Smith and Alfred E. Aarons, "One Umbrella Would Be Big Enough for Two," in *A China Doll* (New York: M. Witmark and Sons, 1904).
48. Robert B. Smith and Alfred E. Aarons, "My Little China Doll," in *A China Doll*, 86–89.
49. Irving Berlin, "Porcelain Maid" (New York: Irving Berlin, Inc., 1922); Robert B. Smith and Bruno Granichstaedten, "When Two Little Hearts Beat Together" (New York: Joseph W. Stern and Co., 1912).
50. Jack E. Slattery, "Chen, My China Girl" (Seattle: Slattery and Suess, 1927).
51. Gus Kahn and Egbert Van Alstyne, "My Dreamy China Lady" (New York: Jerome H. Remick and Co., 1916).
52. Arthur J. Lamb and H. W. Petrie, "Little Peeweet" (Chicago: Petrie Music Co., 1897); A. J. Stasny and Otto Motzan, "In China" (New York: A. J. Stasny Music Co., 1919).
53. Vincent Dattilo, Gene Cullinan, and Thomas R. Murray, "My Chinese Butterfly" (New York: Ansonia Music, 1922); Lee David and Billy Rose, "Chinky Butterfly" (New York: Irving Berlin, Inc., 1925).
54. Aaron S. Hoffman and Andy Lewis, "Pinky Panky Poo" (Chicago: Sol Bloom, 1902); Lynn Cowan and Alex Sullivan, "Fan San" (New York: Broadway Music, 1919).
55. Robert Hood Bowers, "Chinese Lullaby" (New York: G. Schirmer, Inc., 1919).
56. Samuel Shipman and John B. Hymer, *East Is West* (New York: Samuel French, 1924).
57. Roy Turk, Bert Grant, and Cecil Bernard, "Ming Toy" (New York: Waterson, Berlin, and Snyder Co., 1919).
58. Harold Atteridge and Sigmund Romberg, "So Long, Sing Song" (New York: Jerome H. Remick and Co., 1919); Richard C. Norton, *A Chronology of American Musical Theater* (New York: Oxford University Press, 2002), 2:191–192.
59. "Ziegfeld to Start *Ming Toy* Rehearsals," *New York Times*, 10 Sept. 1929, 37; "*East Is West* by Gershwin," *New York Times*, 1 Aug. 1928, 38; George Gershwin and Ira Gershwin, "In the Mandarin's Orchid Garden" (New York: WB Music Corp., 1930).
60. "Miss Bainter's Career," *Washington Post*, 16 Apr. 1922, 56.
61. Alexander Woollcott, "Second Thoughts on First Nights," *New York Times*, 18 Mar. 1917, X5; "*The Willow Tree* a Thing of Beauty," *New York Times*, 7 Mar. 1917, 8.
62. "Fay Bainter's Art," *Washington Post*, 26 Feb. 1922, 56.
63. Shipman and Hymer, *East Is West*, 35.
64. John Corbin, "Drama," *New York Times*, 26 Dec. 1918, 9.
65. Pierre Loti and Judith Gautier, *The Daughter of Heaven*, trans. Ruth Helen Davis (New York: Duffield and Co., 1912).
66. "Finds Fascination in a Chinese Role," *Washington Post*, 16 Mar. 1913, MT3.
67. "Actress and the Woman," *Washington Post*, 2 Apr. 1905, D4.
68. For examples of dangerous Eurasian women, see Valerie Bergére's vaudeville act "Chinese Compensation," the silent film *The Red Lantern* (1919), and the play *East of Suez* (1922). "New Acts This Week," *Variety*, 22 Dec. 1926, 20; "The Screen," *New York Times*, 5 May 1919, 11; "*East of Suez*, Big Melodrama, Week's Feature," *Washington Post*, 22 Apr. 1923, 60. "Song of Shanghai" (1926) warns all men looking for love to stay away from Lu Song, a seductress who uses music to lure her victims. She is not of mixed descent. Vincent Rose, Richard A. Whiting, and Raymond B. Egan, "Song of Shanghai" (New York: Irving Berlin, Inc., 1926).
69. Brooks Atkinson, "Tempestuous Lenore," *New York Times*, 5 Nov. 1932, 26.
70. See George Warren Currier and D. W. Reeves, "The Ilish Chinaman," in *Gems from*

the Comic Opera "The Mandarin Zune, or Feast of the New Year" (New York: G. W. Currier and D. W. Reeves, 1886), 15–18.

71. Aarim-Heriot, *Chinese Immigrants*, 30–42; Spoehr, "Sambo and the Heathen Chinee," 185–204; Caldwell, "Negroization of the Chinese Stereotype," 123–132.

72. James H. Dormon, "Shaping the Popular Image of Post-Reconstruction American Blacks: The 'Coon Song' Phenomenon of the Gilded Age," *American Quarterly* 40 (Dec. 1988): 450–471; Hamm, *Yesterdays*, 320–321; Crawford, *America's Musical Life*, 487–491.

73. Paul J. Knox, "I Don't Care if I Never Wake Up" (Chicago: Will Rossiter, 1899).

74. Dormon, "'Coon Song' Phenomenon," 461–463.

75. Theodore Morse and Edward Madden, "Ching-a-Ling" (New York: F. B. Haviland Publishing, 1907).

76. Bob Cole and Billy Johnson, "The Wedding of the Chinee and the Coon" (New York: Howley, Haviland, and Co. 1897).

77. Ben Harvey, "Li Hung Chang" (New York: Sol Bloom, 1898).

78. Albert Trahern, "Wing Lee's Rag-Time Clock" (New York: Myell Brothers, 1899).

79. "A Colored Man's Defense," *Elevator,* 21 June 1867, 2. See David J. Hellwig, "Black Reactions to Chinese Immigration and the Anti-Chinese Movement: 1850–1910," *Amerasia* 6 (Fall 1979): 25–44; Leigh Dana Johnsen, "Equal Rights and the 'Heathen Chinee': Black Activism in San Francisco," *Western Historical Quarterly* 11 (Jan. 1980): 57–68; Frank H. Goodyear, "'Beneath the Shadow of her Flag': Philip A. Bell's *The Elevator* and the Struggle for Enfranchisement, 1865–1870," *California History* 77 (Spring 1999): 34–35.

80. Thomas Postlewait, "The Hieroglyphic Stage: American Theatre and Society, Post Civil War to 1945," in *The Cambridge History of American Theatre*, ed. Don B. Wilmeth and Christopher Bigsby (New York: Cambridge University Press, 1998–2000), 2:139.

81. "Dramatic Doings," *New York Dramatic News and Society Journal,* 5 July 1879, 5. See Southern, *Music of Black Americans*, 237–238; Bernard L. Peterson Jr., *Profiles of African American Stage Performers and Theatre People, 1816–1960* (Westport, Conn.: Greenwood Press, 2001), 158.

82. "Variety," *New York Clipper,* 5 Jan. 1884, 713.

83. "Things Theatrical," *Wilke's Spirit of the Times,* 16 Mar. 1861, 32.

84. Lester A. Walton, "Colored Vaudevillians Organize," *New York Age*, 10 June 1909, 6; Lester A. Walton, "Fiddler and Shelton Leave U.B.O. [United Booking Office]," *New York Age*, 26 Sept. 1912, 6; "Tom Brown, Talented Actor Passes Away," *New York Age*, 28 June 1919, 6. For discussions of African Americans in vaudeville, see Brenda Dixon Gottschild, *Waltzing in the Dark: African American Vaudeville and Race Politics during the Swing Era* (New York: Palgrave, 2002); Nadine George-Graves, *The Royalty of Negro Vaudeville: The Whitman Sisters and the Negotiation of Race, Gender, and Class in African American Theater, 1900–1940* (New York: St. Martin's Press, 2000).

85. "Tom Brown, Talented Actor Passes Away," 6.

86. Peterson, *Profiles*, 35–36; Norton, *Chronology of American Musical Theater*, 1:623; David A. Jasen and Gene Jones, *Spreadin' the Rhythm Around: Black Popular Songwriters, 1880–1930* (New York: G. Schirmer, Inc., 1998), 97–99.

87. As with other songs from this period, "The Wedding of the Chinee and the Coon" (1897) contained Chinese musical tokens. Riis, *Just before Jazz*, 26–28.

88. Advertisements, *New York Age*, 18 Jan. 1912, 6.

89. Lester A. Walton, "Theatrical Comment," *New York Age*, 14 Jan. 1909, 6.

90. "A New Cooling Plant," *New York Age*, 22 July 1915, 6; "Tom Brown, Talented Actor Passes Away," 6; Peterson, *Profiles*, 35–36; Riis, *Just before Jazz*, 122–124; Eric Ledell Smith, *Bert Williams: A Biography of the Pioneer Black Comedian* (New York: McFarland, 1992), 114–118.

91. "*Mr. Lode of Koal* on the Road," *New York Age*, 9 Dec. 1909, 6; Bert Williams, "Chink, Chink, Chinaman" (Chicago: Will Rossiter, 1909); Riis, *Just before Jazz*, 122–124.

92. "Chink chink chineeman" and its many derivations appeared in other songs during this period. See Harry Greenbank and Sidney Jones, "Chin Chin Chinaman" (New York: White-Smith Music Publishing, 1896); James F. Hanley, Joe Goodwin, and Ballard MacDonald, "Chin-Chin Chinaman" (New York: Shapiro, Bernstein and Co., 1917).

93. Roger D. Abrahams and Lois Rankin, eds., *Counting-Out Rhymes* (Austin: University of Texas Press, 1980), 131–132; Roger D. Abrahams, ed., *Jump Rope Rhymes: A Dictionary* (Austin: University of Texas Press, 1969), 29–30.

94. Mary Church Terrell, *A Colored Woman in a White World* (1940; reprint, New York: Simon and Schuster, 1996), 23.

95. It was also called "The Chinaman and the Coon." Lester A. Walton, "The Benefit," *New York Age*, 11 June 1908, 6; "This Week's Vaudeville Reviews This Week," *Billboard*, 14 May 1910, 45; 26 Dec. 1914, 10.

96. Peterson, *Profiles*, 60; "New Acts This Week," *Variety*, 9 Sept. 1921, 19.

97. "New Acts This Week," *Variety*, 27 Sept. 1906, 11; advertisements, *New York Age*, 24 Dec. 1908, 6.

98. "This Week's Vaudeville Reviews This Week," *Billboard*, 26 Dec. 1914, 10.

99. "New Acts This Week," *Variety*, 24 Oct. 1919, 20.

100. Tom Fletcher, *One Hundred Years of the Negro in Show Business* (New York: Da Capo Press, 1984), 236.

101. Smith, *Bert Williams*, 41–42; Riis, *Just before Jazz*, 80–82, 91–105, 113–117; Thomas L. Riis, "Introduction," in *The Music and Scripts of "In Dahomey,"* ed. Thomas L. Riis (Madison, Wis.: MUSA, 1996), xxviii.

102. "Theatrical Jottings," *New York Age*, 29 Oct. 1908, 6; "Kelley and Catlin Amuse," *New York Age*, 1 Dec. 1910, 6; "This Week's Vaudeville Reviews This Week," *Billboard*, 18 June 1910, 24; 9 May 1914, 14; "'Dad' Kelly Dead," *New York Age*, 5 Feb. 1921, 6.

103. Walter Carter, *The Coon and the Chink* (New York: Dick and Fitzgerald, 1912).

104. Ibid., 5.

105. There were other performers aside from those mentioned here, such as Harry Fiddler and "Ruby" B. Shelton, who gave Chinese/African American skits in vaudeville from 1908 through 1920. Frank Walker sang "Chop Suey Sue" (1915) in Williams and Walker's *Darkydom*. Riis, *Just before Jazz*, 82, 169, 182–184; Peterson, *Profiles*, 61, 97, 158–159, 233, 275–276.

106. *House-Rent Party* (1946) and *What a Guy* (1939) contained a Chinese laundryman played by Alfred Cortez (One Lung Lee) and Al Curtis (One Lung) (this was perhaps the same person). Juanita Hall portrayed Bloody Mary, a Tonkinese woman, in both the stage (1949) and film (1958) versions of Richard Rodgers and Oscar Hammerstein's *South Pacific*. Alan Gevinson, ed., *Within Our Gates: Ethnicity in American Feature Films, 1911–1960* (Berkeley: University of California Press, 1997), 471, 1125–1126.

CHAPTER 6   THE RISE OF CHINESE AND CHINESE AMERICAN VAUDEVILLIANS

1. Robert W. Snyder, *Voice of the City: Vaudeville and Popular Culture in New York* (New York: Oxford University Press, 1989); Roy Rosenzweig, *Eight Hours for What We Will: Workers and Leisure in an Industrialized City, 1870–1920* (New York: Cambridge University Press, 1983); Lewis A. Erenburg, *Steppin' Out: New York Nightlife*

and the Transformation of American Culture, 1890–1920 (Chicago: University of Chicago Press, 1984).

2. Lee, *Orientals*, 36–37.

3. Commissioner General, Washington, D.C., to Martin Beck, Orpheum Circuit general manager, New York, N.Y., 25 Sept. 1913, box 52, file 903–62, Subject Correspondence, 1906–32, National Archives, Washington, D.C.

4. Lee Tung Foo, box 68, file 64, Chinese Exclusion Acts Case Files, 1880–1960, National Archives, New York, N.Y.

5. Woo, "Chinese Protestants"; Riddle, *Flying Dragons*, 125–126, 203–207; Chinn, *Bridging the Pacific*, 55–56, 125–128, 202–215; Helen Wong Jean, "Playing the Palace Theatre: A Chinese American's Recollections of Vaudeville," *Chinese America: History and Perspectives* 3 (1989): 111–116; Lorraine Dong, "The Forbidden City Legacy and Its Chinese American Women," *Chinese America: History and Perspectives* 6 (1992): 125–148; "The Chinese Fred Astaire and Ginger Rogers: Toy and Wing," in *Tap! The Greatest Tap Dance Stars and Their Stories, 1900–1955*, ed. Rusty E. Frank (New York: Da Capo Press, 1994), 102–110; "Rose Yuen Ow, Cabaret Dancer," in *Unbound Voices: A Documentary History of Chinese Women in San Francisco*, ed. Judy Yung (Berkeley: University of California Press, 1999), 273–280.

6. Margaret Blake Alverson, *Sixty Years of California Song* (San Francisco: Sunset Publishing House, 1913), 161–166; "Remarkable Musical Talent of a Chinese Native Son," *San Francisco Chronicle*, 1898, clippings, Margaret Blake Alverson Papers.

7. Diaries, 1905–1911, Margaret Blake Alverson Papers; Chinn, *Bridging the Pacific*, 55–56, 202–203.

8. "Rose Yuen Ow"; Yow Joe (Chong Yow Haw), file 12017/47447, Case File Investigations Not Resulting in Warrants Proceedings in the San Francisco District and Investigations within the San Francisco District at the Request of Other Service Offices, 1912–1950, National Archives, San Bruno, Calif.

9. Don Fung (Fong) Gue, box 29, file 469, Chinese Exclusion Acts Case Files, 1880–1960, National Archives, New York, N.Y.; Harry Haw (Ho Chee Chong), box 29, file 470, Chinese Exclusion Acts Case Files, 1880–1960, National Archives, New York, N.Y.; Chinn, *Bridging the Pacific*, 203–204, 211–213.

10. Tom (Thomas) Guy Wing, box 34, file 272, Chinese Exclusion Acts Case Files, 1880–1960, National Archives, New York, N.Y.

11. "Ching Ling Foo," clippings, Harvard Theatre Collection.

12. Cynthia L. Nakashima, "Servants of Culture: The Symbolic Role of Mixed-Race Asians in American Discourse," in *The Sum of Our Parts: Mixed-Heritage Asian Americans*, ed. Teresa Williams-León and Cynthia L. Nakashima (Philadelphia: Temple University Press, 2001), 35–47.

13. Inspector in Charge, Buffalo, N.Y., to Commissioner-General of Immigration, Washington, D.C., 10 Feb. 1915, box 1, file 55007/12, Subject Correspondence, 1906–32, National Archives, Washington, D.C.

14. Paul Spickard, "Who Is an Asian? Who Is a Pacific Islander? Monoracialism, Multiracial People, and Asian American Communities," in Williams-León and Nakashima, *Sum of Our Parts*, 13–24.

15. "Joseph Ah Chung Took His Life," *Salem Evening News*, 22 Oct. 1906, 1.

16. James H. Archung, box 6, file 1431, Chinese Exclusion Acts Case Files, 1880–1960, National Archives, New York, N.Y.; Chinn, *Bridging the Pacific*, 55–56, 202–203.

17. Lee Tung Foo, letter to Margaret Blake Alverson, New York, N.Y., 30 Nov. 1915.

18. In 1907, Sing Fong Lee, dubbed the "Chinese Kubelik" (a reference to Czech violinist Jan Kubelik), first appeared in vaudeville wearing a Mandarin-style robe, hat, and queue. His act, much like Lee Tung Foo's Scottish impersonations, did not fit with American ideas of Chinese "fiddle music"—what was often described as the

screeching and squealing of the huqin—but consisted of popular and semi-classical pieces. A critic in San Francisco admired his training and ability but remarked that his costume was a detraction. "There is nothing of the freak about Sing Fong Lee except his costuming, which is the green and yellow of the burlesque 'chink' order. This he should speedily discard in favor of the regulation dress suit. Mr. Lee sports a queue, and if oddity in dressing is desired this appendage dangling in the rear of an evening dress coat would suffice." Eventually, Lee did alter his costume, but instead of following the advice of his critics, he chose to wear the clothes of a laborer from southern China, which fit more with the yellowface tradition and not with the appearance of a skilled violinist. Advertisements, *Billboard*, 12 Oct. 1907, 14; 1 Oct. 1910, 17; "New Acts This Week," *Variety*, 3 Aug. 1907, 13.

19. Diaries, 1905–1906, Margaret Blake Alverson Papers; advertising postcard, Lee Tung Foo, n.d., box 68, file 64, Chinese Exclusion Acts Case Files, 1880–1960, National Archives, New York, N.Y.
20. "This Week's Vaudeville Reviews This Week," *Billboard*, 25 Dec. 1915, 7.
21. Advertisements, *Billboard*, 18 Dec. 1915, 4; Princess Jue Quon Tai, Musicians Collection, 1727–1981, Harry Ransom Humanities Research Center, University of Texas at Austin.
22. "Princess Jue Quon Tai," *Theatre Magazine* 37 (Apr. 1923): 43.
23. "World's Only Chinese Baritone," *Keith's News* (Providence, R.I.), 24 Dec. 1906, 3–4, in clippings, Margaret Blake Alverson Papers.
24. "This Week's Vaudeville Reviews This Week," *Billboard*, 26 Feb. 1916, 7; 5 Aug. 1916, 7.
25. "This Week's Vaudeville Reviews This Week," *Billboard*, 7 Oct. 1916, 67.
26. "New Acts This Week," *Variety*, 29 May 1920, 34.
27. "This Week's Vaudeville Reviews This Week," *Billboard*, 21 Feb. 1914, 10; advertisements, *Billboard*, 18 Dec. 1915, 14.
28. Chinn, *Bridging the Pacific*, 205.
29. Lady Tsen Mei, "Chinese Girl Tells How," *Variety*, 26 Dec. 1919, 21, 101–103; "Josephine Kramer, America's First Chinese Actress," *Virginian-Pilot*, 1 Aug. 1985, D4.
30. "New Acts This Week," *Variety*, 9 May 1919, 21.
31. "This Week's Vaudeville Reviews This Week," *Billboard*, 4 Mar. 1916, 7.
32. "Ching Ling Foo," *New York Tribune*, 29 July 1913, in clippings, Harvard Theatre Collection.
33. Clark, "Chinese of New York," 105–106.
34. A. C. Scott, "China: An Overview," 2:127–138; Ingrid Brainard, "Court and Social Dance before 1800," 5:619–622, both in *International Encyclopedia of Dance*, ed. Selma Jeanne Cohen (New York: Oxford University Press, 1998).
35. Vernon Castle, *Modern Dancing* (New York: Harper and Brothers, 1914); Iris M. Fanger, "Vernon and Irene Castle," in Cohen, *International Encyclopedia of Dance*, 2:78–80.
36. "This Week's Vaudeville Reviews This Week," *Billboard*, 22 Aug. 1914, 11.
37. "This Week's Vaudeville Reviews This Week," *Billboard*, 8 Sept. 1917, 70.
38. "Songs Lee Tung Foo Has Studied," n.d., Margaret Blake Alverson Papers.
39. Al. Piantadosi and Alfred Bryan, "I Didn't Raise My Boy to Be a Soldier" (New York: Teller, Sons and Dorner, 1915).
40. Roy Turk, Jack Smith, and Maceo Pinkard, "Gimme a Little Kiss Will 'Ya' Huh?" (New York: Irving Berlin, Inc., 1926).
41. Lee David and Carey Morgan, "Sipping Cider thru' a Straw" (New York: Joseph W. Stern and Co., 1919).
42. Al. Piantadosi and Jack Glogau, "On the Shores of Italy" (New York: Leo Feist, Inc., 1914).

43. "The *Billboard* Song Chart," *Billboard*, 20 Mar. 1915, 14; "This Week's Vaudeville Reviews This Week," *Billboard*, 25 Dec. 1915, 7; advertisements, *Billboard*, 18 Dec. 1915, 4.
44. Lee Tung Foo, letter to Margaret Blake Alverson, Chicago, Ill., 13 Apr. 1914; Milwaukee, Wis., 14 Oct. 1914; Chicago, Ill., 23 Nov. 1914, all in Margaret Blake Alverson Papers.
45. "This Week's Vaudeville Reviews This Week," *Billboard*, 21 Feb. 1914, 10.
46. "This Week's Vaudeville Reviews This Week," *Billboard*, 21 Dec. 1912, 10. A writer for *Billboard* reported that the Chung Hwa Comedy Four sang the spiritual "Roll Them Bones" (n.d.). "Songs Heard in San Francisco Vaudeville Last Week," *Billboard*, 15 Nov. 1913, 16.
47. Michael Rogin, *Blackface, White Noise: Jewish Immigrants in the Hollywood Melting Pot* (Berkeley: University of California Press, 1996).
48. "New Acts This Week," *Variety*, 13 May 1921, 21; 13 Jan. 1922, 20.
49. "New Acts This Week," *Variety*, 27 Jan. 1922, 21.
50. *Boston Post*, 29 Nov. 1906, clippings, Margaret Blake Alverson Papers.
51. *Pittsburgh Press*, 7 Oct. 1906, clippings, Margaret Blake Alverson Papers.
52. "New Acts This Week," *Variety*, 18 Sept. 1929, 52; Rida Johnson Young, Chauncey Olcott, and Ernest R. Ball, "Mother Machree" (New York: M. Witmark and Sons, 1910).
53. "This Week's Vaudeville Reviews This Week," *Billboard*, 5 Aug. 1917, 7; affidavit of Mrs. Poldi Long, Lafayette, Ind., 13 Jan. 1918, box 725, file 53854, Subject Correspondence, 1906–32, National Archives, Washington, D.C.; George S. Emmerson, "Great Britain: Scottish Folk and Traditional Dance," in Cohen, *International Encyclopedia of Dance*, 3:243–250.
54. "This Week's Vaudeville Reviews This Week," *Billboard*, 27 Nov. 1915, 10. Lee Tung Foo reported to Alverson that Jue had many technical problems with her singing. "Well, I heard that 'Princess' Jue Juon Tai last week at the Palace N.Y.C. and she didn't go at all and she has no expression in her songs and can't phrase, breathed between syllables, 'Poor Annie Laurie' ["Bonnie Annie Laurie" (1909)] was killed by her." Lee Tung Foo, letter to Margaret Blake Alverson, Newark, N.J., 28 Dec. 1915, Margaret Blake Alverson Papers.
55. "This Week's Vaudeville Reviews This Week," *Billboard*, 9 Nov. 1912, 43.
56. "This Week's Vaudeville Reviews This Week," *Billboard*, 26 Feb. 1916, 7.
57. Lee Tung Foo, letter to Margaret Blake Alverson, Chicago, Ill., 19 May 1914, Margaret Blake Alverson Papers.
58. Lee Tung Foo, letter to Margaret Blake Alverson, Chicago, Ill., 19 Mar. 1914, Margaret Blake Alverson Papers.
59. Lee Tung Foo, letter to Margaret Blake Alverson, Janesville, Wis., 25 Sept. 1914, Margaret Blake Alverson Papers.
60. There follows a list of Chinese and Chinese Americans acts that I have not discussed here. For some, I found only their names or brief reviews. This list may include different names for the same group; in some cases, these could be Filipino performers posing as Chinese. The acts are: A Peek at Pekin, Au San Lu and Boys, Ben Nee One, Chang's Mandarins, Chin Chee Toy, Chinese Castles, Chinese Jazz Trio, Chinese Musical Entertainers, Ching Fu Lee, Chong, Five Ching Lo Maids, Gee Sun Ki (in Joseph E. Howard's "Musical Revue"), Grace Moy, Hong Fong, Imperial Chinese Trio, J. Lopaz's Chinese Band, Joe Wong and Co., Jiu Fung, Lady Lo Wah, Lee Hop and Company, Ling Joey, Lotus Lee, Lydia Loi Hoi Tsehn, Mamie Ling and Tommy Long, Nee Wong, Pickard's Chinese Syncopators (Pickard's Ling Ting Foo Act), Prince Wong, Princess Tai Tai (Nai Tai Tai), Sam Lee, Shanghai Trio, Tai Sing Ling, Tock and Toy, and Toy Ling Foo.
61. Arthur Dong, *Forbidden City, U.S.A.* (Los Angeles: DeepFocus Productions, 1989).

CONCLUSION

1. Alain Boubil, Claude-Michel Schönberg, and Richard Maltby Jr., sleeve notes to *Miss Saigon* (London: Geffen Records, 1988).
2. Kondo, *About Face*, 227–234; Shimakawa, *National Abjection*, 43–56; Lee, *Performing Asian America*, 15, 163; Ella Shohat, "The Struggle over Representation: Casting, Coalitions, and the Politics of Identification," in *Late Imperial Culture*, ed. Román de la Campa, E. Ann Kaplan, and Michael Sprinker (New York: Verso, 1995), 166–178.
3. Kondo, *About Face*; Shimakawa, *National Abjection*; Lee, *Performing Asian America*; Shohat, "Struggle over Representation."
4. Renu Sehgal and Jeff Yang, "A Movement of Parts: Asian American Activism, 10 Years after Vincent Chin," *A. Magazine*, 30 Apr. 1992, 8.
5. Richard Griffith and Arthur Mayer, *The Movies* (New York: Simon and Schuster, 1957), 108.
6. Frank Chin, "Kung Fu Is Unfair to Chinese," *New York Times*, 24 Mar. 1974, 137; Eugene Franklin Wong, *On Visual Media Racism: Asians in the American Motion Pictures* (New York: Arno Press, 1978), 46; "Asian-American Actors Fight for Jobs and Image," *New York Times*, 3 June 1973, 65; Benjamin Lin, "Adhesive Tape Orientals," *Bridge* 2 (Feb. 1973): 7–10; Buck Wong, "Toward an Asian American Theater Form," *Bridge* 2 (June 1973): 41–44; Irvin Paik, "The East West Players: The First Ten Are the Hardest," *Neworld* 1 (Winter 1975): 31–35.
7. News, *Bridge* 1 (July/Aug. 1972): 34; 1 (Mar./Apr. 1972): 39.
8. Yoko Yoshikawa, "The Heat Is on *Miss Saigon* Coalition: Organizing across Race and Sexuality," in *The State of Asian America: Activism and Resistance in the 1990s*, ed. Karin Aguilar–San Juan (Boston: South End Press, 1994), 278.
9. Gina Marchetti, *Romance and the "Yellow Peril": Race, Sex, and Discursive Strategies in Hollywood Fiction* (Berkeley: University of California Press, 1993), 83; Lee, *Orientals*, 1–14.
10. "Chinese Plays, Real and False," *Literary Digest*, 13 Mar. 1920, 35.
11. Paul K. Whang, "Boycotting American Movies," *World Tomorrow* 13 (Aug. 1930): 339–340.

Index

About the Author

Born and raised in New Hampshire, Krystyn Moon is an assistant professor at Georgia State University in Atlanta, where she teaches U.S. cultural history and Asian American history. This is her first book.